CAMPUS
ARCHITECTURE

CAMPUS ARCHITECTURE

BUILDING IN THE GROVES OF ACADEME

RICHARD P. DOBER, AICP

McGraw-Hill

New York San Francisco Washington, D.C. Auckland Bogotá
Caracas Lisbon London Madrid Mexico City Milan
Montreal New Delhi San Juan Singapore
Sydney Tokyo Toronto

Library of Congress Cataloging-in-Publication Data

Dober, Richard P.
    Campus architecture : building in the groves of academe / Richard
P. Dober.
            p.   cm.
    Includes bibliographical references and index.
    ISBN 0-07-017185-8
    1. College buildings—Designs and plans.   2. Campus planning.
3. College facilities—Planning.   I. Title.
LB3223.D599   1996
378.1`96`2—dc20   95-53779
                                                                    CIP

1 2 3 4 5 6 7 8 9 0   KGP/KGP   9 0 1 0 9 8 7 6

ISBN 0-07-017185-8

*The sponsoring editor for this book was Wendy Lochner, the editing supervisor was
Jane Palmieri, the designer was Silvers Design, and the production supervisor was
Suzanne W. B. Rapcavage. It was set by Silvers Design.*

Printed and bound by Quebecor/Kingsport.

All photographs by Richard P. Dober unless otherwise credited.

McGraw-Hill books are available at special quantity discounts to use as premiums and sales
promotions, or for use in corporate training programs. For more information, please write to
the Director of Special Sales, McGraw-Hill, 11 West 19th Street, New York, NY 10011. Or
contact your local bookstore.

This book is printed on acid-free paper.

For

HANNAH

and

H.R.S.

CONTENTS

PREFACE

THIS BOOK describes, defines, and documents campus architecture, designs that serve and celebrate uniquely our time, taste, temperament, and technology. Organized to give guidance and inspiration to all responsible for improving and extending the extraordinary physical heritage bestowed by earlier generations on our colleges and universities, the book focuses on building types insufficiently represented in many critical annals and reference works. We record with pleasure for peers and professionals the practicable and the visionary, the process and the product. We underscore the receptivity of the American campus for new ideas as evident in its best campus plans and building designs as well as the emerging commitment to the conservation of architectural legacies and the natural environment.

Obviously a vibrant mix of many influences, campus architecture can be interpreted and explained in many ways. Buildings can be evaluated by their appearance, by how well they function, by their siting, and by their contribution to their overall physical environment. Stretching over time as they do, a selection of campus buildings can also be construed and narrated as a history of building technology, or interior design, or theory actualized. A book elucidating the works of great people—a Michelin-like guide to memorable places—this book is not, though reference is and should be made to landmark structures and sites. Some of these are the quirky and quaint residue of lost causes, both the degeneration of traditional architecture and the demise of modern idioms. Buildings of originality and substance will get their due, as well as examples they inspired, a few unremembered because they are in the hinterland and have been less exposed to publicity. Threaded through the exposition will be a plea for campus landscapes, the consummate companion of admirable buildings. Pieced together, our amalgamation and assimilation of definitions and descriptions is intended to yield an efficacious synthesis which may disclose precedents and principles useful in shaping future campus architecture.

Critical judgments and recommendations, aside, for the casual reader and professional alike, our account should also give cause to appreciate college and university architecture as a three-dimensional record of aesthetic achievement, ranking with agoras, forums, cathedrals, capitols, opera houses, and railroad stations as cultural monuments indicative of their period and its aspirations. Some of the documentation we will cite will also include a critical gloss on the parade of styles. Our view of the march by is necessarily selective, not encyclopedic. Of special interest is the emergence of mid-twentieth-century Modern architecture as a suitable vehicle to serve and support the extraordinary growth in higher education which occurred in the same years (and the prelude and aftermath). How propitious? Noted one knowledgeable observer in 1930: "But let us look back at the university buildings, anywhere, everywhere, even the ones being built today; and unfortunately we will know that no breath of Modern rationalization has disturbed the dust back where learning begins." The sequence and impact of change in attitude and substance surround the core of our discussion.

Here, then, is one leading question: If diversity and variety are desirable traits, are there features that all good college and university buildings share in common—transcendental features that are associated with campus architecture? That question is at the core of our inquiry and suggested design direction. After examining building types and their features, we will then attempt to establish a definition of campus architecture which fits the overview of cause and effect and changing circumstances. This, in turn, leads to descriptions of paradigms and exemplary projects. Among thousands of possible case examples, those chosen were selected to chronicle typical situations, a range of functions and geographic areas, a variety of institutions, and an assortment of amenities and ambiance. The commentary is salted with quotes which reveal intransigent intentions and transitory convictions—how delightful and instructive to observe and appreciate the shifting sands of aesthetic canons, how marvelous to see colleges and universities providing the cause and venue for innovation and invention, how rewarding to experience the great work *noveau et anciens ensemble.* Throughout we give evidence that colleges and universities will continue to be patrons, providers, and proprietors of campus architecture. Forty percent of the American population has spent one or more years on campus, a percentage likely to increase (that statistic alone supports the subject's importance).

This chronicle is followed by a discussion and outline of the essential procedures for creating new campus architecture and reconstructing legacy buildings and sites. The material includes homage to the variety and vitality of existing bastions of authenticity as well as comments on some schemes whose design expectations were never (or not yet) realized. In addition to new buildings and sites, the representative group of projects also covers the revitalization and regeneration of older structures and landscapes. Having matured, most American campuses will not remain vital if they neglect to maintain their hard-won architectural heritage, both the built environment and binding greenery. We conclude with sources and an index.

Campus Architecture also completes the author's trilogy, almost 40 years in the making. The first work, *Campus Planning,* laid out methods for melding the new and old constituent components of a campus plan so each would contribute to an overall development concept. *Campus Design* indicated how such concepts could be infused with a distinctive sense of institutional purpose and locale through place making and place marking. *Campus Architecture* gives guidance and support for paradigms and projects—buildings, landscapes, and site features, which, through systematic planning, programming, design, and construction, connect the broader visions of institutional purpose and place with three-dimensional specificity. It is hoped that all three books will serve as an illuminating account of how the planning and design professions affected higher education during a historic growth period and will encourage others to articulate and disseminate in the years ahead additional ideas and concepts about campus development as an environmental art, charged with social and cultural significance and worthy of the special efforts that such architecture requires from all who participate in its formulation.

Richard P. Dober, AICP

ACKNOWLEDGMENTS

Arthur J. Lidsky and Charles A. Craig provided a place, encouragement, and many reasons for starting and completing this book. Professional colleagues and institutional staff responded generously and promptly to my request for information, photos, and drawings. Given their busy lives and many demands on their time and their other obligations, I am particularly grateful to the following: Elizabeth Ahern (Finegold, Alexander + Associates, Inc.); Calvert W. Audrain (Art Institute of Chicago); James Baird (Holabird & Root); Jean Marie Bath (Hardy Holzman Pfeiffer Associates); Peter Blankman (Union College); Stanley G. Boles (Boora Architects); Kate Brannelly (Earl R. Flansburgh + Associates, Inc.); Ignacio F. Bunster-Ossa (Wallace Roberts & Todd); Sandy Burrows (Lycoming College); Ian Caldwell (Imperial College of London); Jill Capanna (Anshen + Allen); Dixi Carrillo (EDAW, Inc.); Lois Carleton (Sir Norman Foster and Partners); Ginger Hall Carnes (Palo Alto College); Perry Chapman (Sasaki Associates, Inc.); Karen Clark (The Colorado College); Cami Colarossi (Goucher College); Geralyn M. Comeau (Shepley Bulfinch Richardson Abbott); Roger Courtney (EDAW, Inc.); Keith Covey (Carleton College); Alan K. Cubbage (Drake University); Charles E. Dagit, Jr. (Dagit • Saylor Architects); William D'Elia (Kaplan • McLaughlin • Diaz); Ann Dumas (Perkins & Will); Janet L. Durkin (Smith College); Esherick Homsey Dodge & Davis; Brian Falk (High House Studio); Laurence H. Fauber; Moe Finegold (Finegold, Alexander & Associates, Inc.); Ira Fink (Ira Fink and Associates); Robert D. Flanigan, Jr. (Spelman College); John Giboney (Pomona College); Kenneth A. Gifford (State University Construction Fund); Janis D. Gleason (Emory University); Karen Handle (Wabash College); Patrick C. Harrington (Boora Architects); Jennifer Harris (Pasanella + Klein, Stolzman + Berg); Kevin Hart (Simon Martin-Vegue Winklestein Moris); Paul Helpern (Helpern Architects); Kevin Herd (The University of Iowa); Clint Hewitt (University of Minnesota); Bonnie J. Hill (Hamline University); Indiana University; Greg Johnson (The University of Iowa); M. Elaine Justus (Benedictine

College); Cindy Keig (Oklahoma State University); Kent State University; Billy Kingsley (Vanderbilt University); Arvid Klein (Pasanella + Klein, Stolzman + Berg); Barbara Lago (The University of Mississippi); Julie Liffrig (University of Maryland at College Park); David J. Loftus (Portland State University); Michael A. Macewicz (Clark University); Rodolfo Machado (Machado and Silvetti Associates, Inc.); Eugene J. Mackey III (Mackey Mitchell Associates); Greg Marshall (Rice University); Frederick W. Mayer (University of Michigan); Grover C. Meetze, Jr. (Little & Associates Architects); Linda C. Michaels (Kenyon College); Marita Miller (Bowdoin College); Susan Millhouse (Kaplan • McLaughlin • Diaz); Dell Mitchell (Perry • Dean • Rogers & Partners, Architects); Maryville College; Leslie E. Morris (Elmira College); James T. Murphy (Illinois College); Joan E. Nelson (Stubbins Associates, Inc.); David J. Neuman (Stanford University); Ron Nief (Middlebury College); Nina Pascale (William Turnbull Associates); Jeanne E. Pasqualini (Connecticut College); Tom Payette (Payette Associates); Tom F. Peters (Lehigh University); Jessica Pieters (Baylor University); Elaine E. Pittaluga (Washington University in St. Louis); Marianna K. Preston (University of Delaware); Rensselaer Polytechnic Institute; Kristin Rojcewicz (Hardy Holzman Pfeiffer Associates); Vicki Kayser Rugo (Sasaki Associates Inc.); Philip R. Scaffidi (Scaffidi & Moore); O. Robert Simha (Massachusetts Institute of Technology); Cliff Silver (Concordia University); Linda L. Steele (Hollins College); Elizabeth Stirling (Rock Valley College); Chris Stratton (Franklin Pierce College); Diane Strauss (The University of North Carolina at Chapel Hill); Charles N. Tseckares (Childs Bertman Tseckares Inc.); Ursinus College; Patti Valentine (Saint Mary's College); Felipe Vasquez (University of California, Irvine); Mrs. Terry Walters (Furman University); Jan Watts (The University of Akron); Linda L. Weber (Leonard Parker Associates Architects, Inc.); William Jewell College; Diane Wilson (University of Nebraska, Lincoln); Carol Wooten (Brown University); Graham Wyatt (Robert Stern Architects); Gerrit Zwart (Shepley Bulfinch Richardson Abbott).

At Dober, Lidsky, Craig and Associates, colleagues Dorothy Atwood, Mary Bush-Brown, George Mathey, and Pekio Vergotis were most helpful in securing information and cheering the work onward. Karen Berchtold and Dori Mottola made major contributions in getting the manuscript and graphics ready for the publisher. At McGraw-Hill, Joel Stein and Wendy Lochner served as senior editors and supported this effort from the beginning, and Jane Palmieri served as senior editing supervisor; Chuck Hutchinson's sound advice was crucial and always available as the book took shape.

As they have in the past, my wife Lee and children Patrick and Claire gave comfort and encouragement throughout the book's genesis and completion. Their constructive and uplifting comments and queries brought energy to an occasionally sagging author. The book is dedicated to Howard R. Swearer, mentor and friend, and to Mary Hannah Dober, Class of 2016. If all goes well, her generation's life on campus will be better, one hopes, because her grandfather persuaded family, friends, and colleagues to assist in creating this book. I thank you all, those specifically mentioned and others whose names and contributions I may have inadvertently overlooked.

CHAPTER 1

PROSPECTUS

...To enlarge shrunken souls, enliven dying
spirits, and enlighten dim eyes...
                                    Peter Shaffer

MODERN CAMPUS ARCHITECTURE: PRELUDE AND PROMISE

Modern here, in particular, refers to the period, work, and influences of Walter
Gropius, Ludwig Mies van der Rohe, and Eliel Saarinen and the legion of practi-
tioner-teachers, students, and professionals associated with them after World War II.
These three trees, their several branches and many leaves (and sometimes a few
viable and complementary grafts such as Louis Kahn and Jose Lluis Sert) produced
a body of accomplished work, in quantity and quality, unparalleled in higher education. During those formative decades, rejecting bland and worn out conceptions
of traditional styles, the main body of college and university designers found,
embraced, and articulated a visual language which soon gained universal acceptance
as a signal and emblem of institutional vitality. If the first crop were hesitant her-
alds of new attitudes, less convincing than the rhetoric that stimulated their genesis, the second crop displays an elegant range of shapes and forms whose visual
delight would remind us of the attractions such designs had for those seeking a
neoteric expression for new institutions, as well as older colleges and universities
expanding with vision and vigor to educate a seemingly ever larger percentage of
the college-age population.

   As to prelude, the aesthetic adventure called Modern, applied to educational
buildings on the American scene, does not begin significantly, however, with higher

---

MASSACHUSETTS HALL, HARVARD UNIVERSITY, 1718. *(facing page, top)* *(Source: Harvard University)*

ARIZONA STATE UNIVERSITY, FINE ARTS CENTER, 1988, ANTOINE PREDOCK. *(facing page, bottom)*
Campus buildings stretched over two and a half centuries, celebrations of time, taste, and technology. The
American higher education spectrum was informed by ideas from other countries, as well as homegrown
concepts. In combination, the variety and diversity are testimony to the vitality of the institutions served
and symbolized by architecture and a tribute to designers engaged in expressing aesthetically the forces
of continuity and change.

education buildings, with some notable exceptions, such as Joseph Urban's New School for Social Research (New York City). There, an unconventional curriculum was wrapped in an architecture unlike almost all educational buildings from that period. These anomalies aside, the records would suggest that the prize for being first in enabling the Modern aesthetic to be built extensively belongs to elementary and secondary school architects and their clients. John Irwin Bright (Chairman, American Institute of Architecture, Committee on School Buildings) saw the future clearly, writing in 1929, "Beauty...is present in an arrangement of plan which reduces waste of motion and leads to economy in mass. It can be further defined as the proper regard relationship of form and function...a commonsense adjustment of the building to the needs for which it is erected."

George Howe and William Lescaze were the first to bring into fruition "modernist commitments to educational and architectural experimentation." Their Oak Lane School project (Pennsylvania, 1929), conceived and built in five months, gained prominence as the first Modern school building in the United States. Nominated by the press as the "Le Corbusier of America," Lescaze's Oak Lane work and a subsequent school in Croton, New York, were characterized as "Clean surfaces and simplified detail. ...Exterior...a direct expression of the interior. ...Large areas of floor space develop into bold, flat-decked masses unencumbered by overpowering roofs...openings distributed where required with freedom gained by the use of steel."

Examining the trends in 1939, Talbot F. Hamlin found California to be the hatchery and nest for the "most radical experiments in school design," with western architects more "daring in their attack on the school problem than their eastern colleagues." Hamlin cited Franklin and Kump's elementary school (Fresno, California, 1938), with its "generous glass areas and its human and personal scale." The low-lying, flat-roof structure, white trim, and entrance portico supported by two steel poles was a photogenic statement of the Modern canon. Equally so, was Richard Neutra's Experimental School for the Los Angeles Board of Education. The side facing the lawn demonstrated Neutra's belief that "The new materials and structural methods available today permit, when used unadulterated, a natural and more intimate relation to the out-of-doors and a consequent full benefit of its health factors." Neutra discovered his building components, he once said, in "*Sweets Catalogue*, a building supply source for architects and engineers...(industrial products) as inspiring as a healthy forest to a Norwegian carpenter." The factory-fabricated components, "plentiful in America," were the "raw materials for a certain technical style of construction," which Neutra advocated. Influential educators saw his designs as "an architecture which children can really understand and love." Critics praised "the liberating feeling, which is the 'forte' of all modern design in space." School boards also discovered that "Modern was cheaper than traditional" styles, a politically pleasing circumstance in the Depression years. That aspect was not left unarticulated in pressing Modern on the unpersuaded.

Sheldon Cheney's *The New World Architecture* (AMS Press, New York, 1930) abbreviates and states enthusiastically the source and character of the design emancipation, "an architectural revolution more fundamental than any in seven centuries." For Cheney, "a new reach has been made toward a strictly rational twentieth century beauty-in-building." The physical attributes he listed were: "geometric simplicity, absolute honesty in the use of materials...total independence from known styles of decoration, a new massiveness and precision; clean lines, hard edges, sanitary smoothness." Ironically, Modern's liberating aesthetic would come from Europe at a time when totalitarian governments were being formed and solidified; ironically, the Modern architectural language, attractive to young American school designers, had its origin in their own country. "American grain elevators, silos, power plants, and automobile factories," were to the Europeans, remarked Cheney, " strong examples of direct thinking and creative handling of new materials in response to new needs." Happy to see Modern being considered for schoolhouse architecture, Cheney was appalled at higher education's reception of the new ideas. "Where one might easily expect some independence...from the falsities and prejudices of warmed-over Italian-French culture," one finds, "deceit, servile-mindedness, and picking at the bones of antiquity."

Royce Hall, the University of California, Los Angeles, flagship building, circa 1927, was his *bete noire*. "A joke," he disclaimed, "not without tragic deeper implications, that for a hundred years the modern-living Californians are to be saddled at one of their highest cultural institutions, with these cramped relics of medieval picturesqueness, instead of machine-like buildings, open and suggestive of the functions they serve." Parenthetically, the *California Monthly* (1929) reported that "The Chemistry and Physics buildings (built at the same time as Royce), of course, are finished plainly, in strict accordance with the needs of the sciences which will be housed in them. They were designed as laboratory buildings of the most modern and practical type, without waste of time or money on decoration which would be useless and inappropriate."

Compare then the early Modern school buildings and two of their first collegiate counterparts, with their self-evident visual relationships, and construction in the most unlikely geographic locales. In a casual visit to Maryville College, fifteen miles from Knoxville, Tennessee, one discovers the 1950 Fine Arts Building. Amidst a jumble of buildings, whose indeterminate character leaves no lasting impression as significant architecture, the design stands out as an authentic rendering of hard-edge, flat-roof, steel-frame, glass-paned linearity—no compromises with, or references to, earlier traditional styles. About the same time, at Indiana University, a new student dining hall asserts and announces Modern's arrival at a public institution where architectural imagination had not yet advanced as far as the curriculum being offered or the quality of research and community service.

Cause and effect? Critic Frank G. Lopez (1950) proposed that "Familiarity breeds acceptance." Yesterday's surprise designs, i.e., Modern, "scarcely causes a raised eyebrow today, particularly since the war." Retrospectively, though America had come of age politically, and its ascendancy as a world leader in the plastic arts was increasingly manifest, higher education did not rush to adopt the mantle of Modern architecture. Some of this reluctance was the simple fact that many of the first Modern campus buildings were not well executed. Experimental detailing, construction practices atypical for the region, an unusual mix of materials—all these real-life factors affected construction quality and design receptivity. Sophisticated judgment was not required to recognize a bumbling Modern campus building.

FOWLER ELEMENTARY SCHOOL, FRESNO, CALIFORNIA, 1938. FRANKLIN AND KUMP, JR. ARCHITECTS. *(top) The conventional ornamented, stylistic school gives way to a new vocabulary of rooms and materials. Modern architecture with its openness and simplicity would seem to be welcomed and pleasing in the doldrums of the Depression. Lower cost than traditional designs was a secondary justification. Significantly, Kump would later design that extraordinary engagement of buildings and landscapes at Foothills Community College.*

EXPERIMENTAL PUBLIC SCHOOL, LOS ANGELES BOARD OF EDUCATION, 1939. RICHARD NEUTRA. *(bottom) Thought by some to be a "radical imposition on teachers and staff," the project was admired pedagogically for its elimination of fixed seating, corridors, and stairways. Hundreds of schools constructed in the post–World War II boom emulated many of Neutra's expressions of Modern architecture.*

MARYVILLE COLLEGE, FINE ARTS CENTER, 1950. SCHWIEKER AND ELTING. *(top) Flat roof, utilitarian, unadorned, with an unmistaken resemblance to schoolhouse architecture. There were no attempts to harmonize the building with nearby structures. The design was a declarative sentence: a curriculum devoted to the arts should be sheltered in a building that itself is a work of Modern art. Such occurring in the hinterlands when it did is one of the features of American higher education: an unexpected bubbling to the surface of designs audacious for their time and place. (Source: Maryville College)*

ROGERS II DORMITORY DINING HALL, INDIANA UNIVERSITY, 1946. *(bottom) Designed by Burns and James as a graduate student dining hall, the concrete-slab, cement block painted exterior, aluminum-frame windows, and protruding flat, hard-edge roof are the signatures of early Modern. An opening day brochure stated these "were some of the finest student housing units to be found anywhere—scientifically planned for maximum health and comfort. The dining hall, a popular social center is the last word in modern construction." Noted the Indianapolis Star Magazine, "the days of drab, dull dormitories are on their way out if Indiana University's Rogers II is any indication. It looks more like an expensive, sea-side resort hotel." (Source: Indiana University)*

ROYCE HALL, UNIVERSITY OF CALIFORNIA, LOS ANGELES (C. 1927). *(right) "Cramped relic of medieval picturesqueness" or not, the building symbolizes the confidence of a rising public university. Stylistic connotations aside, the spatila qualities and textured surfaces are a delight in an environment of sanitized second-rate Modern buildings. A noble building, of weight and consequence as a period piece.*

MUNDANE, MALADROIT CAMPUS BUILDINGS. *(below) When cheapened by expediency and indifference, they cast a long shadow on the Modern's receptivity and longevity as a style celebrating the expansion of American higher education. The paltry landscape and awkward site development are an indictable offense, if such were subject to enforcable laws and regulations.*

ST. BENEDICT'S COLLEGE, ATCHINSON, KANSAS. *(facing page, top and bottom) Fine traditional and firm Modern. (Source: St. Benedict's College)*

Equally disheartening were the feeble attempts at landscape, in the beginning, that is, for later works would be magnificent representations of this communal art. Diffidently, apologetically, at the launch of Modern, A. R. Nichols, ASLA (1931) stated: "America has learned to build beautiful and efficient school buildings. She is, however, still in the process of learning to place these buildings in a proper setting...missing is landscape development...the opportunity for mental recreation...the creation of an environment that reflects the desire for beauty in all things." Two decades later, Garrett Eckbo would stake out the landscape architect's province, assistance in the creation of the "unified picture or environmental experience, a completely synthesized composite of all physical elements as they are seen together at one or more times." The ideal of composite, the blending of landscapes and buildings, will be examined later as a major factor in defining campus architecture.

The idea that a Modern building was "an instrument of education, a machine for learning" also stirred fears about its intrinsic merits as a style for campuses that gave special regard to and promoted traditional values and routines through architecture. How tenacious was the hold of tradition when the professional literature and practice were encouraging a design journey whose destination had not yet been fully identified? At St. Benedict's College, Atchinson, Kansas, conventional Tudor Gothic had fostered and furthered the institution's ideals. The College's 1910 administration building, with its sculptured facade, could be read by the initiated as being the essence of collegiate life. The carved figures represented "scholarly monks, a host of whom had distinguished themselves in the fields of arts and sciences." Whereas these gestures to history informed the earlier design, the footsteps of the Modern could be heard in the 1930 campus expansion.

The dichotomy and tension of recognizing modern technology and materials and the holding power of symbolic values, architecturally expressed, comes into view at St. Benedict's with a clarity that exposes the uncertainty implicit in seeking a new design direction. The dean responsible for guiding the College's new construction (1929) urged a "blending of the best features of modern methods...with the chief characteristics of the different periods, retaining as much as possible their original symbolic significance." The College informed its public that the designs were "wall-bearing construction. ...All floor slabs are of reinforced concrete. ...The roofs are all of steel and tile...all interior door frames are steel...hot water heating...plumbing and piping arranged for accessibility. ...The aim throughout the building was to reduce maintenance to a minimum and assure perfect comfort in

UNIVERSITY OF MIAMI, 1945. ROBERT LAW WEED, ARCHITECTS. *(facing page, top) The first post–World War II American campus constructed extensively in the Modern architectural style. (Source: University of Miami)*

SAINT JOHN'S UNIVERSITY, COLLEGEVILLE, MINNESOTA, STUDENT DORMITORY, 1953. MARCEL BREUER AND HAMILTON SMITH. *(facing page, bottom) From semitropical Florida to cold winter Minnesota the studied, white geometric facades were recognizably Modern architecture. Breuer's doorway was a masterwork of simple materials composed like a bas-relief, a sculptural beauty of light and shadow captured in Shin Koyama's photo. Images such as these were published around the world, accelerating the interest in and acceptance of the canon as appropriate for college and university buildings. (Source: Marcel Breuer and Hamilton Smith)*

all seasons." The massiveness of the structure was intended to embody the ideas of "defense, safety, permanency." The exterior expression was to be arranged as a three-dimensional case study of "the ideals, aspirations, and the culture dominant at the period of their construction." Medieval models could rationalize quixotic design decisions. Wrote the College's representative, in explaining unique aspects of the 1930 scheme, "in earlier times...residence quarters for the retainers, the workmen, and the artisans...were usually constructed from the left-over material, which was poorer in quality and in architectural design than the main buildings." Thus the use of exterior brick was rationalized in the designs, "of the extreme north wing, the quarters for the kitchen attendants."

Within three decades historicism was on the shelf. Benedictine institutions such as Saint John's University (Collegeville, Minnesota) were truly building in the style of the time. The Atchinson campus, now Benedictine College, itself soon after had a reasonable version of Modern wrapped around "one of the largest Catholic under-graduate libraries in the country...with a rare books collection that is the envy of any on the east coast."

Calming the agitated, and espousing the new at the time of transition, an influential publication indicated that the question of style (traditional versus Modern) was "not a question of glorifying the functional aspects. ...Harmony among campus buildings is not a matter of repetition of existing forms and details, but may be achieved by skillful handling of materials, texture, color, and siting...contrast can be an asset to many a dull campus—particularly when the ivy sheds its leaves." While the metaphor was botanically unlikely, the idea of simple Modern being an antidote for dull Georgian and dismal Gothic gained acceptance, especially when the distance between good and bad traditional architecture was palpably evident, though there were not yet sufficient Modern buildings to set critical standards and expectations.

Economies in construction were a factor in acceptance, as noted earlier. Professional journals argued that a "building lacking the complex surface ornament of Collegiate Gothic costs relatively less" than its Modern counterpart. Praising Philip Johnson's designs for the new Trinity College campus (1952), the treasurer saw the project "whipping high building costs without sacrificing values of function, quality and beauty." Ironically, the St. Benedict's 1930 scheme was defended as an organic design. Like its medieval counterpart it had design features and sufficient architectural complexity to permit starting or stopping construction "at such time or times as (the building committee) finances dictated" without the loss of design integrity. Like minimal sculpture, some of the better Modern buildings did not have this inherent quality. Marcel Breuer's work (see p. 9) seems complete as built, and would seem less if some piece were missing. Neutra's and similar work were not so constrained.

To reiterate a point worth making again, the economics of Modern had a promotional appeal that is not to be lost in an historic appreciation of aesthetic philosophy. Neutra demonstrated that convincingly in an astonishing group of 150 schoolhouses he designed for the Commonwealth of Puerto Rico from 1943 to 1945. There, the cost of simulating pseudo-Spanish Colonial architecture was impractical and imprudent. Neutra's concepts for utilizing standardized building components beneficially matched need and resources. He also divided the educational program into modularized spaces and configured these into elements which could be assembled "in different arrangements for different sites." His philosophy, models, and drawings inspired those working at the new site for the University of Miami. "Uncorseted by yesterday's bi-axial symmetry, (the University) was able to develop a site plan suitable for contemporary architectural treatment," editorialized the *Architectural Forum* (1945), thus bringing into being the first American campus constructed extensively in the Modern style.

EMERGENCE, DECLINE, AND ENIGMA

A nation that has many new buildings to erect and plenty of money to spend upon them is sure to develop characteristic architecture. It may be good or bad or simply commonplace, but nothing can prevent its being clearly expressive of the tastes, culture, ideals, and capacities of the Nation. The style of the new buildings will be an index of its artistic taste; the purposes for which they are erected will reveal dominant interests and illustrate the character of its civilization....Recent foreign observers have expressed amazement at the magnitude, number, buildings, equipment, endowments of our universities....No one, indeed who studies the record can fail to be impressed.

A. D. Hamlin
Architectural Record, *1906*

...these persons will admit that of the money that has been spent and is being spent throughout this country for college buildings, but a small portion goes to produce those of real architectural worth, nay even of practical convenience...how heavily our institutions are encumbered with archaic buildings, poorly designed and even worse built, monumental annoyances, the kind of blot upon the scene that evokes the unholy impulse in some secret breast to pray for fire.

Charles Z. Klauder and Herbert C. Wise
College Architecture in America, *1929*

On many campuses where modern architecture has already taken root, the new buildings have been received enthusiastically by the people who use them most— students and faculty. This apparent ease of acceptance on the part of the academic community augers well for the future. If at times the pace of architectural progress seems painfully slow, encouragement may be had from the thought that today's college students are the donors, trustees, alumni, and clients of tomorrow.

Harold D. Hauf
Architectural Record, *1950*

A group of buildings at Baylor University typifies the national scene after World War II, as American higher education began a surge that increased enrollments fivefold, created more than a thousand new campuses, and added about a hundred thousand new buildings to the campus inventory. During that surge, inexorably, countrywide, the novelty called Modern became the quotidian style, the acceptable norm, and, having run its course, made room in attitude and appraisal for a later generation to devise new ideas and concepts. Early Modern purged the system. Middle Modern, with its move away from sanitary surfaces and interest in textured

PAT NEFF HALL, BAYLOR UNIVERSITY. *(top)*
*A reasonable interpretation of collegiate
Georgian. (Source: Baylor University)*

D. K. MARTIN HALL, BAYLOR UNIVERSITY.
*(bottom) Feeble attempts at using the Modern
idioms. (Source: Baylor University)*

COLLINS HALL, BAYLOR UNIVERSITY. *(facing
page, left) The style invalidated, expediency
reigns. (Source: Baylor University)*

**NEW SCHOOL FOR SOCIAL RESEARCH,
1930.** *(facing page, right) Joseph Urban's
landmark structure, the first important Modern
higher education building in the United States.
Not all were happy with the result. Philip
Johnson thought it " an illusion of a building in
the International Style rather than a building
resulting from a genuine application of the new
principles."*

THE NEW SCHOOL

LOWER-CASE SANS SERIF. *(above) Typography, furnishings, textiles, new designs reinforced the Modern canon, creating in the best projects a memorable visual unity and in the worse cases a sense that severity perhaps rose more from economic necessity than taste.*

BIOLOGY INSTITUTE, UNIVERSITY OF PARIS, 1930. *(right) Germane Debre's exquisite version of Modern architecture, planned collegially, and constructed on a tight site; simple forms, limited materials. A seminal project, overlooked by most historians and commentators, deserving citation as a top-ten significant university design.*

and sculptured effects, demonstrated the range of possibilities. Late Modern, with more elaboration and segmentation of building forms, laid the foundations for today's contemporary campus design and architecture. About this evolution, more will be written later.

At the launch, Baylor and many institutions were an aesthetic vacuum waiting to be filled with something better than the bland and wornout traditional styles which expediency was imposing relentlessly in response to immediate needs for expansion. The University's flagship building, Pat Neff Hall, is a standard and reasonable late-nineteenth-century example of Collegiate Georgian. The design concept was a programmatically sound solution for enclosing general university functions, serene in its composition and secure in its symbolism. In D. K. Martin Hall (1953) the decline is evident in the paste-on treatment of reductive columns to establish symmetry and the brickwork to suggest a visual relationship to the older building. Collins Hall three years later shows the ultimate impoverishment of a once-vibrant architectural form and the indifference to and ignorance of other possibilities both in the United States and abroad. In contrast, Germane Debre's Biology Institute, University of Paris, 1930, stands as a master work of Modern brick architecture and a seminal building in collegial facility planning. Working with a committee of 30 academics, each with unique laboratory requirements (including a constant-temperature laboratory 40 feet underground and roof-top botanical garden), Debre organized the building into a handsomely scaled composition of eight interlocking volumes. The window patterns and simplicity in detailing were harbingers of an aesthetic that would fill the American campuses with thousands of Modern buildings, few better than Debre's.

Though not guided by the architectural equivalent of a Papal bull, it was generally understood that, with Modern, simplification was the new norm. Although some campus buildings were affected by the last gasp of regional, romantic revivalism from the 1920s (Moorish in Florida, Spanish in southwest Texas and California, Neo-Georgian in the Northeast), and forms of Classicism were not disdained, the architectural ideas seeded in journals and museum exhibitions germinated abundantly and pervasively. Peeling and paring decoration, using concrete poured and planked, bolting factory-made porcelain-green panels to steel frames, such modern strokes were understood to have social and cultural meaning—away with the past, welcome the new. And so too, in the parallel arts, figurative wall decor and campus sculpture gave way to abstraction. Textiles abandoned embellishment for linear patterns. The typography used on campus signs dropped serifs for modern type faces. Stuffed sofas and Victorian desks were replaced with Formica and molded plywood Scandinavian furniture. The interior of a dormitory room in the 1960s was as different from the 1930s as was the building that enclosed it.

Kansas State University—a middle-America institution, geographically, intellectually, and culturally—illuminates the shifts in aesthetic attitudes and the resulting changes in built forms over a century. At the beginning of public higher education, schoolhouse architecture was proportionately enlarged for collegiate purposes and encased in cut limestone found in the region. Peaked roofs and doorways were reminiscent of courthouses and libraries of the same vintage and district. A century later we find, on the Kansas State campus for example, a cluster of buildings with flat roofs, and hard-edge building forms, with varying combinations of solid masonry walls and glass in idioms recognizably the Modern era. Some of the Kansas State buildings are compromised by stylistic indeterminacy, i.e., designs not sufficiently independent of the earlier generation, nor complete statements of the new idiom. Fortunately, the use of cut limestone straddles a century of campus design; the materials were a placemarking gesture that connected the generations symbolically and visually.

Materials bind and separate time and aesthetics in architectural design. At William and Mary College brick architecture is the visual link connecting generations of buildings in variegated interpretations of the founder's Georgian architecture. Modular, baked clay is thus the defining component of the campus design. Southward, at Duke University, with a tweedy textured stone associated with Collegiate Gothic, provides the palette for continuity in exterior expressions. Westward, in Albuquerque, New Mexico, an adobelike surface gives buildings at the University of New Mexico a distinctive design accent. On the Pacific rim, at Stanford University, the red tile roofs and amber surfaces of the first buildings serve as the design continuum for structures that are visually differentiated by function and architectural taste at their inception.

New life for old forms has many attractions for institutions devoted to continuity and change. But well selected materials alone, of course, do not determine an

Nineteenth-century Kansas courthouse. *(right)*

Nineteenth-century University of Kansas. *(below) Courthouses and universities are cut from the same cloth but stacked and arranged individually in response to function and the architect's determination to give each a desirable distinction in the style of the era. (Source: University of Kansas)*

Nineteenth-century Kansas State University. *(facing page, top)*

1960 Kansas State University. *(facing page, bottom) Roof lines and walls, from complexity to simplicity, signaling changes in building technology and aesthetic forms. Cut-stone provides the melding, merging, generation-binding architectural element, inducing a memorable sense of place.*

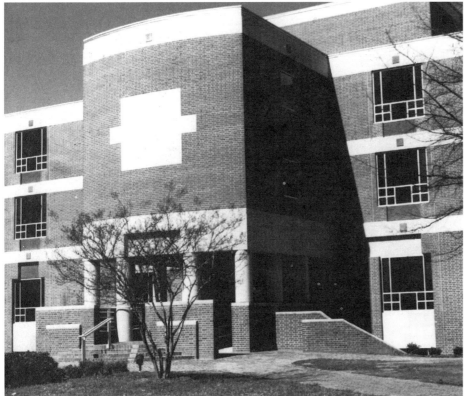

DETAIL, WILLIAM AND MARY UNIVERSITY. *(facing page, top)* *Seventeenth-century design, possibly Christopher Wren.*

DETAIL, STADIUM GATE, WILLIAM AND MARY UNIVERSITY, 1930. *(facing page, bottom)*

DETAIL, STUDENT HOUSING, WILLIAM AND MARY UNIVERSITY, 1970. *(above)*

DETAIL, LIBRARY EXPANSION, WILLIAM AND MARY UNIVERSITY, 1980. *(left)* *Brick architecture, with varying interpretations and homage to the seventeenth-century icon building, provides a fascinating spectrum of changes in taste and design direction. The aesthetic impulses satisfied architecturally over the years are instructive in their variety and continuity; some solutions stale and others refreshing.*

DETAIL, TOWER ELEMENT, MUHLENBERG COLLEGE LIBRARY. *(right) With the opening of a new library in 1991, this 1920s homage to educational values and traditions has been recently redesigned as an administrative office and classroom building. (Source: Muhlenberg College)*

TOM TOWER, CHRIST CHURCH COLLEGE, OXFORD, SEVENTEENTH CENTURY. *(bottom) Designed by Christopher Wren, the form and detailing have inspired numerous renditions of Collegiate Gothic, that which Matlack Prices fairly called the "illusions of the charm and historic association of scholastic architecture." From Princeton's greens to the swamps of Houston, Texas (Rice University), to the heights overlooking Puget Sound (University of Washington), the style's advocates and designers constructed extraordinary architecture-as-stagecraft. For site composition, facades, enticing spaces inside and out, few Modern or contemporary designs equal Collegiate Gothic tactile beauty.*

adequate architectural solution. Bricks can be piled up in abstract forms or arranged to meet the expected canon of a traditional style. Once, Collegiate Georgian was regulated "as that of a sonnet or a Shakespearean stanza, and the artist has liberty in only certain directions, and must not violate the laws." Audacious designers, playing with the forms or in battle with creative urges, will tweak the laws (such as they are) for different ends, sometimes in faithful emulation of traditional architecture and at other times as gestures to the past. As depicted in the sample of William and Mary facades, given a range of buildings constructed over several centuries in brick, coded and connected to the tradition, there will be winners and losers.

The Kansas and William and Mary buildings are indicative of a cycle of influence and exchange that occurs periodically in designing campus buildings. Ideas from the past, or near present, are summoned to serve and minister the future, summonses extraordinarily rich in their physical texture and semiotics. These ideas appeal as documents of aspiration and cultural attitudes, such as Muhlenberg College's version of Christopher Wren's Tom Tower, Christ Church, Oxford. Here a reverential architectural style pays homage to values linked with historic educational institutions and their physical forms. Arguably, the interpretations of traditional styles rise and become popular because they are honest manifestations of their period and values, then decline in critical regard when sentiment more than purpose keeps the style in favor, and then rise again in revival and reinterpretation. The second resurrection may be an earnest attempt to provide visual continuity, a disdain for the current situation, or, retrogressively, a cautionary sentimental reaction:

> *And always keep a hold of Nurse*
> *For fear of finding something worse.*
>
> H. Belloc

Modern architecture was proclaimed as sentiment-free; *honesty* was its intended essence. On first appearance some feared its iconoclastic novelty "which has caused such havoc elsewhere and which produces such undesired results wherever its tendencies are being felt today," editorialized *Architectural Record.* At the same time, 1925, other magazine commentators were inspired by Modern "buildings with severe lines attained along with what seem to be economical uses of material and labor." Like traditional styles that had crossed the Atlantic—Georgian, Gothic, Spanish Renaissance—the Modern idiom could be and was reinterpreted in homage to the originator's values, with varying degrees of honesty and sentimentality. The transposition seems manifest in Mies van der Rohe's dialog with glass and steel at the Illinois Institute of Technology (1950), Philip Johnson's variant (University of Saint Thomas, 1957), Arne Jacobson's rendition (Saint Catherine College, Oxford, 1960), Bush-Brown, Gailey & Heffernan's Library (Georgia Institute of Technology, 1957), and Murphy and Mackey's Monsanto Laboratory of the Life Sciences (Washington University, 1965). All metamorphise a design theme beautifully introduced by Le Corbusier and Pierre Jenneret for the Swiss Student Hostel, Paris 1932. Here, as James Gibbs did for Collegiate Georgian in the eighteenth century, Corbu established a vocabulary of forms and materials (masonry framing,

Swiss student hostel, University of Paris, 1932. Le Corbusier and Pierre Jenneret. *(facing page, top)*

Saint Catherine College, Oxford, housing, 1960. Arne Jacobson. *(facing page, bottom)*

Illinois Institute of Technology, classroom, 1950. Mies van der Rohe. *(below)*

University of Saint Thomas, classroom, 1957. Philip Johnson. *(bottom)* *(Source: University of Saint Thomas; photographer: Frank L.. Miller)*

GEORGIA INSTITUTE OF TECHNOLOGY, LIBRARY, 1957. BUSH-BROWN, GAILEY AND HEFFERNAN. *(facing page, top) (Source: Georgia Institute of Technology)*

WASHINGTON UNIVERSITY, LABORATORY OF LIFE SCIENCES, 1965. MURPHY AND MACKEY. *(facing page, bottom) (Source: Washington University)*

VANDERBILT UNIVERSITY, PSYCHOLOGY LABORATORY AND CLASSROOM, 1987. THE STUBBINS ASSOCIATES, INC. *(above) Gone by the late 1980s were the flat, geometric facades of early and middle Modern. Leading architects favored designs in context. In this instance aspects of the older Vanderbilt buildings were utilized, including rusticated base and cornice and deep shadowed punctured brick wall. (Source: Vanderbilt University; photographer: Bill Kingsley)*

LYCOMING COLLEGE, SCIENCE BUILDING, 1990. HAYLES LARGE ARCHITECTS. *(left) The modulated structural bay is broken at the end to give the facade a pronounced inflection. Hard edges are softened. (Source: Lycoming College)*

minimal detailing, and the calibrated curtain wall) used worldwide in twentieth-century college and university architecture. When honesty faded into sentiment, some of the later work did not have the vitality of the originals. And as a style, recent award-winning college and university work suggests its current displacement by other idioms.

Sentiment versus honesty fuels the age-long debate between those who are content with continuance and those itchy for something new, advocacies that color discernment and animate campus decision making. The paradox of seeking approval for being among the first in line (and thus being a valuable three-dimensional cultural statement, regardless of execution) versus being an adroit example (but a quotidian version of an older style) gives many accounts of how campus buildings come into being an enigmatic flavor uniquely their own. Ever at play are human instincts and judgments. The more controversial the building, and however praised on first arrival, the more likely it seems "destined, as the vacillating reputations of buildings before it can testify, to fall in and out of favor," said critic Joseph Hudnut. Compare Lowell House (Harvard University, 1938) and Canady House (Harvard University, 1978). Lowell fills the Cambridge skyline and streetscape with exultant Collegiate Georgian—a tribute to Colonial times. The cupola, fenestration patterns, red brick and white wood, the massing, the substance, and the detailing look attractive in all seasons. Canady House is a praiseworthy example of stripped-down Modern, with a severity so stark that it might be argued it comes closer to the Puritan values of Harvard's founders than the splendid stagecraft architecture which is Lowell House.

Lowell is sentiment, Canady is honesty. In a collegial setting who determines the preferment, and why? Trustees, donors, review committees, staff—the process and procedures of collegiality and shared governance—give considerable time and effort to vetting designs as they evolve from a preliminary interpretation of the program to construction drawings. Those influencing design decisions are usually aware of precedence in styles and their succession. Abstracting and categorizing an enormous group of buildings constructed the past 40 years, the discerning observer, seeking some order, should be able to see that form follows function, ferment follows form, and fusion follows ferment, i.e., the progression from early Modern to late Modern. At the start of the chain we have simple buildings dictated by programmatic requirements and an adherence to Modern's initial credo. A search and desire for a more elaborate visual expression (ferment) brings into being buildings with textured surfaces and sculptured effects. Late Modern (i.e., fusion) recalls the sanitized surfaces of early Modern and/or seeks and expresses in shapes and forms selected aspects—but it is not a literal emulation—of traditional buildings and materials. Fusion irks purists, is dismissed by critics who see it as a failure to advance a new aesthetic, and delights connoisseurs of the idiosyncratic. Ever present among the disdainful, at each stage, is the expectation that some larger design concept will eventually mediate Hudnut's "discordant notes of abandoned trails of different kinds of architecture" or failing in that regard that building additions, or greater density, would obscure the tours de force that later generations find tours de farce.

Three libraries, each about a decade apart, help visualize these differences. The Crosby Library (Gonzaga University) is a standard version of early Modern with

LOWELL HOUSE, HARVARD UNIVERSITY, 1929. *(left) Stagecraft Collegiate Georgian produced by Coolidge, Shepley, Bulfinch and Abbott and incorporating centuries of nostalgia and sentiment for an architectural setting that commands the Cambridge skyline.*

CANADY HALL, HARVARD UNIVERSITY, 1972. EZRA EHRENKRANTZ. *(below) An honest building in expressing time and technology and in fitting into the Harvard Yard's brick architecture. In the background, another essay in sentimentality, Memorial Hall, 1866 to 1878. An ambitious project, an exceptional building, now being restored for honest reasons (the best architecture of its period and the scene of extraordinary historic events, meetings, and personalities).*

its plain surfaces and three joined boxes: the major functional space, the rectangular and pronounced entrance component, and the utilitarian enclosure plopped on a flat roof. The Clark University Library disaggregates a number of internal functions and expresses them in an exterior organization recognizably not traditional and not early Modern. As ferment, this example continues to be a heady brew. The Kenyon College Library makes a convincing gesture to Collegiate Gothic and Modern antecedents in its fusion of shapes, smooth surfaces, and exterior materials. All three buildings are part of a planetary system called *libraries*. Functions and internal space organization are comparable, but each is as different perceptibly as Saturn, Venus, and Mars.

Does the architecture of higher education follow some logical order of cause and effect, which if stated and understood could sharpen discernment, give direction for fostering new architecture, and help establish the aesthetic ground rules for conserving an architectural heritage worth protection? When does it become obvious that a style has lost its vitality? Surveying the scene in 1926, architect James W. O'Connor was convinced that "important buildings of today, certainly, cannot look as banal or as absurd fifty years from now as similar buildings of fifty years ago look today. It is more, too, than a mere matter of changing fashions. We sincerely believe that our architecture is better intrinsically than ever before." Of the projects he cited in the *Architectural Forum*, none would be listed these days as buildings worth direct emulation. All—with their studied massing, generous configurations, and textured detailing—are worthy of preservation and reuse as legacy buildings.

GONZAGA UNIVERSITY, LIBRARY. *(right) By the 1960s the early Modern boxlike architecture had achieved status and recognition as the suitable expression for a central campus building. Quotidian versions could be found coast-to-coast; the familiar had not yet declined into disfavor. (Source: Gonzaga University)*

CLARK UNIVERSITY, LIBRARY. *(facing page, top) In this iconoclastic work from the 1970s, architect John Johanson disaggregated forms and features, keeping the simplicity of materials but with aesthetic ferment that brought into question other early Modern's tenets. The principle of form following function was endangered by idiosyncratic designs. Architecturally Pandora's box was opened. Modern passed into history as its first advocates lost status as leading-edge designers. (Source: Clark University)*

KENYON COLLEGE, LIBRARY, 1980. SHEPLEY, BULFINCH, RICHARDSON AND ABBOTT. *(facing page, bottom) Designers and clients calmed the ferment with designs that combined the simplicity of early Modern and the visual character of adjacent campus buildings, i.e., architecture in context. The fusion was an appealing antidote to the severity of early Modern and the extreme expressions of fermented designs. (Source: Shepley, Bulfinch, Richardson and Abbott)*

Good design counts. Good designs endure. Illuminating then are the side-by-side examples, maladroit extensions to older buildings, where the mantle of being Modern is insufficient to disguise an opportunity to join new and old with harmony and subtlety that does honor to both.

A series of buildings at the University of Washington, Seattle demonstrates the hazards of designs inaugurated with laudable aims and doomed by ineptitude in handling the canons, and the aftermath, when better hands and eyes are engaged to elevate building design to architecture. Illustrated on page 31 is the University's 1920s art building. A sentimental rendition of collegiate Gothic, the structure is pleasantly proportioned and detailed, textured, intelligently inserted on its site, with a welcoming portal—characteristic of a good campus building irrespective of style.

Sircd in the late 1950s, the University's drama-TV building encapsulates a relatively new art form in an unambiguously Modern building. The design was intended to signal progress in both curriculum and architecture. The signal is strong in rejecting collegiate Gothic, in repulsing faux detailing from monastic sources, in flattening the roof, in sharpening the hard-edge corners of the facades. It is adventuresome in attempting to express visual connections with the textured brick fabric, white trim, and the abstracted Gothic window. The awkward massing, the ill-proportioned and ungainly placement of windows and doors—seemingly factory components, not crafted—and the meager front door are clues as to why these kinds of interpretations of Modern gained few enthusiasts for its continuance, once the style served as a purge for traditional styles.

More convincing, better architecture is Edward Larrabee Barnes's Allen Library (1991)—high-quality fusion, with its shapes and forms and subtle masonry detailing. The front door is easy to find. The tilting wing is an iconic touch,

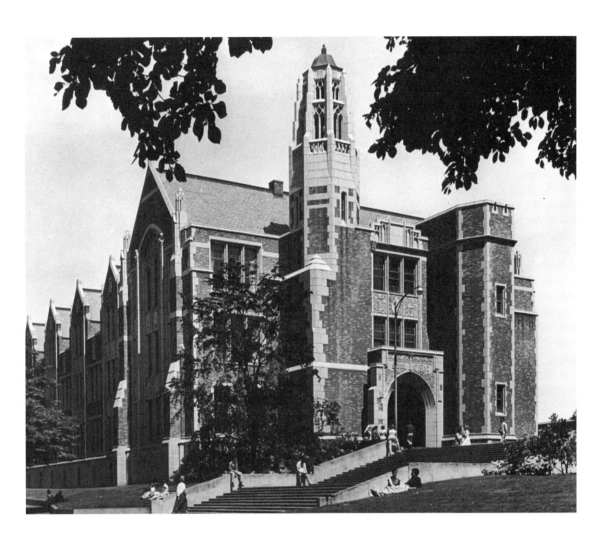

THE ALLEGORY OF UNCERTAINTY. *(facing page)* *A functionally reasonable building solution, burdened with an architectural expression of new and old in a severe contrasting conjunction that favors neither.*

UNIVERSITY OF WASHINGTON, SEATTLE, 1920S ART BUILDING. *(above)* *High-style Collegiate Gothic.*

UNIVERSITY OF WASHINGTON, SEATTLE, 1950S DRAMA-TV BUILDING. *(left)* *An honest gesture of early Modern but dull and unconvincing in execution.*

UNIVERSITY OF WASHINGTON, SEATTLE, LIBRARY, 1991. EDWARD LARRABEE BARNES. *(top) Shapes, forms, and subtle masonry detailing combine attractive visual features from the collegiate Gothic and the simplicity and directness of the Modern canon. (Source: Edward Larrabee Barnes; photographer: Mary Levin)*

UNIVERSITY OF WASHINGTON, SEATTLE, PHYSICS/ASTRONOMY, 1994. CESAR PELLI. *(bottom) The vocabulary of contemporary design—disaggregated but linked forms, with materials reminiscent of older campus buildings—the ensemble becoming an emphatic one-only design. (Source: Cesar Pelli; photographer: Mary Levin)*

AUDITORIUM, NEW YORK UNIVERSITY, c. 1957. MARCEL BREUER. *(top)* *(Source: Marcel Breuer)*
AUDITORIUM, EASTERN MICHIGAN STATE UNIVERSITY, c. 1957. *(bottom)* *Architecture versus a building, both in the Modern architecture idiom: simplicity in materials and hard-edge designs, but evidencing the visual differences between a building (quotidian and dull) and architecture (capricious and vibrant). Topographic changes give Breuer's work an additional panache, which is no excuse for the Eastern Michigan vacuous site and building composition.*

which appears in many campus buildings as a signal, if not symbol, of late-twentieth-century architecture. Cesar Pelli's physics/astronomy building (1994) relies less on shapes that recall the past and more on materials. In both instances the University has achieved a desired goal: buildings uniquely shaped by program, distinctive in their design features but joined in a family resemblance to other University structures.

Contemporary campus architecture (a phrase we apply to recent works from the mid-1980s onward) struggles with finding solutions of this quality. On one hand, there is an anxious affection for sentimental but skillful interpretations of an accomplished past. On the other hand, there is an attraction, but ambivalence, for encouraging honest attempts to pioneer a new route. With the winds of critical regard and institutional choice blowing from many directions, the ship called decision making needs a rudder. We offer one, recalling and illustrating two versions of a university auditorium built in the early 1960s in the Modern idiom. At New York University, Marcel Breuer's concept scintillated with the forms and materials associated with the style. Coterminously, another version of a Modern auditorium at Eastern Michigan University gave evidence that any style rendered without skill is a design to be rejected, however enticing its doctrinal basis or patron's bias toward encouraging a new direction.

SELECTIONS AND EMPHASES

The shuttlecock of continuity and change in campus architecture, in response to program requirements, cultural attitudes, and aesthetic values, weaves an interesting and generally multitextured fabric on most campuses. Through collegial processes the dreams and ambitions for a striving architecture are often settled by requisite matters such as funding and communal tastes—the fate of typical campus architecture. Intellectually, higher education depends on balancing the forces of continuity and change, a fundamental we will revisit in defining a campus architecture rooted in reality and imagination. We will see the results of the warp and woof, continuity and change, in the grand schemes, individual projects, and the fragments and pieces that constitute memorable campus architecture.

Understandably, in our overview and selected projects, judgments must hop, skip, and jump through time. What was the design intention at genesis? What is the current assessment? What do the cited examples offer for the future? While scanning a spectrum of college and university buildings, our answers to these leading questions may be different, instance by instance. Where answers are congruous (good then and good now), the diadem of regard and respect should be apparent in the commentary and captions. In the main, we prefer that groups of campus buildings be likened to an orchestra, not a collection of instruments. Solos should sustain and carry the score forward, not be an interruption and occasion for expressing technical skill. However, there are times and places for the virtuosic, the startling and unexpected, which genius sometimes evokes to shake up the mundane and expected. We will suggest when, where, and how such agitation might be welcomed.

Unquestionably, campuses exhibit an inherent capacity for growth, renewal, and revitalization; elevating, ennobling, enlarging, enriching ideas and interests.

"Gathered here are the forces which move humanity and make history...conspicuous monuments...that mark the progress of civilization...that fit new thoughts to new conditions," wrote landscape architect Ernest E. Walker, Jr. (1936) in an early appreciation applicable to today's circumstances. Walker advocated an understanding of the "topographic individuality of the site" and "the position of all objects of natural and historic interest within...generating points round which (an) ultimate scheme of development will crystallize...the perfect orchestration of Nature, Art, and Science." Good architecture has been doomed by inattention to Walker's dictum. So too, of significant consequence in the robust years of our focal period, were attitudes about site development, especially landscapes. "Consult the genius of the place...and as you work, it designs," wrote Alexander Pope in an expository poem with advice that remains cogent and relevant for all seeking appropriate designs. Illustrated on page 37 is a lesson worth noting. At the University of Denver, University Hall and University Library, two fine, late-nineteenth-century designs, have remained awkwardly positioned and inadequately landscaped from their opening date, to the detriment of the overall campus design and their individual building character. In contrast, genial and expectant, the faculty and students are shown gathered to march up the hill to the new temple of learning superbly worked into the terrain, Kentucky State College, 1911. By the end of the century the ambitious and well-sited architecture had a settled look and a commanding presence. Here is a fine image of place—location, building, legend—which the Hilltoppers now celebrate, eponymic, on T-shirts and campus banners. The architectural command? Meld structure and site with a sensitive examination of how each will contribute to the betterment of the other.

As a theme articulated more fully later, buildings and greenery intermeshed is the defining characteristic of campus architecture. An honored tradition in the evolution of campus development—indeed the essence of great college and university architecture, the occasional neglect of this basic principle has diminished design concepts and projects otherwise commendable. Landscapes and terrain are, or should be, consequential influences on the architectural design. No ground is neutral, all have some tangible quality worth finding and using. Generally building sites are accepted as they are and integrated into the overall design or mediated. The smaller the campus the more likely the latter will require careful determinations, there being less space to maneuver or carve out grandiose prospects and landscape features.

In either instance, large campuses or small, one witnessed and remembers two polar approaches to the challenges and opportunities of site development at the time when higher education was expanding and Modern architecture was its servant: those who visualized their designs as essentially free-standing objects, and those who saw them as being situated in some larger and articulated milieu. The attitudes can be seen in how designers worked up their ideas in models and drawings. Looking back, should we be surprised that air-brush drawings produced a building concept as light-weight as the medium or that certain popular and prevailing stylized site drawings failed to capture and express the continuum of terrain and building—the specificity of place, that good architecture possesses in every style, period, and region? Building designs judged best of their times in the 1950s

Opening Day, Kentucky State College, 1911. *(right) The college assembled to march up the hill and to celebrate its new building. The melding of site and structure produced a landmark design and provided the institution with its image and institutional eponym: The Hilltoppers.*

Kentucky State College. *(below) Landscape matured, the building and site are now engaged as campus architecture in a satisfying site solution and service as institutional symbol.*

University of Denver, c. 1890. *(facing page, top)*
Ferrum Junior College, c. 1960. *(facing page, bottom) Splendid and dismal building designs doomed by indifference or uninformed site sensitivity.*

UNIVERSITY HALL   No.298   UNIVERSITY LIBRARY

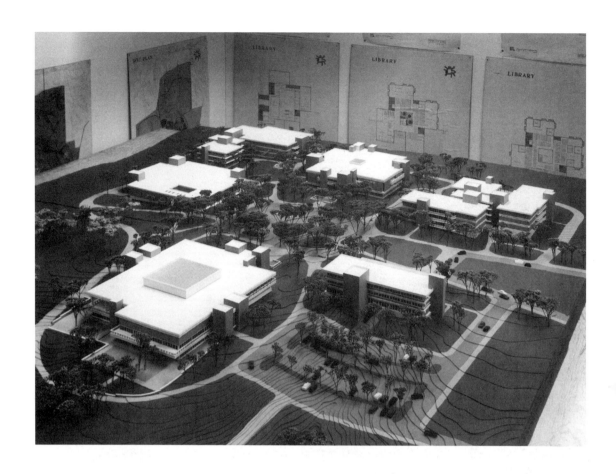

and 1960s were studied works in all dimensions. Leading offices encouraged collaboration between all who might affect the outcome: campus planners, facility programmers, building design, site engineers, landscape architects. Later, informed by the environmental movement of the 1970s, the integrative view of building and site design endures as a basic principle.

The issue of tools, techniques, and collaborative efforts that assist design conceptualization is no second-tier consideration given the arrival and application of computerization. For as has happened occasionally in all architectural periods, a fascination with the modes of expression may warp a designer's interest in problem solving and generate schemes which are enticing as graphic art and exterior expression but devoid of connection to specific needs, site, and heritage. Worrisome—with the advent of computer-assisted design—is the architectural equivalent of the sound-bite, a few exterior gimmicks that convey a recognition of a fad and fashion at the expense of and as substitute for a more reasoned and comprehensive design analysis and outcome.

However, computerization offers an exciting potential for quickly melding data and information from many sources. Intricate and physically complicated campus buildings can be modeled to determine, evaluate, and then revise inexpensively the detailing and spatial relationship of building components previously left unexamined, given the fees and time available in typical office practice. Graphic systems can merge site reality with the designer's imaginative future through three-dimensional pictorialization that heretofore was almost inexpressible. Multiple explorations of alternatives, using the speed and complexity of the computer, become especially meaningful for mature campuses with their rich fabric subject to alteration with in-fill projects, the clarification of circulation routes, and the reshaping

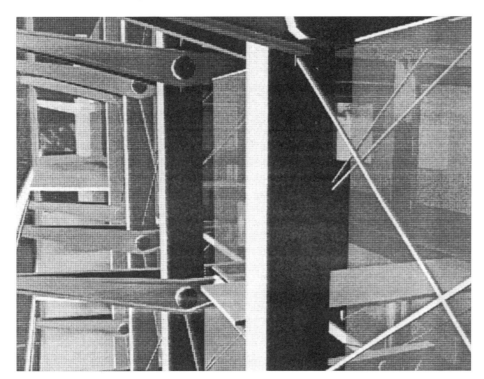

THREE-DIMENSIONAL REPRESENTATION 1950 TO 1960. *(facing page, top and bottom) The better architectural firms were able to help their clients and members of their design teams to see and evaluate the three-dimensional consequences of site character and its landscape potential. Disillusioning and disabling were feeble attempts to display such relationships.*

COMPUTER-GENERATED BUILDING DESIGN STUDY, BOSTON ARCHITECTURAL CENTER, 1995. TROY RANDALL. *(left) Plans, section elevations, cut-away views, site arrangements— computer modeling enable the designer to explore an extraordinary range of possibilities and on completion of the design to create presentations that previous media and techniques could not. (Source: Boston Architectural Center)*

of open space patterns. Variations in massing and facade treatment, the simulation of moving through the proposed spaces—all these are within economic reach of the computer-assisted designer. Campus landscapes, too, can be shown in "before" and "after" versions, seemingly real-life.

Whether traditionally drawn or computerized, images of place that communicate and reflect site realities help raise confidence in the project conceptualization, and, as confidence rises, projects get built—within limits, of course. Whether a sensitive handling of topography and a gorgeous landscape would have produced a more graceful setting for the Gerhard Hall, University of Mississippi, or helped other comparable expedient designs, scaleless and forbidding, cannot be ascertained after the fact. But in such instances of dismal and dull architecture, one should never discount the redemptive powers of a building addition, as in the singular and striking physical recreation annex at Middlebury College and the more complicated and ingenuous Carleton College Library expansion.

The core of the current Carleton College Library was constructed in 1955 with a building design and site concept that neither forecasted a desirable trend nor engendered a fondness among those who had to look at and use the building. By 1980, Carleton had risen to the top of the heap nationally among independent, residential colleges, acquiring the "largest collection of books in an undergraduate institution between Ohio and the West Coast," but a collection rapidly disintegrating due to "lack of air-conditioning in the summer (and) dry, uneven heat in the winter." Further, the building was disastrous in terms of heat loss, lighting, leaky roof, improper glazing, the types of functional space available and their relationship to each other, and building circulation. At the front door the physical image of moat and drawbridge, truncated facade, and the visceral sense that structure was slipping down the sloping terrain were additional features earning attention. Given the compelling physical conditions and the necessity of providing reasonable accommodations for a prestigious faculty and highly qualified and motivated student body, the issue of library improvement could not be postponed.

Led by the administration, monitored by a building committee, the library's technical experts conducted and completed programmatic and physical studies that indicated that the existing library could be reconstructed, and with new space become a contemporary library, uncompromised functionally, at less cost than a new building. Of great advantage was the library's central location, and a site that permitted the construction of a new entrance and sandwichlike additions on two sides—redemptive architecture. What once had been a dreary lobby became a dramatic, well-lit public space that gave access to interiors that were rearranged and furnished to "provide an atmosphere that is conducive to study, encourages schol-

SITE REALITY AND CONSEQUENCES.

GERHARD HALL, UNIVERSITY OF MISSISSIPPI, STUDENT HOUSING, C. 1960. *(facing page, top)*
Post–World War II campus buildings often suffered from inadequate site development, though admittedly some would garner no kudos even if well situated and landscaped. (Source: University of Mississippi)

REDEMPTIVE ARCHITECTURE, MIDDLEBURY COLLEGE, 1989. *(facing page, bottom)* Moser, Pilon,
Nelson's sparkling contemporary addition to the bland Memorial Field House. The fitness center's glass walls overlook the nearby play fields and distant views of the Green Mountains. (Source: Middlebury College)

arly pursuits, and fosters the academic excellence that is the primary goal of the College."

The two projects (and others to be cited) illustrate significant changes in attitudes and approaches in architectural design on mature campuses at the end of the twentieth century. In these instances, qualitative improvements not large enough to warrant new building were realized through expansion. The attachments are designed to give relief to the plain and ordinary, to help the larger building work better programmatically, to overcome design or space deficiencies which earlier budget-cutting measures imposed, or to take advantage of a central site for higher utilization. These additions also signal an embracement of a new campus aesthetic that can be unfurled as a banner of institutional progress, that which the British now call "accretional modernism," a revolution in taste that captures the past but does not destroy, as in Graham Gund's radiant solution to Mount Holyoke College's library expansion.

Of the same "redemptive" spirit is Frank Gehry's Information and Computer Sciences Engineering Research facility at the University of California, Irvine (1985), not an addition, but a pivot for turning in a new direction. Gehry's Irvine

CARLETON COLLEGE LIBRARY, 1956. MAGNEY, TUSLER AND SETTER. *(top)* *One of the first college libraries in the Modern style in the Midwest. Three boxes and moat, four floors, cascading down hill; at the time audacious architecture. (Source: Carleton College Archives)*

CARLETON COLLEGE LIBRARY EXPANSION, 1983. SOVIK MATHRE SATHRUM QUANBECK AND DONLYN LYNDON. *(bottom)* *The front door character is dramatically changed with the moat removed, with new space and renovated space bringing the library into the twenty-first century. Brickwork recalls visually other buildings in the vicinity. (Source: Carleton College)*

building can also be read as a historically important dividing line between the last burst of Modern and the profusion of different styles that followed at campuses wanting a change in appearance and canon. Carefully planned as a new campus in 1960, the first stylistic imprint at Irvine was a series of bulky, white concrete structures arranged along spokes that intersected at a central park. As conceptualized by William Periera the sugar-cube building designs were popular in the 1950s coast-to-coast. The Charlotte College (North Carolina) version made great calendar art, a pristine beauty extensively publicized as a striking, honest, declarative rejection of vestiges or homage to traditional styles. Their holding power as an acceptable design, however, proved to be ephemeral.

"Monumental, Parthenon-modern," judged critic Leon Whiteson, condensing the plus and minus of what was considered at Irvine on opening day an architectural triumph. Irvine became a new campus with a distinctive ambiance in a hurry. Seemingly floating in parched greensward, the buildings in the original architectural composition were, however, unconnected to any readily appreciable overall campus design concept—except as an abstraction in the master plan drawing. In a relatively short time, their bland features were excoriated as symptomatic of a style in its terminal stages, totally unsuitable for a university seeking a competitive image intellectually and visually. "We need a different sort of architecture here," commented one Irvine administrator; "it's time for highly individual and resourceful designers," said another. Hence, Gehry.

A small building spatially (18,000 square feet), a big building aesthetically, Gehry's design presaged the new attitudes about what should constitute campus architecture at Irvine. His three pavilions solution shelter classrooms, engineering laboratories, and administrative spaces, respectively. The architect's signature-style can be found in the minimal massing and mundane materials and the ramps, stairways, canopied porch, and the mix of glass panes, galvanized metal, and multicolored surfaces. If the new architecture were intended to be a shock therapy for the ills of 1960 Modern, then Gehry succeeded. "I don't have to like it," stated Irvine Chancellor Jack Petalson, accepting the furor that the building's design engendered, as long as "people come to see" the architecture as a welcoming signal for empowering the new attitudes. In scanning Irvine's architectural evolution, one speculates whether in time the first Modern buildings and the immediate chronological successors at Irvine might meld in the public's eye into one aesthetic phase—as did variations of Victorian architecture. If so, is the idea of visual unity in twenty-first-century campus design plausible, possible, pleasing, pretentious?

In one of those anecdotes so becoming to higher education, Periera, advising the University as master plan consultant, is reported to have favored Gehry's scheme, saying "Its time for the next generation to have its say." His counsel was respected, and in the decade since Irvine has commissioned a cadre of designers who have given the University the reputation of promoting and building audaciously and provocatively in contemporary styles definitely not Modern as usually defined.

One may expect many more such examples such as the Middlebury, Mount Holyoke, and Carleton additions in the coming years as budgets dictate the economy of an appendage and tastes encourage modifications in the original building appearance. To a significant extent the once-praised simplicity of some Modern

CHARLOTTE COLLEGE, NORTH CAROLINA, C. 1960. A. G. O'DELL, JR. *(top)* *(Source: A. G. O'Dell, Jr.)*

UNIVERSITY OF CALIFORNIA, IRVINE, C. 1960. WILLIAM PERIERA. *(bottom)*

University of California, Irvine, 1985.
Frank Gehry. *(above left)* *(Source: University of California)*
California State University, Fullerton, c. 1980. *(above right)*
University of California, Irvine, 1985.
Frank Gehry. *(right)* *(Source: University of California)*

The Fullerton building evokes the attractive simplicity of early Modern, functions enclosed in one form. The Irvine building disaggregates and expresses the activities individually. Compared to the earlier development the client achieved his objective for Irvine: "a different sort of architecture."

campus architecture may be subject to Gothicization, an old term for new symmetries, piecemeal additions and protuberances, odd angles and decorative exterior effects analogous to that which queens, princes, and magnates did to Romanesque architecture in Europe and, later, the impositions and changes made by their Baroque successors to their elders' earlier masterworks. Some argue that these approaches are a fine antidote to Modernism's extremes; others would claim the conflation of styles reflects higher education's usual reluctance to venture into an artistic realm not sufficiently defined among peers and patrons as beneficial and appropriate for colleges and universities. As to the latter, events at Irvine would indicate that occasionally a change in direction may yield widespread benefits: signally a competitive, public presence and support gained for designs which otherwise might not be considered. If shedding an image was the objective, then Irvine succeeded. In the first half of the 1990s Irvine was the campus to visit, to see, and to enjoy as a pinnacle of architecture, California unfettered—nonpatrician buildings with plentiful panache, polish, and pulchritude.

As noted, the irresistible urge to invent, innovate, and improve architecturally runs deep in institutions dedicated to creating and finding knowledge and promoting change—causes and effects we will trace more elaborately later. Always, of course, that urge does not have to be fulfilled at the price of abusing the physical heritage. Some mediation in campus designs and buildings can also be achieved through new landscapes. Greening the campus for visual and symbolic reasons can have many advantages: completing a design concept by extending the building design themes through site development, creating a new look in the building surrounds, and/or planting the landscape as an armature and context for a full-range of projected architectural solutions not yet ready for implementation. Thus, from the sidelines, one observes with admiration particularly those colleges and universities that promote a continuity in campus design with new buildings developed in tandem with new greenery. With the binding landscape, the ensemble emerges as a comprehensive and expressive environmental experience. Without a suitable site and setting, a building is not architecture. We will see how such can be accomplished.

REVITALIZATION, RESTORATION, REGENERATION

The campus expresses (architecturally) something about the quality of its academic life, as well as its role as a citizen of the community in which it is located. The campus also represents many different things to various groups of people who live, learn, teach, or visit there. It plays the role of home, museum, place of employment, social center, park, arena for dissent, and forum for the search for truth. All these functions must be designed not only for today but also for the future.

Roger B. Finch
Rensselaer Polytechnic Institute, 1971

Architecture, like politics, is very much "the art of the possible." Dons may live in ivory towers, but they do not often build them. So in universities...architecture is always a compromise between the visionary and the practicable.

Howard Colvin
Unbuilt Oxford, 1983

In the main, most of the 15 million students projected for American campuses in the first decade of the twenty-first century will be educated on the existing 3600 campuses. The physical settings that serve this population will be improved in several ways. Existing buildings will be restored and rehabilitated, many with additions and wings that alter their appearance for functional and aesthetic reasons—again, redemptive architecture. A significant and impressive group of new buildings will be constructed so as to complete long-range plans as well as to replace structures beyond salvage and to help institutions compete for and retain students and faculty, in order to maintain pace with peers and/or to symbolize institutional advancement. The architectural improvements will trigger a renewed interest in campus landscape.

Undergirding and overarching the more visible and changing aspects of architecture as art will be the confirmation of an ideal: function shaping form. The Modern movement claimed this as an essential tenet in its creed. All great architecture has been similarly informed. Cathedrals, churches, and chapels changed in response to new rites and rituals. Late-twentieth-century hospitals and prisons are different from their ancient predecessors because new attitudes, routines, and technology require new solutions, which functional architecture handles best. Let the inside be arranged for purpose; let the outside proclaim its locale and situation; and then let the design expression signify institutional aesthetics as determined by the times, culture, and collegiality—such seems a reasonable stance.

Of course, as to what will constitute appropriate campus architecture, beyond being a three-dimensional paean to institutional purpose, place, and ambitions—constructed on a satisfactory site—there will be no lack of opinions, or examples of the fit and the fitful. One generation's great and extraordinary building may be seen by another generation as an exercise in aesthetic futility. Ironically, in recent years, the rapidity of change in design innovations seems to have outpaced the ability of professional criticism to summarize cause and effect into a unified theory that at least explains, if not evaluates, what is occurring. Nonetheless in the histories of campus development and in current events one can trace the flowering of architecture of higher education, the weeds, the buds, and nosegays, i.e., edifices misplaced in their environment, ideas in process and not fully realized, and collections of buildings lovely in every aspect that counts. We will examine that garden to screen out and digest ideas worth applying in emulation or in devising new architecture. From this information some simple methods will be synthesized which, when applied, will give every project thus conceived a chance to flourish for its own reasons and at the same time contribute to, and be fortified by, its surrounding physical setting. For convenience and coverage, most examples will be shown in terms of their exterior appearance.

What follows is an overview of college and university construction so as to recognize and apprehend typical building types, trends, and complexity. As indicated earlier, the sampling is selective; necessarily, inasmuch as each type itself could fill a book of descriptions and evaluations. The examples chosen highlight seminal concepts, their changing character, and the present-day situation with regard to programmatic issues which are affecting building and site design. The sampling enables us to trace, again, how traditional architecture gave way to austere Modern designs. Thus, generic simplicity was followed by a period of elaboration in external appearances, then fragmentation of the building into connected pieces and/or the warping and bending of plan form to escape from the earlier generation's box and rectangle solutions, and/or extrusions and extensions that are witty or worldly elements that give a building a uniqueness it might not otherwise possess. Along the way we will see the rise and fall of current-wall architecture and the imposition and then rejection of poured concrete—the latter an allegory of the Modern transformed into brutal expressionism, whose hard-edge declarations now have few admirers. As indicated, such styles were succeeded in many places by an interest in mining and mimicking traditional designs, under the rubric and rationale of joining new and old with architecture in context. These were most successful when rich-fabric nineteenth-century Collegiate Georgian, Collegiate Gothic, and Victorian buildings inspired a transferable design vocabulary. The Challange?

Viewed comprehensively, architectural concepts and styles visible in the panorama of college and university buildings, within one lifetime, seem to have an ever-shortening life cycle. Response to functional requirements is one cause, adjustments in institutional missions another, fashion a third. Further, the purgative value of rejecting quotidian work in anticipation and preparation for a design direction not yet imagined, or for nurturing another and better round of revivals and reinterpretations, cannot be ignored or discounted in understanding how college and university buildings come into being. Above all, there is the verity that architecture is the tangible record of cultural human progress or retrogression. If the buildings of higher education this past century are Joseph Hudnut's "human documents casting a remorseless light on the civilization of the times and on the quality of mind of their creators," then campus architecture, with its extraordinary variety, has been a faithful expression of the goal of enlarging and diversifying higher education.

How much so? Admittedly critical judgment can be warped and strained by reading into designs connotations and meanings never intended. And as we will see, the architect's own words may not explain sufficiently the final results. But surely William George Tight's path-finding effort to establish a regional architecture at the University of New Mexico (an amalgam of native and Spanish Colonial features) must rank high as a three-dimensional expression of his wish to have all the state's population see the University as a welcoming place for diverse interests, sexes, races, and creeds. Tight lost his presidency fighting that cause. His first designs (the University heating plant) were as naive as his political sense. Later John Gaw Meem demonstrated the art of architecture in his elegant versions of Tight's Pueblo style, and detail counts, as Meem demonstrated on the Albuquerque campus. Thus the recent lobby at the Wriston Art Center (Lawrence University) is fine architecture and a welcoming beacon and invitation for all to enter and enjoy the arts as participants or observers. An early view of Princeton substantiates the claim that *openness* is a time-tested quality of commendable and appropriate campus architecture. How disappointing to see such qualities lost in or forgotten in grand designs as well as smaller projects.

HEATING PLANT, UNIVERSITY OF NEW MEXICO, c. 1898. WILLIAM GEORGE TIGHT, PRESIDENT AND DESIGNER. *(right) In the Jeffersonian tradition: an architecture to serve and symbolize the people. (Source: University archives, courtesy of Joe C. McKinney)*

LOBBY DETAIL, LAWRENCE UNIVERSITY, 1992. CENTERBROOK ARCHITECTS. *(bottom) For the punditic, a design loaded with contemporary design codes. For everyone, an inviting, welcoming, and attractive ambiance. (Source: Lawrence University)*

PRINCETON UNIVERSITY, 1838. *(facing page, top) A welcoming view of campus buildings and greenery. (Source: Princeton University)*

UNIVERSITY OF KANSAS, 1960. *(facing page, bottom) A building for the arts, with some aspects of art missing. (Source: University of Kansas)*

CHAPTER 2

BUILDING TYPES

It may be reasonably inferred that buildings already in existence in any and all
periods, having had similar requirements with those that occur in present problems,
will have created and used so-called styles which have in them architectural
expression of value at all times for work of the same kind.

C. Howard Walker
Expression—the Collegiate Style, *1931*

Stretched along the road that separates it from the medical buildings is the long, low,
steel, glass and brick home of the natural sciences laboratories. Nestled against this
brick and steel spine, lie vestiges of science past. On one side the old physics building,
large and austere with a red tile roof slowly turning black, and tall, narrow windows
that belie the high ceiling dark rooms within...around the mall punctuated at one
end...lie the squat, functional, ceramic brick and concrete buildings of the engineering
and management schools, almost defiantly ugly as though to emphasize that
appearances are secondary to reality...(adjacent) Gothic stone buildings beside
awkward Victorian red brick construction...home for the humanities and social
sciences...Beyond is the flashy, contemporary law school building, its black one-way
windows revealing as little inside as a state trooper's sun glasses.

David Kolb
The Modern American College, *1981*

A "building" is defined as a roofed structure for temporary or permanent shelter of
persons, animals, plants, materials or equipment.

Postsecondary Education Facilities
Inventory and Classification Manual,
Washington 1992

FUNCTIONAL DIVERSIFICATION

That fount of all plausible explication, the eleventh edition of the *Encyclopedia Britannia*, says that "the end of building is convenience; the end of architecture as an art is beauty, grandeur, unity and power." Old Main, Kenyon College (1827) (illustrated on page 55), and the previously cited Memorial Hall (1872), Royce Hall (1929), and Breuer's work at St. John's University (1953) meet those expectations. Modern architecture was heralded as the logical end of that progression. The canon would guide all designers to useful and attractive solutions; philosophically one style would fit all conditions. Its simplicity, however, was deceptive. Unfortunately, propelled by expediency, many institutions in the two decades following World War II constructed stodgy solutions and specious structures disguised and puffed as Modern architecture. Not atypical, from that period, is the Lafayette College Science Building (illustrated on page 55), which displays aspects of the Modern idiom and may exemplify functionality. However, by any standard it hardly represents the art of architecture, though touted originally as an "adventuresome design," stripped as the building was of the iconic detailing of older styles. Other buildings from the early 1950s, once truly rousing, ground-breaking Modern designs, are now also relegated to footnotes in historic surveys. Some, good designs for their times, hold attention because of their association with their designer, such as Eero Saarinen's Divinity School building and chapel at Drake University. And there are a few tantalizing period pieces, neither traditional nor Modern, such as the Hollins College Chapel, a quirky rendition of Collegiate Georgian. Like Wordsworth's "authentic tidings of invisible things," the 1958 design could be read retrospectively as a prelude to post-Modern architecture, à la Michael Graves.

In scanning a sample of Modern campus buildings built from 1945 to 1970, and in reading skewering screeds such as David Kolb's impressions of Case-Western University, the phrase *Modern* is more a slogan of emancipation from traditional styles rather than the title for a rigorous codification of design terms and appearances. Diversity reigned and reigns. As early as 1931, *Architectural Forum* writer Kenneth K. Stowell editorialized that in higher education, "Uniformity of product is no longer the object being sought. The mediocrity of mass production of graduates gives way to developing individuals to realize as fully as possible their potentialities, mental, physical, social and spiritual. The environment (sic) atmosphere and facilities provided are considered as important as the subjects in the curriculum. The architecture must be in accord with and contribute to those educational aims." Here, then, was the educational argument for setting aside introspective traditional styles and adopting open-ended Modern. Unquestionably some designers would and did use the aspects of the Modern canon as a license for pursuing quotidian nontraditional work; others would accept the canon as a departure point for a striving level of creative interpretation. Astutely, Antony Part, British Ministry of Education, captured the alpha and omega of swarming but mediocre emulation as well as sparkling solo flights. During his year-long tour and evaluation of American architecture in 1950–1951, Part saw "Fashion...raising the level of performance, but also holding experimentation within narrow limits....The truth seems to be that the modern building, being a more individual affair in every respect than its predecessors, requires a greater degree of skill in the designer to make it successful." True then, and true now, particularly when examining the exceptional variety of building types that constitute campus architecture.

At the start of higher education in North America, functions and buildings were simple: housing, chapel, classroom, library, dining, and a suite of rooms for the administration, usually the president and bursar, occasionally all sheltered under one roof. Pictured on page 57 is Texas Christian University's oldest building, circa 1878; another illustration is a view of the inaugural building at Southern Methodist University, constructed a number of years later, Jeffersonian in spirit and form. These nostalgic photos expose the hard times which many institution's faced in giving shape and substance to the founder's aspirations. Some failed, most succeeded. The landscape surrounding and approaching SMU's flagship building (now

OLD MAIN, KENYON COLLEGE, 1827. *(top) (Source: Kenyon College)*
SCIENCE BUILDING, LAFAYETTE COLLEGE, C. 1960. *(bottom) (Source: Lafayette College)*
Two projects in visual contrast, separated by a century of technology and an eon of taste and skill, displaying the perceptible differences between architecture and a building.

Dedham Hall) grew gracefully, and the building has been restored and reconstructed several times for varying academic activities. TCU's first structure is now only an archival memory.

Not all began impoverished. Kenyon College's Old Main, for example, was substantial architecture by any benchmark. Architecturally one of the best from the first assortment crop was Benjamin Latrobe's Old West (Dickinson College, 1803). His detailing and materials have been copied or interpreted in several later Dickinson buildings, a visual continuity that strengthens and ennobles the Dickinson campus design. The custom of shared space continues today in Massachusetts Hall (1713), with the Harvard University president's offices on the lower floors and student bedrooms above, an anachronistic homage to the past at the world's richest university; the custom endures in Swarthmore College's Parish Hall (1865), where the functional mix is maintained as a symbolic statement of institutional integrity.

College size was, of course, the major determinant in configuring multifunction buildings. One building served all at the start, then growth in enrollment, diversification in subject matter, and then many buildings, or incremental expansion. The latter has generated some visually fascinating architecture. Center Hall, Wabash College (1854–1871) was designed and built in three phases, each to help keep the academic activities under one roof. An historic example of the Italian Renaissance Villa Revival style, the building originally included "library, Chemical Laboratory, Science Lecture Room, literary societies, and chapel." The "villa" design is a good example of style as signal. The building size and location impressed on the Indiana community the College's presence and functions and its determination to be recognized as a contemporary institution with its choice of style, at that time unique. How steadfast such signals? Gradually new buildings were erected for the sciences and the library, none in the villa mode, which had gone out of fashion. A 1926 campus plan study determined that the "historic development of campus and community" would be best expressed architecturally by "Early American of the Classical Period." The architect's sketches and notes showed how Center Hall could be transformed to send new signals, "at small cost by changes to the roof and tower." It would be, the designer wrote, "an interesting example of how, through careful architectural study, an existing building of permanent value can be preserved." The Depression stilled the creative thought. Center Hall has been remodeled several times inside. The exterior remains intact, preserved as originally designed, as it should be as an honest example of regional period architecture.

Today, typically, each prime college and university activity is encased in one or more of its own buildings. Thus Illinois College, established in 1829, grew from 1 building to 23. Promoted as a prototype of a small New England College campus transplanted to the Mid-west, the school currently enrolls 900 students. The college expansion can be read qualitatively and quantitatively in an air view drawing of its period architecture: roofs, facades, materials. Not all signals are on the exterior. The latest at Illinois College is "a multi-purpose learning center, [which] features a dramatic atrium, a college living room." Modest in scale, important in their locale, the two Wabash and Illinois buildings are examples of architecture as an institutional time clock. Situated among many buildings, the overlay of function

TEXAS CHRISTIAN UNIVERSITY, C. 1878. *(top) Start-up building. (Source: Texas Christian University)*
UNIVERSITY OF VIRGINIA, C. 1948. *(bottom left) (Source: Library of Congress)*
SOUTHERN METHODIST UNIVERSITY, C. 1915. *(bottom right) First architecture. Two from Texas, architectural evidence of varying degrees of success in obtaining funds for the initial construction; both landmarks of faith and confidence in higher education. The SMU vista and building form obviously owe origin to Jefferson's Charlottesville campus.*

Drake University, chapel and classroom, c. 1958. Saarinen and Swan. *(above)*
(Source: Drake University)
Chapel, Hollins College, c. 1958. *(right)*
(Source: Hollins College)
Same period, disparate aesthetics. Drake a forgotten masterwork. Hollins, perhaps a design worth reconsidering as a harbinger of Post-Modern.

Center Hall, Wabash College, 1854 to 1870. William Tinsley. *(facing page, top)* An *historic Indiana college building, now a national landmark, a rare existing example of the Italianate-Villa style. Frequently remodeled, the exterior remains, through fortunate circumstances, as envisioned a century ago. (Source: Wabash College)*

Center Hall, proposed modernization, c. 1930. *(facing page, bottom) Redemptive architecture, architect's arrogance, changing cultural values? Designer Jens Fredrick Larson believed a new look would best communicate 1930 collegiate purpose and local tastes. The Depression postponed implementation. The idea was not later pursued. How vulnerable are Modern classics? When should conservation of heritage override functional necessity and rational maintenance decisions, or a groundswell of changing architectural taste?*

and fashion in these buildings reinforces not only the site-specific sense of place but also announces what cultural and aesthetic values were important when the buildings were constructed. Of large, single-purpose structures, two by Perkins and Will (shown on pages 62 and 63) exemplify how site and context may help determine external appearances and demonstrate how skilled hands can avoid the curse of signature architecture. The latter misfortune occurs when the creativity of a fashionable designer is commissioned to produce a building recognizably his or her style but otherwise deficient in conceptualization. The remedy is care and caution in defining project function, size, site, budget, and expectations.

We turn now to examining variations in building types so as to see and appreciate a source of architectural distinction, i.e., functional diversification. As to categorizing and describing building types by function, *prime activity* are key words, inasmuch as many campus buildings continue to be multipurpose. As one would expect, the range of activities has expanded. For example, a working group organized to classify college and university facilities (National Center for Educational Statistics, 1992) identified about 60 discrete kinds of functional spaces (rooms) associated with postsecondary education buildings. Sixteen such functions appear in a sample survey of early-nineteenth-century buildings. Fifty-four functions appear in a comparable group of late-twentieth-century buildings on the same campuses. No surprises here. As we have seen, higher education became more diverse and differentiated in teaching, research, and community service, and so too did its architecture. The comments that follow, necessarily selective and abbreviated, illuminate the diversity and shed light on current issues and solutions. For convenience in description, we begin with athletic and physical recreation facilities.

ATHLETIC AND PHYSICAL RECREATION

At Brown University athletic and physical recreation functions once could be housed in a single building. By 1990 a full range of sports and recreation would require separate facilities for swimming, basketball, ice hockey, and a multipurpose field house, each with a distinctive appearance and form. Professional journals as early as 1926 acknowledge "that the architect has a real problem in planning such an exacting building." The *Architectural Forum* (1931) published a "practical compilation of the modern trends in planning, design and construction of buildings for intercollegiate athletics." How helpful? Apparently the subsequent battle of style versus function left mortal wounds. The American Athletic Institute (1947) deplored "the tragic prevalence of errors in the construction of facilities." Because of such things as "the absence or ignorance of desirable standards, the failure of designers and program specialists to pool their knowledge, the policy of false economy and the tendency to imitate grievous mistakes have been made and repeated. The result has been monstrosities that have persisted for generations."

Be that as it may, the programmatic aspects of such buildings were soon settled authoritatively, leaving the design response to stretch the architect's imagination. A checklist prepared by the American Athletic Institute (1970) addressed the earlier deficiencies, setting criteria for 27 indoor activities requiring specialized spaces. Each had their regulated criteria for the size and configuration of interior spaces.

The Campus

Illinois College is trees, grass, brick paths, and classic buildings, both old and new. The architecture skillfully blends old New England with the best contemporary styles. Recent construction includes the Kirby Learning Center, Mundinger Hall and the renovation of Sturtevant Hall.

ILLINOIS COLLEGE, 1995 CAMPUS DEVELOPMENT. *(top) As the college grew and educational purposes changed, buildings increased in number and were diversified functionally. The campus is an architectural clock, tracking the evolution of taste and technology. The generation-binding design theme: a site composition and landscape developed in homage to New England campus design paradigms. (Source: Illinois College)*

ILLINOIS COLLEGE, ATRIUM, KIRBY LEARNING CENTER, 1992. STONE, MARRACCINI, PATERSON. *(bottom) Another click on the architectural clock, with an interior demonstrating further diversification of building types and styles. (Source: Illinois College)*

NORTHWESTERN UNIVERSITY, TARRY RESEARCH AND EDUCATION BUILDING, SCHOOL OF MEDICINE, 1990. PERKINS AND WILL. *Biomedical research, clinical studies, and basic sciences are enclosed in a 17-story, 272,000-square-foot edifice in downtown Chicago. The low element to the building's right is a steel and glass atrium, giving access to the new and adjacent university buildings. The architect's challenge, designing a distinctive new high-rise in Chicago, ranks with rowing backward across the Atlantic in a wash-tub. The Perkins and Will solution is a dignified essay in limestone, painted aluminum wall, and glass. The elements, an echo of older skyscrapers, denote a sense of place and are sufficiently varied to express contemporary design ideas. Most important, the building's interiors were engineered and organized to meet biomedical teaching and research standards. Flexibility—the key to building longevity—is optimized through a central vertical utility shaft, threaded through the structure like a tree trunk and extended limbs. (Source: Perkins and Will)*

CATHOLIC UNIVERSITY, VITREOUS STATE LABORATORY, 1986. PERKINS AND WILL. *The five-story, 93,000-square-foot scientific facility is devoted to research in novel glass technologies. The public side of the building gives a strong edge to a paved campus open space. The glass, metal, and panel materials are in keeping with the building purpose. The forms and composition of the facade are intended to suggest the classical features of the surrounding buildings—granite Romanesque. A precast panel, lightly textured and solid granite at the base, provide the visual connection. The seating and lighting elements reinforce the allusion. Not visible are the engineering solutions for energy conservation and the handling of low-level radiation and other exacting environmental requirements for glass surface catalysis and experiments with optic fibers. (Source: Perkins and Will)*

And stretch the imagination must, because of the awesome dimensions of the building type: 55 percent of all space in the facilities will require high ceilings for basketball, volleyball, badminton, tennis, and gymnastics, experts say.

Spanning of tall, voluminous space, free of columns, has stimulated audacious structural solutions. The first nontraditional designs after World War II unfortunately had a lumpen quality and were often miserably sited. As at Montana State College, the potential of a graceful surrounding landscape and relationships to the central campus was lost in the need to get as much parking as close to the front entrance as possible and the fear, not unfounded, that the new structure, the first modern university building of its kind in the region, would overwhelm its neighbors. Questionable as to being a style suitable for modern times, the earlier traditional gymnasium and field house solutions did possess a commanding presence and visual character worth admiration, especially when trees, paving, and path arrangements could help scale down elephantine structures and connect them visually and functionally to nearby play fields and adjacent campus buildings.

Facility designs at the University of Iowa summarize evolving institutional attitudes about athletics, recreation, and physical education and the corresponding design concepts. When erected in 1926, the University of Iowa field house was the "largest structure of its kind in the world...5.5 million cubic feet of space...seating 12,000." Its fate reveals two trends: a new facility was constructed for varsity athletics and spectator sports; the old building was remodeled in 1985 for general recreation and physical education; to this was added, in 1989, a second recreational facility the size of a conventional college gym. The result is equal time and space for both men and women team sports and substantial facilities for students, faculty, and staff. The original field house and addition are brick boxes, more building than architecture. The new sports arena nestles into the ground, its size disguised, its frontage scaled to human dimension, its facade announcing hints of its ingenious interior structural system.

Land available and surrounding ambiance, not scale mediation, was the affecting design consideration at Georgetown University, a field house extensively built below grade with the roof engineered for play fields. Multiple use, the image of being "leading edge," and the economy of construction led Elmira College to construct three linked geodesic domes in 1972. Should Buckminster Fuller require a monument, these will do: gymnasium, hockey, and field house situated in a greensward. The gym encloses the acre and a half of courts, lockers, offices, and classrooms. The field house was expected "to host stamp shows to horse shows when not being used for field and track events." Such multiuse has helped rationalize the costs of constructing many new, large, indoor spectator facilities. Those bothered by what they perceive to be the "dangers of big-time athletic" programs are assuaged with the notion that the local basketball arena will be used for convocations, special events, and performances that might not otherwise be possible indoors on campus.

As to stimulating new thoughts about leading edge architecture, revealing, cogent, and still timely is Henry Noble McCracken's 1928 study of "suitable concepts" for a new facility at Vassar College, where he was president, leading the charge for a comprehensive sports and recreation program. McCracken was concerned with the notion that too often sports are seen as the province of "the specialized athlete rather

PAYNE WHITNEY GYMNASIUM, YALE UNIVERSITY, C. 1925. *(left) John Russell Pope's ennoblement of Eli competition and sweat.*

ATHLETIC BUILDING. MONTANA STATE COLLEGE, C. 1956. *(below) An emphatic example of early Modern architecture giving form and subsistence to high-span athletic buildings. The lumpen qualities might be forgiven for its commitment to break away from traditional styles that turned gymnasiums into cathedrals, as in Yale's Whitney Gymnasium. However, the crude site development shows an opportunity lost for an epitome of campus architecture, i.e., a landscape that scaled the building to human dimensions and connected the site to the nearby central campus.*

than for the whole community." He hoped that a new kind of building would encourage greater participation. "Games," he said, "are a happy combination of wit and will, strength and agility. Cooperation and organized attack upon problems are taught, together with the control of temper and the sublimation of suppressed desires." It was his goal that "after a generation or two had grown up under the stimulation of (his proposed gymnasia) we may be as fond of sports as the English." After studying "over thirty gymnasia," McCracken advocated "the drafting of plans for a facility at Vassar based on the idea of a country club." The 1990 student recreation center at Vanderbilt University measures up to that ideal. The scheme includes a lap pool, racquetball and squash courts, jogging track, and climbing wall, and "spa-type natatorium." The exterior "reinforces the heritage of the Vanderbilt brick and limestone buildings with contemporary materials." In contrast to a visual heritage, McCracken advocated "a building design suggesting an English manor and farm outbuildings" which would bring the various "sports spaces into a harmonious architectural relationship." Admirably, Helmut Jahn's athletic facility, Saint Mary's College, Indiana (1977), required no cultural or stylistic allusion, with its antilumpen configuration, elegant detailing, and contemporary materials.

On the horizon are innovative facilities which are "apt to be new applications and new combinations of previously tried elements," for the building type has not exhausted its run programmatically or physically. Some old advice from Fiske Kimball (1930) thus remains germane, "there are certain definite principles and certain definite trends which produce inevitable similarities and differences in all cases. For this reason knowledge of what has been done and what is being done elsewhere is of inestimable benefit to those in charge of new projects of this kind." With additional facilities on the horizon, appropriate, then, are some concluding words about the fate of redundant gymnasia whose architectural character and campus history merit preservation and adaptation for new uses. Possibilities range from a campus center (Carleton College's version is commendable in every respect) to Brown University's proposed conversion of its historic Sayles gymnasium into special function classrooms. In both instances the exteriors are kept intact in tribute to history and the interiors changed to satisfy new needs.

CLASSROOMS AND FACULTY OFFICES

The Brown proposal reflects the retooling of classroom space occurring at most institutions. This is happening for two reasons. Higher education is recognizing important differences in learning and teaching styles associated with specific disciplines. Computers and communications technology are altering conventional time

UNIVERSITY OF IOWA. *(facing page, top)* *The 1926 building and 1989 addition. Big boxes above ground. (Source: University of Iowa)*

UNIVERSITY OF IOWA, CARVER HAWKEYE-ARENA. CRSS; THE DURANT GROUP; GEIGER ASSOCIATES. *(facing page, bottom)* *A splendid team effort in placing a large 13,200-seat practice and performance facility in a natural ravine, providing at the entrance level a design human in scale, contemporary in materials, and expressive in its articulation of the space frame. (Source: University of Iowa)*

ST. MARY'S COLLEGE, INDIANA, 1977.
HELMUT JAHN. *(facing page, top) (Source: St. Mary's College)*

ELMIRA COLLEGE, GEODESIC DOMES, 1970.
HASKELL, CONNOR & FROST. *(facing page, bottom) (Source: Elmira College)*

SAYLES GYMNASIUM, 1912. *(right) Originally constructed for Pembroke College at Brown University, the interior of the historic structure is scheduled to be reconstructed as a twenty-first-century classroom. (Source: Brown University)*

SPELMAN COLLEGE, COSBY ACADEMIC CENTER, 1995. DE JONG ARCHITECTS. *(below) Designed to fit the Spelman ambiance, to gather and serve the humanities, to combine traditional modes of teaching with oncoming information technology. (Source: Spelman College)*

and space practices and modes of teaching and learning. The traditional inventory of classroom spaces is being modified in terms of size, configuration, environmental conditions, furnishings, and equipment. The 1992 Massachusetts Institute of Technology Bechtel classroom illuminates the design horizon with its extraordinary range of electronic devices arranged to encourage faculty use of the new devices and in turn to adapt them to personal teaching styles.

Lock-step, these trends are also affecting faculty office designs, which are becoming communications centers for receiving and sending knowledge electronically as well as venues for those face-to-face conversations and meetings—the essence of collegiality and educational exchanges—for which machines are no substitute. Locationally, classrooms and faculty offices are likely to continue to be distributed throughout campus in clusters identified with the discipline, department, or division and occasionally grouped as a campuswide facility for efficiency in scheduling and experimentation with emerging technology. Thus, Spelman College's Cosby Academic Center (1994) gathers the humanities into one location with contemporary architecture that recalls the older Spelman buildings. But, might these trends generate a new building type? Most everyone on campus, at some point in the daily routine, is in a classroom or faculty office. Could function, materials, and teaching technology combine to induce a distinctive design and style? Once this was the hope of those advocating Modern architecture. Traditional designs were a "sauce," said the critics, that gave functionally differentiated buildings an unwelcome uniform resemblance. Collegiate Gothic could be applied equally to chapels and heating plants, classrooms and gymnasium. Fine for the past, they explained, but not for higher education's new age. The expectations were that function *would* blossom into a new style. But the Modern idiom was all too soon trapped by its own canon. By the late 1950s, good examples of a classroom building and a dormitory, conceived as Modern, located a thousand miles apart, from different hands, could barely be distinguished in general appearance from each other. Traditional or Modern, or something else, whether viable *campus architecture* requires a distinctive style in the future, and what that might be, is an issue obviously germane to our inquiry.

VISUAL AND PERFORMING ARTS

Facilities for the arts are reliable indicators of the maturation of American higher education and the vitality of diversified architecture. Curricula and programs have evolved from "appreciation" to "hands on" experience. Fifty years ago there were few such buildings, telltale marks of an uncertain culture. By the 1970s buildings for the arts could lay claim to being architecturally ubiquitous and among the campuses' most accomplished works. Dartmouth's Hopkins Center physically and

---

MODERN ARCHITECTURE: THE CANON AT ITS PEAK. *(facing page, top and bottom) Two award-winning buildings constructed 1955 to 1960. A classroom building and student housing, located a thousand miles apart, designed by different hands and firms; confident and persuasive renditions of an important but now dated style.*

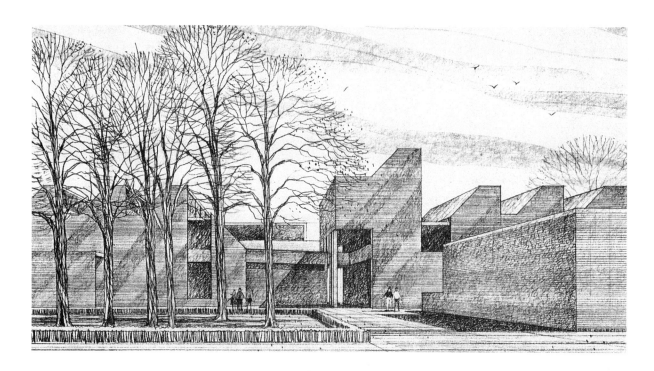

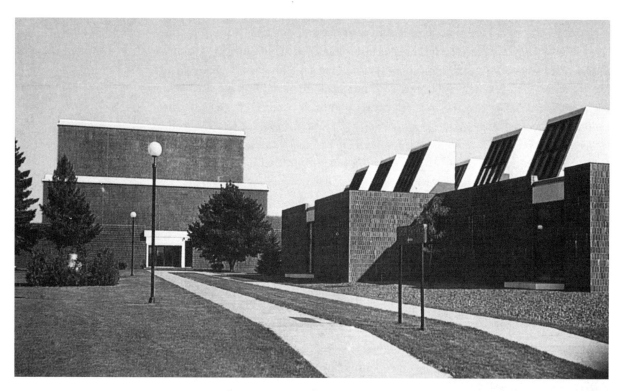

STATE UNIVERSITY OF NEW YORK, PURCHASE, VISUAL ARTS INSTRUCTION FACILITY, 1971. *(top) The Architect's Collaborative version of the then popular Modern architectural style, with forms and shapes associated with arts facilities, with minimal articulation of the facade.*

ST. BENEDICTA ARTS CENTER, COLLEGE OF ST. BENEDICT, 1962. HAMMEL, GREEN, ABRAHAMSON. *(bottom) All the arts under one roof: practice, performance, creation, display. A landmark design in the history of Modern collegiate architecture, including flexibility in space use, acoustics, and building systems. (Source: College of St. Benedict)*

philosophically brought the arts into the middle of campus life. The Krannert Center (University of Illinois, Urbana-Champaign) was as imposing as Lincoln Center. New campuses, such as the State University of New York, Purchase, and older campuses such as the College of Saint Benedict (Minnesota) sponsored and built facilities that epitomized Modern architecture in the 1960s. The designs were manifest discourses of function influencing form, and simple materials melding disparate structures into a visual unity. Architecturally, the designs signal the arts coming of age in America—reflecting, we think, the nation's ascendancy as a world political power and aesthetic leader and the willingness of higher education to afford students avocational opportunities and vocational training within a college and university curriculum, as well as conservatory level training. Thus, painters such as Mark Rothko and Burgoyne Diller taught not in an art school, but at a liberal arts institution, Brooklyn College. Goucher College operates a renowned modern dance program. Columbia University filled its faculty ranks with internationally respected composers. Webster College stages a summer opera season that draws audiences and critical acclaim worldwide. Few conservatories could equal the faculty and facilities at the University of Indiana.

Today every campus has a wing, a building, or a group of buildings devoted to some aspect of understanding, learning, experiencing, or doing art, dance, theater, music, and the kindred arts and crafts. In the hinterland, many are town-gown cultural centers, routinely offering concerts, recitals, films, lectures, dance and theater productions, and art exhibitions. Studios, galleries, practice rooms, performance spaces—the technical requirements for good architecture are demanding, space configurations and relationships exacting, and the design expression an opportunity for introducing architectural concepts that extend and celebrate the aesthetic experience such buildings enclose. These are unique buildings. Sloppy and expedient planning would be disastrous. As critic Mildred F. Schmertz explained in vetting the Krannert scheme, one notes with appreciation if not awe, "five different facilities each of the optimum size and shape for the types of performance housed...whose intrinsic interest is not diminished by the fact that (once constructed) complexes such as these will probably never be built again."

Examining a cluster of visual and performing arts buildings, one appreciates the importance of a well-formulated facility program and the designation of a prime site. These themselves do not, of course, determine the architectural outcomes. Good architecture communicates values and attitudes, as well as time and place, through the arrangement of forms and site composition, massing and materials. How such is devised is part of the art of architecture. And the results will differ from age to age. Design proposals submitted for the University of Maryland, College Park, arts center (1994) exemplify how a singular statement of requirements can yield an enticing range of possibilities. A significant competition, the range of possibilities generated by the Maryland designers taken together can be read as a catalog of contemporary architectural concepts. The client requirements included concert hall, recital hall, proscenium and experimental theater, dance studio, library, classrooms, restaurant, and amphitheater. In the solutions submitted straight-line calibrated site arrangements or all-under-one-roof concepts have been dismissed in favor of combinations of buildings, building segments, roof shapes,

UNIVERSITY OF MARYLAND CENTER FOR THE PERFORMING ARTS, 1994 COMPETITION. *One program, one site, varying solutions. Textbook examples of contemporary design attitudes about building forms and site composition. Shown are four of the six submissions.* (Source: University of Maryland)

ANTOINE PREDOCK. *(top)*

MOORE RUBLE YUDELL. *(bottom) The winning proposal.*

PEI COBB FREED AND PARTNERS. *(top)*

CESAR PELLI AND ASSOCIATES. *(bottom)*

FURMAN UNIVERSITY, ROE ART BUILDING, 1985. PERRY DEAN ROGERS AND PARTNERS.
The campus image is informed by Collegiate Georgian, a Palladian style favored in the region and well utilized by the University in older buildings such as the James B. Duke Library (right). Pediment, portico, and brick materials are the signature features from the older structures reorganized in the fashionable and faultless facade of the new building. Interestingly, the same firm was responsible for both buildings. (Source: Furman University)

courtyards, and landscapes. Where one might find a Beaux Arts classical essay of dominant and subordinated elements, complexity reigns. The Pei Cobb Freed and Partners scheme reads like a modern Roman forum, Cesar Pelli's connected halls, a market place for the arts, and Antoine Predock's architecture as sculpture. In these works, all is not revealed in one glance. Each hold's the promise of sequenced visual surprises as one moves through the site, a visceral overture and introduction to the aesthetic experiences inside the buildings—potentially splendid campus architecture. The winning scheme (Moore Ruble Yudell) was selected by the jury because "It promises a rich mix of humanly scaled forms and spaces...humanism in architecture as opposed to pure abstraction."

Delightful are those campus buildings which serve the arts without compromise to interior functional requirements, span generations symbolically, are architecturally distinctive, and pay harmonious homage to their predecessors. Thus the fine arts facility at Furman University (with its roof shape, portico, and materials) stands out as a superior work from the 1980s, recalling without insult older Furman structures less refined in their formation. The principle of design continuity with generation differences is exquisitely handled in James Stirling's Cornell University project. Located at the seam of campus and community, the design epitomizes place making and place marking. Function informs shapes, the site affects location and building connections. Materials and detailing are inspired and drawn from the nearby architecture, educational and vernacular, aesthetic and commercial. Collegiate arts centers in small towns also carry the charge of being local cultural centers. As venues for events, ceremonies, performances, their sites must be part of the campus pedestrian precinct as well as accessible to the outside public through conveniently placed parking. Thus these arts buildings are significant design opportunities for arranging buildings, circulation patterns, and landscape elements into an overall design that serves as a public ceremonial and/or memorial portal to the campus.

CAMPUS CENTERS

As with a library, the college and university without a campus center would be exceptional. Extracurricular activities converge and are sheltered in the campus center, serving young and old. Conceived as wholesome alternatives to the attractions that the seedier aspects of town and city life held for undergraduates, and then envisioned as places to nurture collegiality as institutions grew larger and the population more diverse; promoted as proper memorials for the alumnus and benefactors, and then transformed from student enclaves to campus unions serving the entire community—campus centers are now multifunctional buildings charged to serve and symbolize all aspects of campus life. Older students often use the center as a social club, as a study lounge, as a place to experience campus life when such appeals to their interests. For younger people contact and involvement with peers in the campus center helps provide knowledge and perspective on differing backgrounds, values, lifestyles, interests. Whereas this process occurs in well-designed campus housing, the campus center is the main venue in terms of numbers of people involved, and the programs and ambiance serving the bold, the shy, the introspective, the articulate. A "hot button" topic is keeping students on campus for

SAN FRANCISCO STATE UNIVERSITY, CAMPUS CENTER, 1970. PARTRIDGE & KEATING. *(facing page, top) An intriguing solution that summarizes the spirited designs of the 1970s, when clients were willing to extend a free hand for innovation and invention. (Source: San Francisco State University)*

FRANKLIN PIERCE COLLEGE, CAMPUS CENTER, 1986. SWAIN ASSOCIATES. *(facing page, bottom) Forms and shapes are reminiscent of regional agricultural architecture. The design elements are organized to establish a skyline image associated with marvelous views to and from the building. A clever interior circulation scheme provides patrons and visitors a delightful sequence of spatial experiences and activity choices. (Source: Franklin Pierce College)*

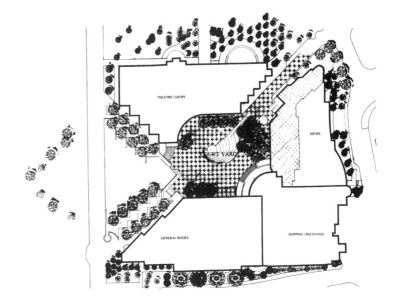

UNIVERSITY OF CALIFORNIA, SAN DIEGO, PRICE CAMPUS CENTER, 1992. KAPLAN, McLAUGLIN, DIAZ, ARCHITECTS. *(this page, top and bottom) A dramatic piazza, framed by two campus center buildings, bookstore, and food court. The piazza is traversed by a major campus walk, carrying pedestrian traffic into and through the central space. The conjunction of paved areas and a greensward create a beguiling visual setting that attracts students and enlivens the campus scene. The food services building includes "roll-up garage-type doors that break down the barrier between inside and outside space." The designers note that "sales in the bookstore and food court are in the highest percentile of all college centers…a testament to the success of the design." (Source: Kaplan, McLauglin, Diaz, Architects)*

evenings and weekends—a programmatic issue on most campuses with a residential population and a design issue of consequence for campus center life administrators, planners, and architects.

Modest or grandiose, campus centers occupy a central site and are intended to be designed as special buildings reflecting local conditions, customs, needs, and aspirations. The Memorial Student Union at the University of Missouri, Columbia, is indicative of how such came into being. It was started in 1926 with a Memorial Tower, Tudor Gothic style, for university students who died in World War I. But sentiment could not induce additional expenditures. Two activity wings, which would have constituted the center proper, were delayed for three decades "due to fund-raising difficulties, another world war, and spiraling construction costs." Enrollment growth after World War II gave further cause for a union, and an alert university leadership sustained the political impetus to complete the "cherished dream." Externally, the second-phase design was arranged to match the older Tudor Gothic architecture of the shrinelike Tower, but by then the design model was dated and the results bland and enervated. The Missouri building is a landmark structure ending the era of romance with traditional styles and forms but not the idea of arranging the constituent elements of a campus center to rise upward and mark and celebrate time and place.

Campus centers at San Francisco State University (1974), Franklin Pierce College (1985), and Emory University (1986) illustrate differences in design expression, varying functional concepts, the codification of aesthetic values, the influence of geography, and site treatment. All three conform to programmatic principles found in successful campus centers: typically some combination of six basic functions—bookstore, dining, meeting rooms, post office, social spaces, and student organization rooms. The best buildings are designed to encourage people to circulate through the interior spaces so as to see the ongoing activities and choose to participate; this often requires an audacious building design and crossroads location. In this regard, the San Francisco building has few equals; in appearance, it was as if Le Corbusier and the architect of a Mayan temple had collaborated on a competition entry arranged to catch the jury's attention. Roofscape, surrounding plaza, and building combine to generate San Francisco's unique form.

Designing and redesigning centers as a progression of diverse spatial and activity experiences does not require a large building to be successful, a principle well expressed in the Franklin Pierce College campus center. Bookstore and post office anchor either end of the circulation spine, which, running end to end on the south side, and well fenestrated, provides picturesque views to the lake beyond. The spine gives access to all the main activity areas, with the spatial sequence arranged to take advantage of the varying levels fitted into the hillside topography. The design merges contemporary architecture with regional features; the structural profile suggesting rural barns and the shingles local materials. A five-story tower provides a viewing platform to the surrounding landscape. The tower's physical profile and height—a gesture to, but not imitation of, rural New England silos—furnishes a place-marking, skyline element recognized locally as a college symbol.

The most significant recent changes in campus centers have been in the type and appearance of food services. About 1980 it was generally recognized that the oncoming generation of students would not be satisfied with conventional, static, minimal-choice, limited-hours dining. Further, many campus centers from the 1960s were showing their inevitable obsolescence and their stale decor. Food courts and food malls became the central theme in new buildings and renovations. What dining professions call "the full service, central kitchen," was used to make ready food for the campus equivalent of delis, cafes, salad bars, ethnic food stations, mall-like courts as well as traditional snack bars and dining rooms. Emory's solution is unique in its terraced dining and dramatic melding of new and old spaces.

Some campuses are held in bondage by their rural site and have to use the campus center for activities, goods, and services otherwise not available in the immediate environs. Fortunately, we think, are those institutions that have a surrounding ambiance that enlarges the choices available for participation in campus life by having a surrounding district attuned to college and university routines and needs. The bazaars at the gateway of the University of Istanbul; the cafes and book stalls enfolding the Sorbonne; the English town markets interleaved with the colleges at Cambridge and Oxford; Harvard Square, Telegraph Avenue at Berkeley, and Thayer Street at Brown—these are enclaves of private enterprise, with memorable activities and physical forms. They are not substitutes for campus centers but supplements. The University of California, San Diego's Price Center (bookstores, shops, eating facilities, piazza) captures the best of Berkeley or Harvard Square and retains the advantages of onsite building location. Brown University took a two-prong approach, restoring and revitalizing Faunce Hall (an early-twentieth-century campus center of historic importance) in response to current student and faculty programs and activities and promoted a cooperative effort with the neighboring commercial interests to help keep Thayer Street economically viable, safe, and visually pleasant.

For Beloit College, "saving the heritage" meant reconstructing a Burham and Root masterpiece, originally designed for the sciences in 1893. The building lay fallow from 1967 until 1985—too historic to destroy and seemingly too expensive to

BELOIT COLLEGE, HISTORIC SCIENCE BUILDING SAVED AND CONVERTED INTO CAMPUS CENTER, **1989. C. EDWARD WARE, ASSOCIATES, ARCHITECTS.** *(Source: Beloit College)*

EMORY UNIVERSITY, MEMORIAL UNION, C. 1926. HENRY HORNBOSTEL. (*above***)** *Henry Hornbostel established a significant design image for Emory University in the 1920s, an Italianate palazzo style, inspired, it has been said, by the site's red clay soil, topography, and pine trees, which reminded him of Tuscany. The campus center, shown here, was designed as a memorial to university alumni. Though the building became decrepit and outmoded, there was strong sentiment for its continuation as a central campus building.*

EMORY UNIVERSITY, R. HOWARD DOBBS UNIVERSITY CENTER, 1986. JOHN PORTMAN AND ASSOCIATES. *(facing page, top) A stellar designer of the architecture of hospitality, John Portman devised a contemporary solution that not only saved the old building but gave the image-inducing facade a dramatic setting. The new section, shown, contains post office, bookstore, lounges, dining and ballroom, kitchen, and support spaces. The older section was reconstructed for student activity and operational offices, social space, film theater, and legitimate theater. (Source: Emory University)*

THE TERRACE. *(facing page, bottom) The juncture of new and old has been configured into a terrace for informal dining and socializing. The steps of the older building can serve as a stage for special events. The concept is said to be inspired by the Vicenza's Teatro Olimpico. Assertive new architecture and calm classical: The combination offers something for everybody, and, with its programmatic synergy and serendipity, truly a formula for a successful campus center. (Source: Emory University)*

convert to some other use. With student recruitment and retention pivoting on having an improved campus center, in tandem with the College's cultivation of benefactors appreciative of the building's design significance, reconstruction became tenable. The typical range of campus center functions were adroitly fitted into the large spaces in the original structure. The impressive wooden framing uncovered during the work was restored as an interior design theme.

SUPPORT FACILITIES

Like all institutions, higher education has certain predictable routines—administration, recordkeeping, physical plant operations, i.e., support facilities. The structures serving and symbolizing those activities need not be mundane and can in fact glow with creative interpretations. All building types can be architecture, if a client insists; thus a Princeton University parking deck and the heating plant at Scarborough College become three-dimensional art. The visual expression for the admissions functions and administrative routines, for example, may vary from the plain vanilla of an 1890 New England mill building converted by the University of New Hampshire as a satellite facility (1988) to Connecticut College's (1990) elaborate and elegant Admissions House.

Having surveyed a group of typical college and university structures by function, three building types have been selected below for extended examination: libraries, laboratories, and housing. We use them to trace further how institutional needs and requirements shift and how architecture responds. Libraries are and have been the pomp and glory edifices in the cities of knowledge. Laboratories, serving science and technology, raise the expectation that the outer expression of the building might be as rational as the activities inside. For many institutions, but not all, the character and quality of campus housing defines its position in the higher education's hierarchy and its commitment to campus life as an experiential contribution to student development or, for married students, faculty, and staff, a service and convenience not available in the local market. The overview includes a gloss on current issues and trends as a way of indicating the ebullience that keeps college and university architecture vital with certainty or vitiated with stale dogma. Several of the designs reviewed below are, or were, considered the best of their time by historians, critics, and journalists and certified as being good architecture by awards given by peers and educational associations. Some are also chosen for illustrative purposes because they show how function, exterior expression, and site development can produce design distinction and differentiation without sacrificing campus heritage. Others are didactic, which with accompanying captions and notes are alert systems for concepts flawed and frail. Again, admittedly, this sweeping view of building types, of course, runs the risk of being an overstated generalization, of missing an example which an encyclopedic treatment would snare, or of being composed of nuances so finite that their importance is lost in minutiae. It is our hope, however, that after circling several pivotal definitions several times throughout the book with examples and comments, the thematic idea and ideal will be readily sensed and appreciated, i.e., the built environment as a sequence of accomplishment: structures, buildings, architecture, campus architecture.

SCARBOROUGH COLLEGE, HEATING PLANT, 1968. JOHN ANDREWS. *(left)*

PRINCETON UNIVERSITY, PARKING STRUCTURE, 1992. MACHADO AND SILVETTI. *(below) The Princeton scheme demonstrates the power and potential of creative designs for a commonplace utilitarian campus structure. John Andrews' design combines engineering and sculpture into an extraordinary campus design element. (Photo: Chuck Choi, courtesy of Rudolpho Machado.)*

UNIVERSITY OF NEW HAMPSHIRE, MANCHESTER CAMPUS. *(right) Entrance area to admissions office, 1890 mill building converted for university functions. A well-located facility that enables the university to contribute to historic conservation of an urban area deserving friendly renewal. (Source: University of New Hampshire)*

CONNECTICUT COLLEGE, ADMISSIONS HOUSE, 1990. GRAHAM GUND AND ASSOCIATES. *(below) Intended to make an immediate impact on students considering admissions to a independent college, saying architecturally: this place is not your large, impersonal public institution. (Source: Connecticut College)*

LIBRARIES

*Not only should the new library (Harvard University) be as perfect in plan
and equipment as a wise and generous expenditure can make it, it should
also, avoiding any display of costliness, possess a beauty of its own, both from
within and without, that it may be a constant source of pleasure and
inspiration to all who use it.*

L. J. May, 1902

*The elevation or facade of a library building should, as far as possible, be in
keeping with the object for which it is erected, although there is always a difficulty
in making the outside characteristic of the use to be made of the interior.*

*It is inevitable that in the absence of special knowledge (of library functions) and
in special devotion to a particular style of edifice, the sentiment of architectural
display should get the upper hand.*

F. J. Burgone
Library Construction, London, 1905

*To plan it, find an able librarian. To construct it, get a skillful architect. To
control both, choose a wise committee. These three, by patient study and debate, can
satisfy taste without sacrificing use—achieving complete and felicitous success.*

Charles C. Soul
How to Plan a Library Building for Library Work, 1912

*Perhaps the surest sign of a first-class architect is his ability to design a building which
is functional and also distinguished architecturally. But no architect can be expected to
accomplish this unless he understands the institution, its objectives, and requirements,
and has a satisfactory program on which to base his work.*

Keyes D. Metcalf
Planning Academic and Research Libraries, 1965

*A golden age of library building appeared imminent. Many of the libraries which
arose were striking pieces of architectural design—adventurous, attractive, original.
Some won prizes—architectural prizes; very few indeed would win prizes awarded
by working librarians....A few, including work by some very distinguished
architects, deserve enrollment in the record of monumental howlers.*

Godfrey Thompson, 1973

*Attending the right graduate school and being published in prestigious places
are still important, but establishing a name for oneself on-line has become the
newest way to gain recognition. I don't see how you can keep up with your
field in any other way. The Internet is probably at least six months ahead of
journals and conferences, and certainly books.*

Veronica S. Panteldis
The Chronicle of Higher Education, November 1994

Enclosing books and bytes, libraries are perhaps the most revealing exhibit of the
functional transformation of knowledge and institutional response architecturally.
From a few volumes locked in closets to be kept from dampness, fire, and wear,

RADCLIFFE CAMERA, 1747. JAMES GIBBS. *(right) An all-time classic, campus landmark, modernized and still used as a library.*

REED LIBRARY, 1965. I. M. PEI AND PARTNERS. *(below) College and university libraries draw the best talent of their time, devising memorable designs. Each architect intends to leave her or his imprint, sometimes, as in this instance, inventing forms and styles that no one would or should copy. The best libraries are not monuments to their designers but team efforts in which the architect and librarian are coauthors of the project. The principle is not new. Its implementation seems daunting. (Source: State University of New York, Fredonia)*

CORNELL UNIVERSITY, CARL A. KROCH LIBRARY, 1992. SHEPLEY, BULFINCH, RICHARDSON AND ABBOTT. *(facing page) Library commissions have always provided client and designer opportunities to devise solutions functionally sound and aesthetically imaginative. Differences in site location, library purpose and size, technology, budget, and skill are affecting factors as can be gleaned in the contrasting configurations of Kroch Library and the examples that follow. (Photo: Jeff Goldberg, courtesy of Shepley, Bulfinch, Richardson and Abbott)*

THE
Heart
& Core
•

CAROLINA'S
LIBRARY

with circulation controlled by the president, libraries soon became the architectural symbols of college and university purpose and progress, monuments to intellectual memory of a monastic past and a tribute to a cyberspace future. Industrialization of knowledge—mass printing of relatively cheap books and periodicals to computerization—was one factor in generating expansion. The inevitable pressures of growth in the size and variety of collections and number of patrons, the professionalization of library service, felicitous collaboration with faculty, and accreditation standards were among the other influences that gave cause for more and better libraries. From the times when books were unchained from abbey walls, every decade has been a golden age for college and university libraries and their architects.

Colleges and university libraries are model meldings of information technology, aesthetics, and campus design. Christopher Wren's Trinity College Library (1690) and Cornell University's Carl A. Kroch Library (1992), three centuries later, are joined by a common theme—spatial qualities that Wren said should "satisfy the eye and impress the imagination." Designed to help conserve a campus open space, the Kroch designers pack 800,000 volumes into a three-level underground structure. The landscaped roof serves as a courtyard. Skylights admit light from above to an atrium, creating spatial effects among the offices, classrooms, and exhibit area that recall Piranesi at his best.

There are more campus library buildings than there are campuses, bearing witness to knowledge growth and specialization and the potential reuse older campus libraries have for continued service for discipline-oriented collections, professional schools, and rare books. Recent projects help illustrate library differences and design distinctions. Giurgola and Mitchell's Davis Library (University of North Carolina) is the large central university facility, an information mall with 2.5 million volumes and the technological capability of tapping electronically library resources worldwide. Hugh N. Jacobson's Gettysburg College library typifies a sculptural approach to building design, the client's desire for a shape and form that signaled institutional advancement. The University of Toronto multimillion-volume library, imposed on a small site, scrupulously well planned, epitomizes the heavy concrete fortress architecture popular at that time.

In contrast to the Toronto scheme, James Stirling's open and light essay in glass and metal—the Cambridge University Faculty History Library (1968), stands out literally in its programmatic premise and its architectural form. Of unique, modern special-purpose library buildings, the chief feature is a contemporary version of the nineteenth-century British Museum reading room. Programmatically the fear of losing books to theft prompted the Cambridge design, as well as the objective of accommodating seminar and lecture rooms and faculty offices under the same

UNIVERSITY OF NORTH CAROLINA, WALTER ROYAL DAVIS LIBRARY, 1984. MITCHELL & GIURGOLA. *(facing page) The largest of the twelve campus libraries. Constructed on a site once a parking lot and funded through the sale of the University-operated utility systems, which had provided telephone service, water, and electricity to town and campus. The banners display publisher's marks (as old as Caxton and as young as the Ashantily Press) from works in the University's Wilson Library. The latter is the predecessor to Davis and is now used for special collections. (Source: University of North Carolina)*

roof as the library. The spatial configuration of the main room is a Stirling-stunner in shape and expansiveness. A control desk is situated above the reading room, like the guard's station in a minimum security prison. The upper floor corridors are glazed to permit continuous scrutiny of the readers and books below.

Unlike any architecture before or since at Cambridge—with its cascading glass facade and elegant detailing and joining of tile, brick, and metal—the building attracts visitors worldwide as an epitome of period design; few come as librarians seeking clues for functional solutions. There are, however, aspects of the Stirling building—the human scale and serendipitous design effects—which the Toronto scheme for all its functionality totally misses and the Gettsyburg scheme sets aside in favor of an heroic, masonry edifice. Whether or not intended by the architect, the upper floors of the Cambridge scheme have become an indoor garden. Flowering plants in pots, arranged informally along the corridors by the nearby faculty, yielded an unexpected treat during a recent January visit. An unconscious gesture to the vistas of buildings and greenery for which the University is famous? Equally beguiling was the prospect of Kings Chapel on the horizon; the kind of enchanting visual dialog which generations of great campus architecture will evoke, a bonus from genius.

As to commanding presence, how much more specific than the instruction given by the St. Louis Library Conference (1869), "that inasmuch as the library is the heart of a university, it should be given a central position from which the other buildings radiate." Bebb & Gould interpreted the principle as a library-cum-cathedral and surrounding medieval town square at the University of Washington, 1926—now one of the landmark open spaces in American campus design. The principle has precedent in Radcliffe Camera (Oxford, 1747), James Gibb's eloquent skyline edifice and one of the first buildings designed and constructed for science collections, and is dramatically restated at Brown University by Warner, Burns, Toan and Lunde. Their high-rise science library—award-winning concrete architecture—soars over the campus and neighborhood. Visible miles away, it anchors one corner of a nascent science quadrangle. Millikin Library, California Institute of Technology, 1978, equally dominates its setting, in this instance quixotic and idiosyncratic as a library and eye-catching as a glitzy slab that sets no trend in function or aesthetics.

Four buildings from the 1950-to-1980 era summarize technical issues and designer's response. At Goucher College, the 1953 library building was erected on the new campus "to occupy a central position, both in the educational program of the college, and in the plan for its physical facilities." Where the site was cramped and building style disguised function, then the desired prominence could be substantiated with a heroic sculpture, announcing building purpose, as on the Holland Library facade, Washington State University. From the same period, the University of Detroit architect states: "the library has been placed at one end of a central mall in a location where it will dominate the entire campus...the exterior design should follow as a straightforward expression of this plan with reliance on choice of materials and careful attention to fenestration making it fit comfortably with its older neighbors." The only real concession to style, wrote designer Paul B. Brown, "is the large cartouche over the main entrance, incorporating the seal of the

University." Walter Netsch's contribution to a golden age of libraries at Northwestern University (1980) was a series of pavilions linked to the existing library, eliciting an architectural critic's kudos, "as a building of crystalline beauty, creating a major icon of twentieth-century architecture."

Praised at their opening dates, neither the Brown, Detroit, nor Northwestern buildings are favored today aesthetically or functionally. Detroit had the last of the closed-stack systems. Brown's verticality and Northwestern's separate pavilions impede rearranging collections, reader and support space, and provision for computerized information technology. Brown's stylistic tower, one of several such university library towers associated with its designer, is an example of one generation's "soaring" becoming another generation's intimidation. The Northwestern building plan and facades are often cited as examples of Modern architecture gone wrong. In these instances what Soul observed as a possible danger at the beginning of the century came to pass: "That the business of planning of a library is specific, technical, and minute; that it is like the planning of other useful structures which can be spoiled by blunders or ignorance, or by sins done in the name of art." Plain-vanilla Goucher survives, still central in location, reasonably adaptable to changing needs, but stylistically dull. The front door design and adjacent site was an opportunity neglected, in terms of creating a significant campus open space at a crossroads location, an opportunity creatively grasped in the University of Missouri's Columbia Law School project.

On the inside of the Missouri scheme, the physical relationship of the three main law functions are a tour de force of expressing function and symbol, and melding these with building circulation, and provision for information technology. As the client wished, and the designer responded, the idea was that justice is given form in spatial character of the courtrooms, service in the functional arrangement of administration suites and offices, and education in the library ambiance. The lobby and plaza has that angular, diagonal slicing that signifies late-twentieth-century institutional design. The stacking and steeping of the latter give the building a distinctive profile, scaling down a massive building and permitting the largest numbers of books and readers to be situated on the plaza level. Brickwork and masonry effects, the light towers, and detailing are reminiscent of adjacent older campus buildings. "Natural light defines and enlivens inside and out," noted a design jury giving the building a prestigious award in the name of the master of such lighting effects in educational buildings, Louis Kahn.

Technology and library design can be seen advancing hand-by-hand, shaping and impacting every aspect of the library's physical development. The introduction of metal stacks (Harvard, 1877) permitted new ways to store and arrange books. The Dewy Decimal system rationalized locations. Small items such as Tonk's shelf-fitting (1870) and the Simplex Indicator (1880) stimulated and required an adjustment in library operations, floor layouts, building circulation. The Tonk device was a metal clasp system that permitted shelves to be lowered or raised for adjustment in book heights. The Simplex Indicator was a graphic device for displaying which books were in the library, borrowed, or missing, the precursor to contemporary computerized circulation systems. Furnishings, too, have been the subject of continuing evolution. The nineteenth-century views about whether tables and chairs

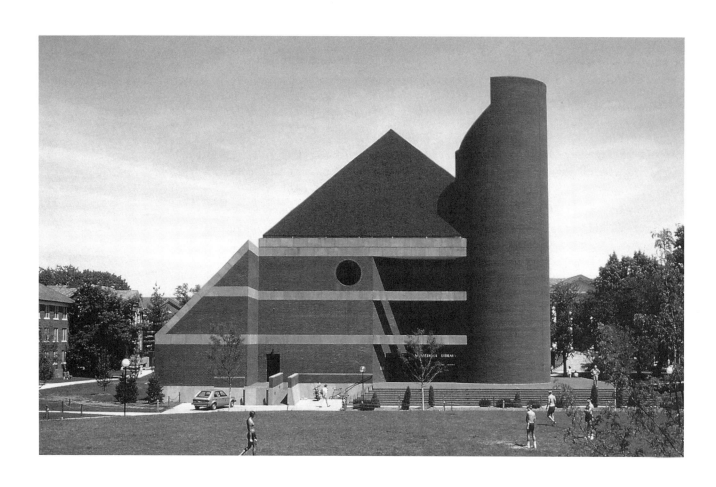

CAMBRIDGE UNIVERSITY, FACULTY OF HISTORY LIBRARY, 1968. JAMES STIRLING, ARCHITECT. *(facing page)* Program objective: *"the building is organized on the principle that there should be close contact between the library and faculty offices (the motivating element of the Faculty of History design and all its parts is the security of the collections)...therefore windows are set into the corridor walls around the upper floors and these appear under the roof lantern...allowing members in the upper parts of the building to look down into the reading area and maintain a visual, but non-intrusive and silent contact, with the Library."* Stirling's crystal palace satisfied the requirements and gave Cambridge a commanding, dramatic modern building. It drew on few precedents, and since has set no direction for any subsequent buildings in its district, nor as an example of library-as-function.

Here, then, in one project is the excitement and despair, too frequently, of critic's and connoisseur's laudable college and university architecture. What does one say of a flawed masterpiece, designed to the client's program objectives, human in scale, a gem, a building worth seeing and experiencing, though not a model in terms of library practices and information technology, and deficient as to energy conservation, maintenance, and operations? A thing of beauty is a joy forever?

GETTYSBURG COLLEGE, LIBRARY LEARNING RESOURCES CENTER, 1981. HUGH NEWELL JACOBSON. *(above)*

UNIVERSITY OF TORONTO, ROBBERS LIBRARY, 1980. WARNER, BURNS, TOAN, LUNDE. *(right)* Small library buildings or large, eminent designers strive to give the library a unique design, thus signaling institutional advancement architecturally. Sometimes the results compromise library functions and long-term expansion, and sometimes they impose a physical form that later generations regret seeing and using.

UNIVERSITY OF WASHINGTON, LIBRARY AS CATHEDRAL, 1926. BEBB & GOULD. *(top)*

BROWN UNIVERSITY, LIBRARY AS TOWER, 1972. WARNER, BURNS, TOAN AND LUNDE. *(bottom left)*

CALIFORNIA INSTITUTE OF TECHNOLOGY, LIBRARY AS BEACON, 1966. SWELLING AND MOODY. *(bottom right)*

should have racks for holding patron's hats are not dissimilar to decisions on providing extra-size lockers for patron's expensive down-filled jackets. Reading carrels once elaborately carved like church pews are now manufactured as electronic work stations.

Arrangements for heating, ventilation, and illumination more than anything else brought campus libraries into the Modern era. Within one generation oil lamps gave way to gas fixtures and gas to electricity. Library journals recorded "scientific discussions of the forms of bulbs, the materials of reflectors, and the forms of shade." Early on (1905), some thought that "the cost of current to serve proper illumination—to enable us to see things without injury or fatiguing the eye, would be prohibitive." Proven economical, and with further modifications, the new electrical lighting systems however soon helped alter architectural forms. As a result, libraries were "able to dispense with uneconomic and narrow reading rooms; very high ceilings and long windows; light wells, skylights, and rotundas; and multitudinous stack windows; all of which had their origins in the earlier necessity of admitting as much light as possible." Energy conservation, lighting for computer screens, and the theme that natural lighting is the "cheeriest, clearest, healthiest, and cheapest" are matters that connect those earlier technical advances with today's topics and interests.

How basic too, the observations of one early-twentieth-century library designer: "Underheating promotes discomfort, coughs, and colds; overheating stupefies staff and readers. More than anything else bad air interferes with clearness and concentration of thought." Good air, wrote a commentator much later, "seems destined to increase the comfort of readers as well as the preservation of library materials." The rapidity in which nineteenth-century library building technology was introduced to mediate all aspects of environmental conditions gave birth to the technical specialist, whose contributions to library design now are as important as they were then. There are "subjects which neither the librarian nor the architect may know all the latest phases, and they really want and must seek skilled information," advised librarian L. B. Marks in 1886. Expert advice is the first line of defense against "howlers," large and small. One responds now with amusement, but then with disdain, to a physical plant manager's solution for energy savings and higher levels of illumination in a main reading room: highway sodium vapor fixtures. The orange glow and noisy rheostat were not kindly received. Professional librarians should "courageously oppose with facts and figures, all efforts to erect buildings not functionally planned," stated William H. Carlson in 1946. Respect for function and technology, he said, does rule out the achievement of "striking architectural effect," or making the library the "show place of the campus, lending dignity to the intellectual center of the institution." Library expansion is a productive occasion for retooling deficient technology, when such is required, an aspect well handled in Graham Gund's extension to the Mount Holyoke Library (shown on page 42) a contemporary design also commendable in its solution to joining new and old.

Thanks to the labors of library masters such as Keyes D. Metcalf, the essential characteristics of college and university libraries, as a building type, can be succinctly stated. Libraries support the academic mission by acquiring, holding, and making accessible books, periodicals, journals, newspapers, and, increasingly, data and information in nonprint formats, both on and off site. The library staff,

WASHINGTON STATE UNIVERSITY, HOLLAND LIBRARY. *(top)* *(Source: Washington State University)*

GOUCHER COLLEGE LIBRARY. *(bottom)* *(Source: Goucher College)*

UNIVERSITY OF MISSOURI, COLUMBIA, LAW SCHOOL LIBRARY. THE LEONARD PARKER ARCHITECTS (P. PROSE). *(Source: The Leonard Parker Architects)*

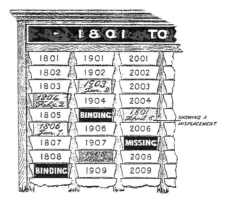

through catalogs and reference works, assist the faculty and students in using the library materials, to guide and connect to other sources. Space, furnishings, and equipment are provided for the library patrons' convenience and comfort when engaged in library activities, independently or in groups. Staff work places are vital for ordering, receiving, preparing, and shelving library materials. As a highly used public building, toilets, telephones, copy machines, and janitorial rooms are required. These are the essential features of all modern campus libraries.

Essential, but not necessarily sufficient. Each library has a constituency and serves a clientele distinctly its own. Not every library will be a depository of public documents, collect prints and drawings, operate a reserve reading, hold and display rare books and manuscripts, give patrons physical access to on-line databases. Thus we see the importance of a facility program to inform library architecture with a complete statement of needs and expectations, the first line of defense against howlers. The second line of defense in achieving a good building is a systematic scrutiny of conceptual drawings and detailed drawings to ensure that the program is correctly interpreted as well as to see and adjust proposed internal physical arrangements, furnishings, and specifications that those operating the libraries know best. The program will mandate certain standards and criteria, such as structural modularity, stack spacing and shelf heights, and floor coverings. It may also lay out in words some design objectives more ephemeral than ceiling heights and lighting levels. One such statement, quoted in the standard reference work by Metcalf (*Planning Academic and Research Library Buildings*, McGraw-Hill, New York, 1965) is well remembered: "As the heart of the University, the library will combine genuine functionalism with aesthetic imagination and avoid every sort of aesthetic falsity, pretentiousness, or slovenliness."

Juxtaposed on page 102 are two libraries, circa 1960, that are true to the intentions stated by Metcalf. Inside they are immediately decipherable instances of his consistent library philosophy, outside, polar expressions architecturally. The common theme is an open, modular library concept first advocated by some young librarians in the 1940s and now accepted as standard practice. Modularity provides for flexible mixing of collections, patron seating, and services from the professional staff. Unlike the earlier fixed-stack concepts, which froze the library to the time of its first construction, shelving and furniture arrangements in modular libraries can be modified in response to changes in collection policies, number of volumes, seating patterns.

The Bennington College Library (illustrated on page 102) is a jewel-box, domestic in scale; 210 seats, about 75,000 volumes, serving a small college located in a rural setting. The Boston University Library, with over a million and a half volumes and seats for 2300 readers, is compressed on an urban site, a landmark structure at the edge of the Charles River. Both buildings assert their modernity, as such was then understood. Size and location obviously affect the two design solutions. Certain architectural features, the ephemeral differences, can also be apprehended and rationalized as design influences. A high-rise wooden structure on a stone base would seem as incongruous for the Boston University land area as would a tough concrete exterior in picturesque, bucolic Vermont. A good building, and these were for their date, is a team effort with a logical division of labor. The librarian was charged with defining function, the architect with creating the design expression, and both with realizing the melding of the two.

As noted, with the specialization and sectorization of knowledge, college and university libraries now outnumber campuses. It is not unusual for a college to have individual buildings for the main collections and the sciences. Music scores and reference books may be held in a dedicated library wing in a performing arts center. Understandably at the university level, professional schools will have their own edifices, with specialized collections and services wrapped in a building that exudes confidence and pride, as does the law school building at the University of Missouri, Columbia, cited earlier.

As to building additions, design attitudes, and, in turn, alternatives, vary considerably. At the Massachusetts Institute of Technology, the prosaic facade of the older complex is broken, and a contemporary architectural expression is introduced to accommodate and herald library expansion for the School for Engineering. A special research library devoted to books focusing on the settlement of North America, the expansion of the John Carter Brown Library earns attention—for the functional integration of new space and old, for the architect's skill in giving a seamless exterior expression of the two, and the University's decision that the cost for crafting and constructing a stylistic faithful addition was worth the effort. The University of Michigan Law School library expansion was solved with an ultra-modern subsurface addition that left the older, traditional facade intact.

Whether there will be any life in any libraries through the twenty-first century, given the expected fundamental alterations in information technology, remains problematic, and the answers obviously will have architectural implications. As J. C. R. Licklider forecast in 1971 (*Libraries of the Future*, Cambridge), "the technology of digital memory is not operating near any fundamental physical limit, and new departures could continue to appear once every decade." More recently, the new and emerging forms of information technology and telecommunications, say some experts, can provide a full range of library resources in computerized formats accessible in any place, at any time. And should Virtual Online University succeed—the "electronic equivalent of an actual classroom"—then new forms of teaching and learning (machines for accumulating and using facts, and people for exchanging opinions and values) may generate and require hybrid forms of class-

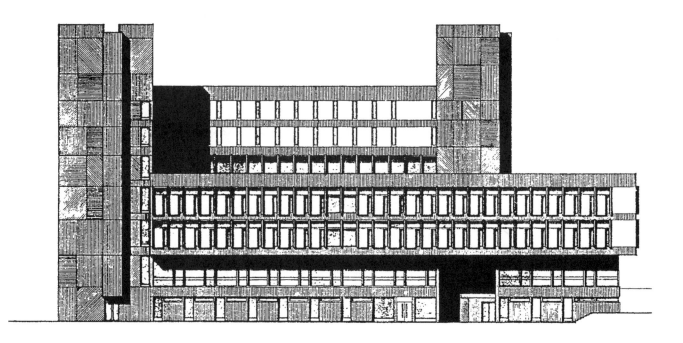

BOSTON UNIVERSITY CENTRAL LIBRARY, 1965. HOYLE, DORAN, AND BERRY WITH SERT, JACKSON AND ASSOCIATES, INC. *(top) One and a half million volumes, with provision for 2300 readers, with its stacked floors and unusual configuration fitted to an urban site. Now a cityscape landmark along the Charles River.*

BENNINGTON COLLEGE, 1959. CARL KOCH AND ASSOCIATES AND PIETRO BELLUSCHI. *(bottom) Planned for 75,000 volumes and 210 reader stations, in a design that reflects the New England countryside. The terrain permitted a clever three-level solution, with the main entrance at the second level, a formula favored by library expert Keyes Metcalf. The modern facade, painted white wood, brick-enclosed courtyard, and stone wall, the sense of place, represent the best visual aspects of the pre-electronic-age small college library.*

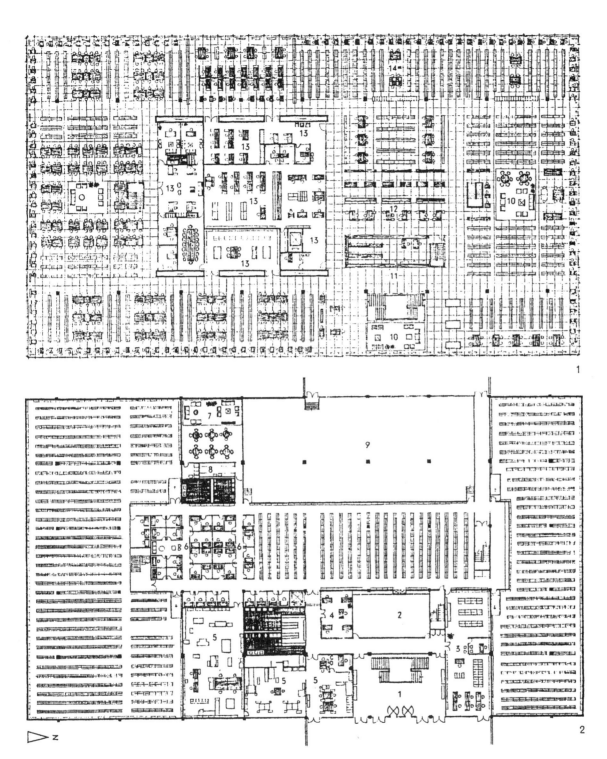

LIBRARY FLOOR PLAN/COMPUTER CHIP, ILLINOIS INSTITUTE OF TECHNOLOGY, 1962. *Floor plans for John Crerar Library, by Skidmore, Owings, Merrill. A superb example of the open-plan research library, with long-range flexibility for rearranging collections, readers, and services. Resembling a computer chip, the graphic may also serve as a metaphor for the astounding changes in information technology. The contents of the library can now be stored on a single disc and transported for use wherever the owner would wish. Not as transportable are the services of a professional librarian to guide the reader through references and to assist bibliographically or to help validate the reliability of information acquired electronically.*

room and library architecture. Conceptually this is not a new idea, if one recalls the functional unitary buildings of the early American colleges—all of education under one roof. The weight of professional opinion, however, leans toward the new information formats as being supplements to, rather than substitutes for, traditional library materials. The predicted future—collections, patrons, staff, technology, service—wrapped in, not warped by, golden-age architecture.

The Reed Library addition, State University of New York, Fredonia, 1994, distills the important aspects of taking existing libraries into the twenty-first century and in doing so staking out important design features which no library—new, expanded, or improved—should neglect: a building which inside and out beckons, welcomes, and encourages one to participate in its offerings and activities.

Designed by Pei and Partners, Reed Library is a classic composition of Modern, sculptural concrete architecture, built in 1965; 90,000 square feet, with no expansion expected or planned and little provision for handicapped accessibility or library automation and electronic information technology. The 45,000-square-foot addition (Pasanella+Klein Stolzman+Berg) presents a different scale and facade treatment to the arriving library patron, while paying homage to the original concept. The exterior materials combine the brick of the older campus and Pei's concrete. New space and old is reorganized for twenty-first-century functions. The interior has the skewing and sweeping spatial arrangements, with the curving walls and slanting architectural elements seen in contemporary 1990 college and university architecture. The curtain wall with spandrel glass, exposed structure and utility systems, nooks and crannies, and occasional informal seating patterns, all help humanize the original 1965 blockhouse architecture.

LABORATORY BUILDINGS

> *A key goal is to improve national literacy in science and mathematics and meet future requirements for trained people in science and engineering. This is essential in an increasingly technological and competitive world.*
>
> D. Allen Bromley, 1990

> *Serendipity—the chance discovery of an idea—is common in the daily practice of science and mathematics. Facilities should support serendipity.*
>
> Project Kaleidoscope, 1991

> *The construction of new laboratory buildings and the renovation of old ones requires close communication between the laboratory users, project engineers, architects, construction engineers, and safety and health experts.*
>
> Louis J. DiBerardinis, 1993

> *Unfunded science and engineering capital needs total $5.7 billion for 515 institutions (of the nation's 3,600 campuses) reporting such information.*
>
> National Science Foundation, 1994

Why do science buildings from the 1920s and 1930s look different from today's architecture? What occurred to transform exterior expression from traditional styles to Modern idioms? Did differentiation in subject matter, pioneering research rou-

STATE UNIVERSITY OF NEW YORK, FREDONIA,
REED LIBRARY ADDITION, 1994.
PASANELLA+KLEIN STOLZMAN+BERG. *(right)*
*Detail of new addition, changing scale and
image, and improving existing library functions
sympathetically. (Source: Pasanella+Klein
Stolzman+Berg)*

STATE UNIVERSITY OF NEW YORK, FREDONIA,
REED LIBRARY, 1965. I. M. PEI AND
PARTNERS. *(below) The apex of the modern
sculptural architecture: assertive and emphatic, a
style not currently in vogue. (Source: I. M. Pei and
Partners)*

STATE UNIVERSITY OF NEW YORK, FREDONIA, REED LIBRARY ADDITION, 1994. PASANELLA+KLEIN STOLZMAN+BERG. *(facing page) The building systems are made visible, the interiors lightened and scaled with structural elements, all expressed as part of the redesign. (Source: Pasanella+Klein Stolzman+Berg)*

UNIVERSITY OF MICHIGAN, LAW SCHOOL ADDITION, 1981. GUNNAR BIRKERTS AND ASSOCIATES. *(above) Underground: 98,000 gross square feet, overall 211,000 gross square feet, new and old. A clever and sensitive solution to expanding a landmark library building whose design features do not admit an economic and functional extension in the same style. The expansion site was a parking lot. The new greensward, an abstraction of the older building's collegiate Gothic, adds another piece of greenery to the University's history of commendable campus landscape development. (Photo: Timothy Hursley, courtesy of the University of Michigan Planning Office)*

tines, or novel modes of teaching stimulate a new architecture as science and technology expanded in the frenzied race to ensure the country's dominant position in international affairs following World War II? We address first the expectation that laboratory buildings will be as rational and studied as the activities they contain and that such rationality will inform good architecture.

The assumption seems tenable historically. Christopher Wren (1689), scientist and architect, applied both skills in designing a superb teaching and demonstration room: "one of the best imagined for seeing, hearing, and for the display of anatomical demonstrations or philosophical experiments upon a table in the middle of the arena." Fitted with audiovisual and computer technology, the room would be suitable today. Pierre Gaudet (*Elements and Theory of Architecture*, 1909) classified science teaching rooms by discipline, suggesting differences in size and shape related to scientific topics. And, more than a half century ago, Larson and Palmer (*Architectural Planning of the American College*, 1933) laid out some guidelines as germane then as now: "lines of demarcation separating sharply the accepted fields (disciplines) are fading out and we frequently find ourselves on the borderlands where they meet and overlap." The authors urged designers "to seek flexibility in a building devoted to science study, and to make the interior arrangements adaptable to changing interests and varying emphases. Adequate provision should also be made for research by both students and faculty, and with the increase of independent study and tutorial plans, for conference and seminar rooms."

World War II is a threshold in examining current programmatic needs and architectural responses. The discoveries and inventions that came from the defense effort (radar, penicillin, atomic energy, electronic computational devices) were stimulated by basic research whose theories and findings soon made their way into the curriculum. This gave cause on every campus for the design and construction of a range of laboratories and support space facilities previously seen only at the most sophisticated technical institutes. During the Cold War and energy crisis, the establishment of national agencies with mandates and budgets to support research offered universities, and some colleges, the reasons and financial resources to design and construct facilities at a phenomenal rate. Private foundations, corporations, and enlightened donors played a significant role in that surge, encouraging and sponsoring some of the best architecture of its time. The output from the labs (trained personnel, ideas, products) fueled the economy and helped move the country into the postindustrial status it now enjoys.

Science and engineering research in fiscal year 1993 ranged from $745 million (Johns Hopkins University) to $64 million (University of Massachusetts, Amherst) at the 100 leading research institutions. The top 26 schools were budgeted at over $200 million each. Funded research was not limited to universities. "The new culture"—emerging science and technology creating an ever-expanding knowledge base—requires undergraduate faculty to keep current with their fields not only through the literature but also through participation in theoretical and applied research. On the best campuses, students share with faculty, "learning science by doing science," giving cause for more and better space. Advanced science and appropriate facilities can thus be found at smaller institutions, such as Oberlin College, with its Kettering Neuroscience Center.

URSINUS COLLEGE, PFAHLER HALL OF SCIENCE. *(left) A sensible version of a traditional style, which for the older generation evokes an image of campus life. (Source: Ursinus College)*

HAMLINE COLLEGE, ROBBINS SCIENCE CENTER, 1990. BWBR, ARCHITECTS. *(below) The oldest college in Minnesota, architecturally notable for several fine collegiate Gothic buildings. The new science building visually connects to the older structures through the selection of exterior materials: sienna brick, red tile roof, limestone trim. The flat roof, hard-edge corners, slit windows, aluminum, and glass honor and indicate twentieth-century precedents; all together a fine rendition of restrained Modern architecture. (Source: Hamline College)*

Examined broadly, design principles and procedures for science buildings apply to engineering and technology structures, with some understandable caveats stated. Among all such buildings there are significant differences in subject matter being studied, in teaching and learning routines, and research. How variable? The National Science Foundation, for example, tracks the intellectual content and facility needs of 43 distinct science and engineering "departments," or disciplines and subject areas, not including the medical sciences and social sciences. From aerospace to zoology each has substantive differences that engender an exceptional and exacting range of building functions, configurations, interior environmental criteria, and building systems requirements. The latter two give rise to the axiom that a good laboratory is a plumbing and ventilation diagram wrapped in an elegant ambiance whose size, structure, and shape are determined by discipline-based instructional practices and investigative protocols.

In scanning National Science Foundation facility documents, two trends are evident: hyperspecialization in facilities as one moves up the scale of higher education, and a tendency on all campuses to expand and gather the sciences and engineering facilities into a discrete development sector for intellectual exchanges, for convenience in operations, for sharing equipment and services. Hyperspecialization engenders building complexity particularly in handling the products and wastes of science and engineering. In these instances, the design, locations, arrangements, and detailing of building components, fixtures, and furnishings are significantly determined by engineering criteria. As a result, the progression of science, engineering, and technology buildings has been awesome in scale and physical representation. From the suite of science laboratories in modern community colleges, in which DNA materials and lasers can be found, to the recent Cyclopean castles of biology research at University of California, Los Angeles, and the Massachusetts Institute of Technology (pages 112 and 116), the functional requirements for teaching and research have and will continue to stimulate a more visually interesting architecture than any other campus building type. Some, such as the engineering buildings at University of Minnesota, are exotic by functional concept, with significant space being underground. Others gain attention for size, as the Biomedical Science Tower, University of Pittsburgh, with 10 acres of enclosed space stacked on a tight site. Stanford University's 1994 science and engineering quad is remarkable for the program thrust, sophistication of building types, and the University's ability to cast out obsolete structures to create suitable sites for significant new buildings. Five "drab buildings from the 1950s and 100 parking spaces" are to be removed to create a major landscape setting for four new teaching and research buildings. The site arrangement is intended to sustain the Stanford tradition of "students in engineering and the sciences interacting with students from the humanities."

STANFORD UNIVERSITY, SCIENCE AND ENGINEERING QUAD, 1994. PEI COBB FREED & PARTNERS.
(facing page) A significant undertaking at a leading research university recognized for the quality of its campus design. Site was cleared of obsolete buildings and parking to create a landscaped setting for three major teaching and research buildings and a high-tech teaching and lecture hall. (Source: Stanford University)

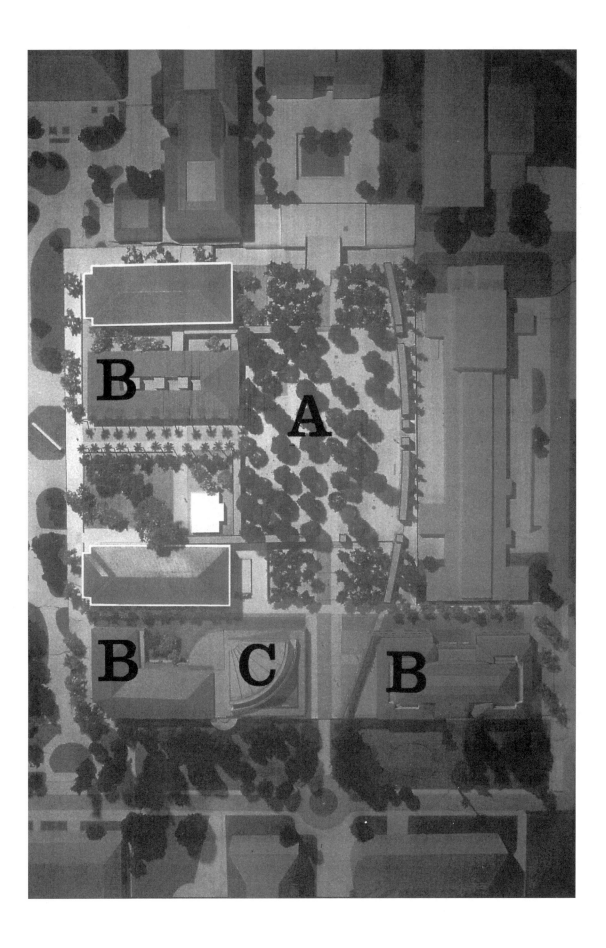

UNIVERSITY OF CALIFORNIA, LOS ANGELES, MOLECULAR SCIENCE BUILDING, 1993. ANSHEN+ALLEN. *An epitome of building rationalization and contemporary campus architecture. A difficult site, a large building (159,000 gross square feet), a demanding program, an assertive and commanding solution. (Photo: T. Hursley, courtesy of Anshen+Allen)*

THE COLORADO COLLEGE, BARNES SCIENCE CENTER, 1988. CLIFFORD S. NAKATA. *(top) (Source: The Colorado College)*

RENSSELAER POLYTECHNIC INSTITUTE, LOW CENTER FOR INDUSTRIAL INNOVATION, 1987. MITCHELL/GIURGOLA. *(bottom left) (Source: Rensselaer Polytechnic Institute)*

UNIVERSITY OF AKRON, COLLEGE OF POLYMER SCIENCE AND ENGINEERING, 1988. RICHARD FLEISCHMAN. *(bottom right) (Source: University of Akron)*

Acknowledging hyperspecialization in building functions at the university level and relatively simpler physical forms for buildings serving the collegiate curriculum, what are the signatures of this building type, i.e., the commonality that comprises a useful generalization? The comments and design implications now noted would seem applicable to most circumstances, i.e., the majority of higher-education laboratory buildings.

Signature 1 is philosophic—each discipline has modes of teaching and research uniquely its own, where clearly one best learns and advances science and engineering by doing science and engineering. Though multiuse spaces are possible, and equipment and support services can be shared, the *doing* requires more space per student than any other scheduled higher-education undertaking. Signature 2 is that all disciplines will stress team activities, with significant amounts of space and time intensively dedicated to singular routines in specialized spaces, large amounts of which must be designed to close tolerances and exacting environmental criteria. Signature 3 is that the desired outcomes to which the buildings are dedicated are fostered by spaces that invite discussions, and interactions, i.e., the socialization and accumulation of the educational and experimental experiences. Finally, signature 4 is the chimera of flexibility in science and technology buildings, whose logic attracts designers forward like a gravitational force, and whose realization (to date) never is sufficiently realizable. The objective is a structure that is functional, reliable, safe on opening day; maintainable during heavy use, and changeable as new needs and requirements dictate.

Procedurally, good laboratory architecture begins by stating clearly the programmatic objectives and physical characteristics of the space components that constitute the project and then confirmation and/or adjustment of the project budget or project size and elements. The start-up methodology is then followed by a determination of the overall internal spatial organization and circulation, site disposition, and external expression. Parenthetically, the design methods applicable to science and engineering are also useful and adaptable to designing any college and university building. The importance of facility programming for libraries was discussed earlier. For example, the generic building type of laboratory being our topic, the comments that follow focus on selective aspects to indicate distinctions and differences. These are building modularity and systems complexity, the visual expression of the exterior walls, and the benefits programmatically and physically of "interactive spaces." The latter's physical expression gives recent laboratory buildings a scale and aesthetic character that critics found missing in what one charitably labeled the "Fort Knox Laboratory Architecture" that climaxed the Modern architectural movement.

MODULARITY, SYSTEMS, AND BUILDING COMPLEXITY. In the 1930s building modularity was shrewdly partnered with pleasure for Modern architectural aesthetics. The Association of Technical Institutions (London) documented the desired trends as early as 1935. The Association promulgated the view that whereas science and engineering technical college buildings "should not be devoid of architectural interest, it is possible to obtain a dignified effect in a simple manner relying upon skillful composition and the judicious employment of modern materials, rather than upon the more elaborate decorative forms associated with past architectural periods." The Association also argued for the presumed economies of Modern architecture, as it was then emerging, noting: "It will be obvious that a considerable saving will be effected by adopting this suggestion." The Association publications also made a strong case for differentiation in building types based on functional variations in environmental requirements. Buildings "should be planned in a simple and orderly manner, as far as possible on a 'Unit' basis, which effects economy in cost and also simplifies subsequent alterations." "Unit" also meant space and construction standardization. Architecturally, the Association's ideas are significant launching points in promoting the causes and benefits of modularity, which in Great Britain reached their aesthetic peak in construction of a new campus for York University, circa 1962. There, employing a regional, prefabricated building system called CLASP, the University was able to construct facilities for 1000 students in 18 months, with a hierarchy of building types, with significant differentiation and flexibility in the interiors of the science buildings, and a visual unity among all the structures on the site. York demonstrated the efficacy of the principle of rational architecture. However, the exterior designs—initially praised for their color, simplicity, and texture—did not take hold as enduring designs. Ironically, a new facility for teaching management was the first to set aside the original designs. The York academics contended that a curriculum devoted to "rational decision-making" deserved an elaborately configured contemporary architectural statement.

Forgotten in many accounts are the precedents for rationalization; one was the first designs for the Massachusetts Institute of Technology's new campus along the Charles River, in Boston. Inside the 1915 scheme, MIT utilized a New England mill planning principles: Large-span spaces could be easily and continuously subdivided. Utilities and mechanical systems could be threaded throughout, accessible and adjustable as needed. Outside, at the beginning, MIT wrapped its east campus in a Roman toga. The Classical idiom was then replaced with Modern designs, when these became popular in the 1950s and 1960s. In the 1970s and 1980s, assertive examples of hard-edge concrete structures extended the Institute's willingness to remain *au courant* architecturally. MIT's latest large building (shown on page 116) straddles several decades of design innovations, and shifts in style, with a structure that has a reasoned resemblance to the other east campus architecture, a visual continuity and heritage the Institute typically prizes, protects, and occasionally misinterprets when the excitement of trendy architecture overcomes studied judgments.

The lure of "new being best" for signifying institutional progress should be judged on a case-by-case basis. At Carnegie-Mellon University, a Modern engineering building intrudes into and destroys a classic campus plan established by Henry Hornbostel, whose sense of grandeur in site composition did not diminish his ability to organize a building facade human in scale and visually interesting. The more recent concrete, blockhouse engineering structure is so out of character and context as to make one wish architecture were biodegradable.

Big and bold doesn't necessarily mean brash and bulky. The Hammel, Green, Abrahamson solution for the University of Minnesota Electrical Engineering/Computer Science Building (1988) placed 40 percent of the building

CARNEGIE-MELLON UNIVERSITY. *(facing page)*
Spring 1994 views of the contrasting architecture. A classical facade inspired by Henry Hornbostel's Beaux Arts training (admittedly marred by window-unit air conditioners) versus a blockhouse intrusion into the major campus open space. The entrance to the older building, human in scale, is a welcoming portal. The bulky concrete form of the newer building sits heavily over the entrance area. In the background, the University of Pittsburgh's Cathedral, designed by Charles Z. Klauder. Taken together, the vista is an instructive example of serendipitous campus design, a panoramic summary of historic architectural aspirations.

MASSACHUSETTS INSTITUTE OF TECHNOLOGY, BUILDING 68—BIOCHEMISTRY, EAST CAMPUS, 1994. GOODY, CLANCY ARCHITECTS. *(above and right) A watershed structure in campus design at an institution whose eastward expansion is a model of sound campus planning and adventuresome architecture. A century of exemplary American higher education buildings can be found in the precinct, produced by the leading architects of their time. These include a candy factory converted into a cancer research center; a swimming pool, metro Boston's first Modern campus building (Lawrence B. Anderson, circa 1940); several Miesian buildings from Skidmore, Owings and Merill; and essays in hard-edge concrete by I. M. Pei (tower building, upper left); among other notables. The Goody, Clancy design is an architectural Rosetta stone. The shapes and textures in their felicitously modulated facade are derived and combined from older campus buildings, and can be read and translated as the architect's code of hierarchy and importance.*

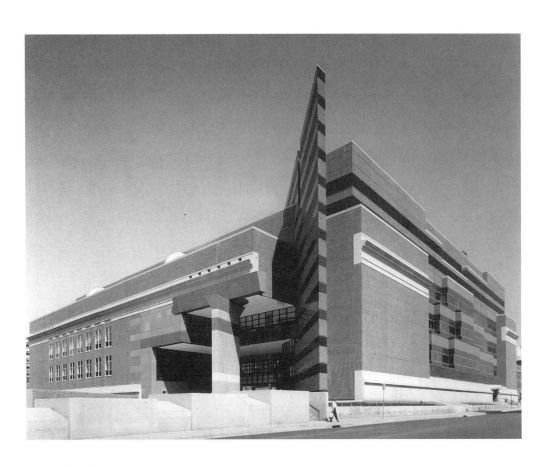

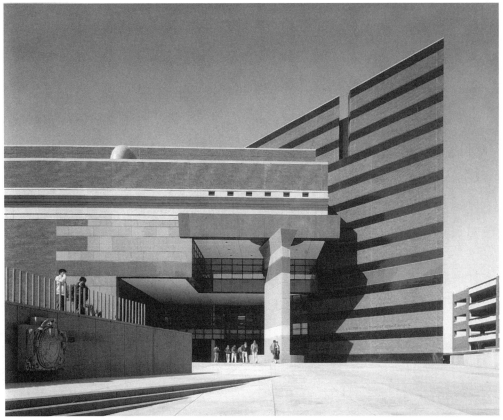

below grade. The visible portion had to establish a strong physical image for the program, and at the same time relate to the existing older buildings (illustrated on page 118). The main portal is inset at the building corner, facing a campus open space, and framed by a heroic composition of structural element and flaring wall. The base is extended at the ground level to form a slanting, greenhouse wall, which admits light to the lower levels. Pedestrian traffic can view interior activities, making the building less ponderous than it seems at a distance. The gestures to context include the horizontal banding pattern and picking up the patterns of stone and brick in the vicinity. Technical requirements included vibration-free rooms, extensive air purification, and, of course, adequate light and ventilation to the below-grade rooms. The building tries to "communicate in three languages" said project designer Bruce Abrahamson, "the classical old one, a language in transition, and one that talks about the future."

In establishing a "language," a legitimate but frustrating objective in laboratory building design is the integration of utility systems and the structure of the building for optimum flexibility; the end product is the ultimate rational science structure. The design features would be systematized, ordered, and arranged with a clear formal hierarchy in spaces and structural frame, with an interior adaptable to change, and an exterior clad with combinations of traditional and contemporary materials that reflect the region and building purpose. The University of California's Molecular Sciences Building comes close to being such paradigm, a blending of function and visual delight. Critic Joseph Giovannini summarized the essential utilitarian features of the UCLA structure when he called it a "giant lung." The 300 hoods, he said, were a "synchronized, extensive system of intake, distribution, and exhaust that constituted an architectural order itself." The "architecture of air" was further complicated in the UCLA project by the necessity of keeping biology and chemistry laboratories separate and distinct, a requirement dramatized in the building plan and massing. (See page 112.)

Understanding and expressing laboratory systems is the port of entry for architecture that serves and symbolizes the building types. Once laboratory rooms, circa 1931, could be "ventilated by a special fan which introduces warm air through openings in the ceiling, foul air being removed through the floor ducts by a separately controlled exhaust." The simple technology posed no challenge for those muffling the technology in Collegiate Georgian and Gothic styles. Engineering was a secondary consideration. Today variations in laboratory architecture are the productive result of collaboration of architects, engineers, and laboratory design specialists concerned about functional solutions for health and safety reasons. Indicative of the challenges is Harvard University's School of Public Health alert list, items which can be found in both college and university laboratories: common use and storage of toxic gases and vapors, unstable chemicals and hazardous solids,

UNIVERSITY OF MINNESOTA ELECTRICAL ENGINEERING/COMPUTER SCIENCE BUILDING, 1988. HAMMEL, GREEN, AND ABRAHAMSON. *(facing page) A large building, with a technically challenging program on a prominent site, breaking the mold of older architecture in the vicinity but remaining in context. The test of the design direction will come when additional structures are sited nearby—in harmony or contrast? (Photos courtesy of C. N. Hewett)*

WILLIAM JEWELL COLLEGE, WHITE SCIENCE CENTER, 1992. *(right) A new piece to an old building; a contemporary design providing a welcoming facade to those passing by and those entering the domain of collegiate science. (Source: William Jewell College)*

HOLLINS COLLEGE, DANA SCIENCE BUILDING, 1967. DOUGLAS ORR, deCOSSY, WINDER AND RANDOLPH FRANTZ & JOHN CHAPPELEAR. *(below) Twenty-five years after its opening, this building was recognized and awarded as a "pleasing oasis of learning...the bold, integrated, flexible design has proved itself repeatedly, as its uses have evolved to meet the changing demands of the sciences at Hollins." (Source: Hollins College)*

ionizing and nonionizing radiation, and natural as well as artificially engineered bio-hazards. The words help measure 50 years of change in building requirements. Building systems (structural, mechanical, ventilation, electrical) thus account for the largest share of the laboratory building budget. Operating costs are the highest per square foot.

The search for flexibility and solutions to building complexity will continue, as it should. Versions of today's pursuit of flexibility and improved technology in science engineering buildings have historic precedents worth recalling, if for no other reason than to inspire further progress. For a culture heavily immersed in science and engineering, it is ironic how little appears about laboratories as a distinctive building type in the literature and chronology of the architecture of higher education. The MIT experience was cited earlier; the Lehigh University Chemical Building (1884) is another deserving attention. A landmark in science building technology, the Lehigh lab is believed to have the "earliest example of contemporary modular bench layout designed to maximize the use of lab space." Now named William H. Chandler Hall, after the Lehigh professor who devised its pioneering features, the building features also include "services piped to each bench station, including gas, steam, vacuum, compressed air, and water...unknown before the construction of Chandler." Chimneylike flues were arranged for fresh air intake, "with steam pipes supplying the radiators...within each chimney flue to heat air, ensuring a positive updraft of exhaust gases."

Curriculum, teaching, and research were "real-world," one enthusiast recollected in tracing how the nineteenth-century Lehigh programs connected lab design and university goals and objectives. "There was a strong industrial flavor to the faculty's interests; the assay course received particular attention. Custom-designed muffle furnaces were mounted at the basement level and were used to teach the milk, butter, fat, oil, and mineral analyses. Assaying, an intense, technique-based summer course enrolled most of the chemistry majors in June, July, and August. Students practically lived in the laboratory while taking this degree track." Chandler also provided space for a small museum, "centrally located" to arouse curiosity and display samples and scientific artifacts used in teaching and research. His functional concepts were suitably translated into architecture by Philadelphia architect Addison Hutton. The building won an award for "innovation" at the 1889 Paris Exposition.

Effective utilization of space, equipment, people—the 1927 Kedzie Chemical Laboratory, Michigan State College (now Michigan State University) addressed these questions effectively. Under Professor Arthur T. Clark's direction, the architects were encouraged to design an "H-shape" building plan that "allows abundant light and cross-circulation of air in each laboratory." Laboratory size "was limited to thirty students, the maximum number that can be taught at one time." For flexibility in assignment, labs were amply designed, serviced, and equipped "to make variations in courses from one semester to another easy of adjustment." The "plumbing was left as accessible as possible, with numerous cleanouts and connections for continuous flushing....Corridor space is reduced to a minimum...offices are conveniently located adjoining the laboratories...(with) hoods and tables for private research, and also small blackboards for private instruction."

LEHIGH UNIVERSITY, CHANDLER CHEMISTRY
LABORATORY, 1884. *(Source: Lehigh University)*

In several decades of laboratory evolution, early Modern architecture continued to rationalize the interiors functionally and stripped the exteriors of all visual references to traditional styles. The "box for science" was first welcomed for its simplicity and then questioned as to its visual impact. Around 1970, expert science facilities consultants, such as Burgess Preston Standley, were encouraging a transformation in design attitudes, a fundamental shift from antiseptic building forms to a more textured architecture. "Science is not a sacred cow, why enclose it in a pyramid," he wrote. "An appealing science center should not be monumental or overpowering, but represent the activities within its walls as intensely human activities...the creative, freely imaginative, nature of science." Standley was appalled by edifices such as the Yale University Kline Biology Tower (1965), where a popular designer, with an audacious concept, overpowered the faculty planning the building. Appalled, because the form cast an inflexible mold and impediment to change, as Yale discovered decades later in studying ways to adapt the building to new needs and requirements. Critics praised Kline as "great skill...its tall, strong form sets up a pleasing and effective relationship with the city, the bounding streets, and the hill it crowns." Perhaps. But, in this and similar instances, Standley and other observers would second William C. Caudill's injunction: "the beauty, integrity, and permanence that a science building deserves should not be a reflection of frozen function, but should derive from the excitement of change that its flexible interior must allow." Dana Science Building (1967) and White Science Center (1992), shown on page 120, demonstrate the realizable objective: "an innovative structure which does not aggressively assert its scientific purpose, but is gracious, humane, and inviting in a manner befitting the traditions of the college."

Again, could the architectural recognition and arrangement of functional systems give rise to a contemporary canon the equivalent of Vassari's classical orders? One might judge successes and failures against a measurable index. Yes and no? True flexibility for the unpredictable needs would probably mean a building design and premium expenditure for which few institutions, if any, would wish to pay. Reasons other than function and economics, of course, also influence the design outcomes in contemporary laboratory buildings. The College of Polymer Science and Polymer Engineering, University of Akron, 1991, glistens in glass, with atriums and laboratories providing "faculty and student researchers with a pleasant laboratory environment with natural light." The building geometry was sculptured to give the discipline a prominent position on the skyline. For comparable reasons—visibility and symbol—the George M. Low Center (Rensselaer Polytechnic Institute, 1987) rears above the campus skyline. Less assertive than either two, and thus perhaps less likely to be dated as passing fashion, is the Barnes Science Building (Colorado College, 1988). The Colorado building merits attention for the gesture made to the adjacent Palmer Hall (1889)—through window shapes and green-colored roof. The Barnes loggia helps modulate the facade with a play of light and shadow welcomed in the mountain sun. The dramatic oculus identifies the front door and illuminates the four-story interior atrium. Positioned in the campus plan to complete a science quadrangle and in conjunction with totally new and reconstructed science space in nearby structures, to which it is physically connected, the building materials and shapes generate an image and sense of place recognizably Colorado College, defining clearly the place for science instruction.

Gathering and clustering the sciences in one location has operational and intellectual benefits. When development occurs over time, what are the architectural choices and effects? Our selection of an illuminating example begins in the late-nineteenth-century when science and technology crossed the threshold of being, in the main, disciplines that could be housed in a suite of rooms or a wing, to teaching and research facilities that required extensive, specialized space. Carleton College archives, circa 1870: "Professor Payne transferred the whole chemistry laboratory to his quarters in a bushel basket, making one trip." A century later, 1960, Carleton sheltered the sciences and mathematics in three structures. Gradually these became dated and beyond economic adaptation for the new curriculum, modes of teaching, and equipment. Within 35 years, the time span of a tenured professor, each of the sciences then had the spatial equivalent of its own building. Biology, chemistry, geology, physics, and psychology were connected in a four-part site arrangement, each piece a forward step from Modern to contemporary architecture. Biology, the last piece, was assigned new space in 1994. Its vacated quarters were reallocated and redesigned for physics and psychology, these latter having less demanding requirements for building systems. Mathematics and computer

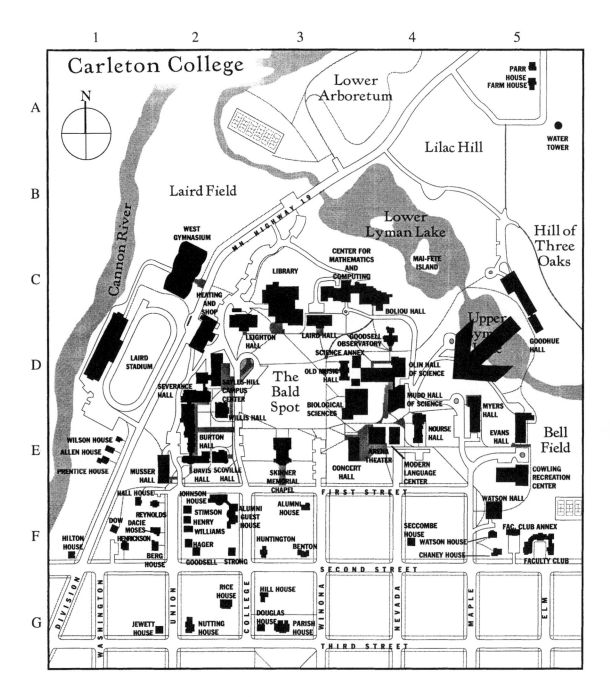

Carleton College

A

B   Laird Field

Lower
Arboretum

Lilac Hill

PARR
HOUSE
FARM HOUSE

WATER
TOWER

C

Cannon River

MN HIGHWAY 19

WEST
GYMNASIUM

Lower
Lyman Lake

Hill of
Three
Oaks

LIBRARY

CENTER FOR
MATHEMATICS
AND
COMPUTING

MAI-FETE
ISLAND

HEATING
AND
SHOP

BOLIOU HALL

Upper
yma

D

LAIRD
STADIUM

LEIGHTON
HALL

LAIRD HALL

SCIENCE ANNEX

GOODSELL
OBSERVATORY

GOODHUE
HALL

OLD MUSIC
HALL

OLIN HALL
OF SCIENCE

SEVERANCE
HALL

SAYLES-HILL
CAMPUS
CENTER

The
Bald
Spot

BIOLOGICAL
SCIENCES

MUDD HALL
OF SCIENCE

MYERS
HALL

E

WILLIS HALL

WILSON HOUSE

ALLEN HOUSE

BURTON
HALL

SKINNER
MEMORIAL
CHAPEL

NOURSE
HALL

EVANS
HALL

Bell
Field

PRENTICE HOUSE

DAVIS SCOVILLE
HALL   HALL

ARENA
THEATER

MODERN
LANGUAGE
CENTER

COWLING
RECREATION
CENTER

MUSSER
HALL

CONCERT
HALL

FIRST STREET

WATSON HALL

F

HALL HOUSE

DOW

REYNOLDS
DACIE
MOSES

HENRICKSON

JOHNSON
HOUSE

STIMSON

HENRY

WILLIAMS

HAGER

ALUMNI
GUEST
HOUSE

ALUMNI
HOUSE

HUNTINGTON

BENTON

SECCOMBE
HOUSE

WATSON HOUSE

CHANEY HOUSE

FAC. CLUB ANNEX

FACULTY CLUB

HILTON
HOUSE

BERG
HOUSE

GOODSELL STRONG

SECOND STREET

G

DIVISION

WASHINGTON

UNION

JEWETT
HOUSE

NUTTING
HOUSE

RICE
HOUSE

COLLEGE

HILL HOUSE

DOUGLAS
HOUSE

PARISH
HOUSE

WINONA

NEVADA

MAPLE

ELM

THIRD STREET

CARLETON COLLEGE, 1995. *(above) An open-quadrangle campus design with a century of architecture and landscapes typically intended to be the best of their period. Lyman Lakes, constructed in the 1920s, ranks nationally as a panoramic vista of exceptional beauty. The views upward from the west, across the Cannon River, reveal a landmark collegiate skyline. The map arrow points to the new science quad, part of the fine-graining of the campus landscapes and the consolidation of the sciences in one location.*

CARLETON COLLEGE, OLIN HALL OF SCIENCE, 1960. *(facing page, top) Minoru Yamasaki's Modern Gothic. (Source: Carleton College Archives)*

CARLETON COLLEGE, SEELEY G. MUDD HALL OF SCIENCE, 1975. SOVIK MATHRE SATHRUM QUANBECK. *(facing page, bottom) Second piece in a phased site development strategy to provide faculty and students with facilities for a top-tier educational program. Each piece has its individual exterior expression, though a family resemblance in the use of exterior brick. The linking and joining of the science buildings on a single site, framing and forming a new quadrangle, establishes the unifying campus architectural theme. (Source: Carleton College)*

sciences were also provided new space nearby. A site closer and connected to the other science disciplines would have been advisable, but existing buildings, not moveable, and mature tree cover, were intractable impediments to a unified functional scheme on a single site.

As to appearance, the 1994 Carleton biology wing will continue a transition away from a landmark older science building. Designed by Minoru Yamasaki (1961), it earned national awards for its attempt to make a functional, stripped-down, brick-box science building into an art form by embellishing the exterior with abstracted forms of an ancient style, "Modern Gothic," Yamasaki called it. The gesture did not gain a foothold on the enduring ladder of styles at the College or elsewhere. Carleton's later science buildings were wrapped in simpler building forms using brick and stone. The science grouping is further unified by a new landscaped open space—a quadrangle that symbolizes collegiality.

Chessboard moves, such as the Carleton College development scheme, will be increasingly commonplace as colleges follow universities in gathering their sciences into one definable area. When the costs and suitability of replacing worn-out and dated laboratory support systems are factored into the facility planning equation, as well as the typical backlog of deferred maintenance and mandated accessibility improvements, then a planning and design strategy that blends old and new, rehabilitated and reallocated space into a unified concept usually proves to be the best functional and economic solution, with self-evident architectural consequences. The amount of new space required in many instances can be satisfied in a building addition. At Macalester College and Pomona College, carefully calibrated in-fill architecture is thus the desired route, with local materials and building scale favored as gestures for design continuity. In all these examples the thrust of improved facilities signals an institutional commitment for a higher-quality science educational experience and concomitantly better facilities. Sometimes however, as at Allegheny College, the key to starting a successful sequence is a new science building (1992), complimenting and adjacent to the older structures, yet in form and detailing clearly commemorating the architecture of its time. The new Allegheny building is also intended to set the design standard for new structures that might be added in this sector of the campus.

Laboratory buildings of the quality illustrated have always been the collaborative efforts of client and designer. Identity, connectedness, contact, and communications among the occupants, an encouragement of synergy and serendipity—these are underlying principles that configure award-winning historic and contemporary laboratory buildings. Mind not that the Lehigh edifice looks like a Victorian orphanage, or that Kedzie, on first glance externally, might resemble a library or large fraternity house, or that the cited recent projects struggle with the challenge of giving related buildings a family resemblance, for the utopian, truly flexible rational building has not been realized. To see, know, and appreciate why designs emerge, appear, and are distinctive and different is to understand a cause and effect in generating architecture. Solutions to internal function stimulated by careful examination of teaching and research activities, team effort designs—these are the commendable lessons to be noted in historic precedents. The external expression may rise from other sources, motivations, and design intentions, as we have seen and will examine again in attitudes about articulating the exterior, "the almighty wall," the "great walls" of memorable college and university laboratory buildings.

THE ALMIGHTY WALL AND GREAT WALLS. Informed by the collaboration of architecture and engineering, an outstanding laboratory building may be recognized by the manner in which the four signatures cited earlier are expressed. In the progression of design innovation after World War II, which seems to have no logical beginning or end on most American campuses, the boxlike, utilitarian, Modern designs have given way to physical forms that are slanted, indented, and bulged to avoid the monotony of the grid. Nonlab spaces are located as joints and connections between the lab assemblages. Differences in exterior materials and variations in fenestration patterns are used to mark differences in interior functions. The outside wall once muted in the Modern idiom speaks assertively in contemporary designs—as in the recent University of Minnesota and MIT examples seen earlier. This aspect deserves further comment, since elevations are vivid and prominent components of campus architecture, and the discussion will lead us through some informative by-ways as to how memorable architecture is created.

Once all laboratory activities could be fit into a conventional building envelope, with undifferentiated architecture such as Bowdoin College's Mary Francis Searles Science Building. The structure at first glance could be read from the exterior as being a nineteenth-century dormitory, or classroom and faculty office building. Searles imparts several lessons about appearance. The building draws attention for its programmatic thrust, the careful modulation of its facade, the changes in exterior color that were made 50 years after the building's completion, and the risks the College took in engaging Henry Vaughn for a project that may have been beyond his competency.

The "Almighty Wall," thus biographer William Morgan subtitled his account of Vaughn's life (MIT Press; Cambridge, MA, 1983). Morgan substantiates Vaughn's reputation for articulating building elevations that meld and merge historic detailing, resulting in a "clear sense of monumentality and controlled taste for textural richness," work that Ralph Adams Cram (master of stagecraft architecture) praised as "an inspiration for young architects who were working towards a more sincere and expressive manner of building." Vaughn's designs were, thought Cram, "infused with thoughtful and scholarly spirit that varies from precedent only enough to give the work life and contemporaneity…thoroughly modern, thoroughly alive." Here, Cram's "modern" is like our "Modern," being a polemic slogan, which like the phrase "good design," is used to defend personal tastes and values, often arbitrary and transitory, against the whims, fancies, and vagaries of the seemingly vulgar and uninformed.

Vaughn had little experience with college buildings. His masterworks, such as the Chapel of Saint Peter and Saint Paul (Saint Paul's School, New Hampshire) were almost entirely ecclesiastical. But with a nudge from a benefactor ready to fund the project, and touting Vaughn's reputation as a designer, the College engaged his services, continuing a tradition of Bowdoin seeking and achieving aspiring architecture from the pantheon of eminent practitioners. Thus, Richard Upjohn's Bowdoin Chapel (1884) is probably the benchmark edifice in revivalist Romanesque style.

McKim, Mead, White's Warner Art Building (1894) was good enough to be commemorated recently with an illustration of its facade on a U.S. Postal Service postcard. Edward Larrabee Barnes' Visual Arts Center (1975) is frequently cited, along with Le Corbusier's building at Harvard, as the yin and yang of contemporary collegiate art instruction buildings. Henry Vaughn's Searles belongs to that illustrious company, with his design "giving lasting substance to the history of the institution." In style Jacobethean, in plan an ingenious functional solution, Searles demonstrates an architectural skill tweaking nuance and variety from every aspect the canon permits, and, praiseworthy, with no compromise to building purpose.

Searles was not a chapel design molded to fit late-nineteenth-century science. To Vaughn's and the College's credit, style did not determine and dominate the building plan. Biology, chemistry, and physics each had its own building entrance and interior spatial identity. The main facade faces the quadrangle, with the north and south ends anchored by two octagonal staircases, functional escape routes for safety, and crenulated as stylistic gestures. Window patterns (with more glass for daylight to the labs than Vaughn originally wished) and the secondary asymmetrical facades reflect functional floor plans and laboratory arrangements. Where Cram would have liked to "tie the anarchy of the past into the order of the present" with an elaborate site plan for buildings and spaces (some from the architect's imagination and not necessarily from well-determined institutional needs), Vaughn was pleased to produce a building that sat on its own site and was complete and satisfying in scale and massing on four sides.

Color and texture were Vaughn's *métier*. The yellow and buff brick was accented by contrasting sandstone, which was used in coursework, turrets, gables, door frames, and carved medallions. Where Vaughn's church detailing would include saints, he decorated his Searles exterior with the scientific paraphernalia, including telescopes and geological hammers. "An essentially utilitarian structure, the one thing Vaughn surely did not want was a bland surface," observes the College's architectural historian, Patricia M. Anderson. In an action that might annoy purists and preservationists, she reports that Vaughn's "original brick was painted red in the 1950s, the better to harmonize with both the oldest and newest Bowdoin buildings." A landmark building, Searles is being given new life as a science building through a physical development strategy that relocates the systems-demanding disciplines therein to new space—contemporary brick architecture—and renovates the older building (Searles) for mathematics and physics.

Walls, especially Great Walls, are billboards for symbolic gestures. Thus Princeton University in the first half of the twentieth century boxed its sciences in collegiate Gothic, following Ralph Adams Cram's advice that the monastic style was "the great cultural influence good art must always be." A. D. F. Hamlin seconded Cram's dicta, writing that "The average American college student is probably somewhat opaque to the penetration of the rays of purely aesthetic influences…he is a good deal of a Philistine; that he is impervious to every aesthetic influence. I do not believe, consciously, or unconsciously, he reacts to his environment." For Cram there was "nothing diffuse, casual, or individualistic" in his Princeton concept (Cram's Collegiate Gothic), "but all is coordinated, controlled by sound law, infused with the impulse of an indestructible tradition that transcends the limits of conti-

nents and centuries." If, in those years, Princeton was in an import mode (the Oxbridge Gothic models), then export was the mode of the latter half of the century. The dichotomy of Nobel prize work in the sciences occurring in retrograde architecture was patently contradictory. Abandoning the "style of the ages," Princeton adopted variations of the Modern to signal institutional advancement, functionally and aesthetically after World War II, and gained a reputation for not being reluctant to try different variations of contemporary design. Wishing to avoid any difficulties in gaining a superior, up-to-date, exterior expression, by a celebrated designer, and at the same time committed to achieving an equally superior interior functional layout, the University used different firms for each aspect. The collaboration worked well. Several Princeton buildings in this spirit became icons for young designers worldwide, notably the Lewis Thomas Laboratory (1985). "The most interesting thing to happen on campus in a long time" said one local observer.

While Princeton was sending Gothic signals, designers for a new engineering school in the Southwest decided sunny and sere Spain would be the source of inspiring architecture for Texas Technological College (now Texas Technological University). Founded in 1924, "the primary objective of the new campus (was) to establish the most modern and most completely equipped textile school in the entire South." Located in the cotton-growing Llano Estado, the College was ushered into the twentieth century with a grandiose development scheme of the kind that folklore couples with Texan ambitions. The main feature was a classical site arrangement, a mile in width and a half-mile in depth, "with its main axis the continuance of a 4-mile boulevard 200 feet wide leading directly from the Courthouse Square in downtown Lubbock…to the future Commencement Hall of the College." The Court of Technology sat within this framework, with the new textile engineering building centered like a baroque palace. "The entire college is in architecture reflecting the Spanish history of the earlier days of Texas. The climate and physical environment of Lubbock are quite similar to those of central Spain," wrote the campus designer William Ward Watkin. The Spanish influence was ritualized on the walls with cartouche, balconies, and carved door frames in a manifestation that a Cervantes might recollect as Iberian regal. Later, the expensive detailing did not survive changes in architectural taste and more stringent building budgets. The great spaces proved to be environmentally uncomfortable, with landscapes difficult to maintain in a dry climate. What did survive, and now joins disparate science and engineering buildings into a singular campus design theme, are the variations on the original tweedy, buff-colored brick and red tile roofs. The first building, a gem of regional architecture, well-proportioned, human in scale, also serves as the benchmark building for local contextual architecture.

Walls being extensive and visually prominent, their constituent materials provide the easiest approach to achieving a family resemblance among buildings or for using architecture to signal a cultural, intellectual, or physical separation from earlier structures in the same vicinity. The silver-gray glass enclosure for Carnegie-Mellon University's Software Engineering Institute (1988) effectively conveys the spirit of a nontraditional building for an emerging technology. The environs have North America's most perplexing conglomerate of disparate collegiate architecture. Interestingly, the reflective glass mirrors the designs of nearby structures, further giving the building a liveliness that these sanitized, machinelike exteriors usually do not possess. The walls of Brown's geochemistry building, from the same period, are made of denser material. The "reflection" of neighborhood context is expressed in the color and texture of the brickwork, the coursing, and laboratory windows,

TEXAS BAROQUE—1924, TEXAS
TECHNOLOGICAL COLLEGE TEXTILE
ENGINEERING BUILDING. WILLIAM WARD,
ARCHITECT. *(above)*

BRICK AS NEIGHBORHOOD CONTEXT—1984.
BROWN UNIVERSITY, GEOCHEMISTRY BUILD-
ING. DAVIS, BRODY & ASSOCIATES. *(right)*

REFLECTING FACADE: AN EPITOME OF
STYLISH-MIRROR ARCHITECTURE—1988,
CARNEGIE-MELLON UNIVERSITY'S SOFTWARE
ENGINEERING INSTITUTE. PETER
BOHLIN+ASSOCIATES. *(below)*

UNIVERSITY OF PENNSYLVANIA, RICHARDS MEDICAL RESEARCH LABORATORIES, 1957. *(right) Louis Kahn's pioneering design for rationalizing "servant and served space." The concept dramatized similar ideas explored in Modern architecture in Europe in the 1930s. Kahn succeeded in finding a client willing to experiment with the forms. Lawrence S. Williams' camera summarized the idea with a photograph that spread Kahn's gospel worldwide. (Source: University of Pennsylvania)*

UNIVERSITY OF MISSISSIPPI, NATIONAL CENTER FOR PHYSICAL ACOUSTICS, 1988. HAINES LUNBERG WAEHLER AND MOCKBEE-COKER-HOWOTH. *(below) Science organized horizontally in a one-story building. All mechanical equipment is located in a wing, isolated from sound-sensitive labs. Offices are located on the exterior wall, to provide a window for researchers and additional sound barrier between the ultra-quiet labs and exterior noise sources. The building facade is a contemporary synthesis of historic campus buildings and materials. (Source: University of Mississippi)*

almost domestic in scale. A third approach to "wall design" involves accenting the utility systems, ventilation stacks, and exhaust hoods (the lungs and the waste disposal organs of high-tech science and engineering) through special encasement or exposure. Of the former, the precedent-setting design is Louis Kahn's Richards Medical Research Laboratories, University of Pennsylvania (1957). Kahn disaggregated building functions into "served" and "servant" spaces. The vertical shafts of the serving utilities stood apart from the lab modules. Slender and higher, they gave the flat-roof architecture a gracefulness that the boxy architecture might not otherwise possess. The 1988 National Acoustics Laboratory (University of Mississippi) is a more recent and successful variation of these functional distinctions expressed architecturally.

Conceptually important for demonstrating Kahn's theory of architectural distinction for "served and serving" spaces, the Richards labs were, however, deficient in other respects, including the problems of daylight flooding experimental areas where illumination was not wanted and the loss of wall space in the extensively fenestrated lab areas. The exposure approach to treating building systems also has had mixed reviews, especially when such solutions are draped down the sides of buildings in an interpretation of the fashionable Centre Pompidou (1972) or in gestures to space-age technology, as if Gene Raymond, the author and draftsman of Flash Gordon, had turned his imagination from twenty-first-century solar system cities to late-twentieth-century science and engineering structures. Nonetheless, the Wellesley College Science Center project (1978) proved that a skillful architect could merge two ends of the century with an inventive blending of adapted space and new space. The College's Gothic science building was renovated for classrooms and offices. New laboratories are packaged into a flexible structure whose facade advertises the building technology. The two are joined by an atrium designed for library functions and enlivened by bridges which cross the space and connect the buildings. More common and acceptable is the undisguised treatment of the fifth facade—the utilitarian roofscape that fascinates with its complicated array of machinery, piping, vents, and apertures, of which the UCLA project (pictured on page 112) is also an edifying example.

Considerations of taste, context, and technology may be emphasized or subordinated in designing Great Walls. Harvard's Mallinckrodt Laboratory (1927) hides its functions inside a brick box whose monumentality is punctuated by a portico said to be a simplified version of Charles Bulfinch's Massachusetts General Hospital. The structure is set back from the street, uninviting, somber, more like a courthouse than an incubator of ideas and training grounds for people who have changed the world. Nearby, the 1979 Sherman Fairchild biochemistry building beautifully scales down a large building with a patterned facade whose rhythm is established by the interior laboratory module. Brick serves as gesture to Harvard's campus design milieu. The facade is softened by wooden panels and balconies that double as emergency exits. Day and night, the activities inside the biochemistry building are visible from the sidewalk. A splendid melding of functional purpose and design logic, palpably and measurably in context with its neighbors, delightfully sited and strung out among other structures from another era, this building, arguably, is Harvard's best twentieth-century building, laboratory or otherwise.

HARVARD UNIVERSITY, SHERMAN FAIRCHILD BIOCHEMISTRY BUILDING, 1979. PAYETTE AND ASSOCIATES INC. *(facing page)*
(Source: Payette and Associates Inc.)
WELLESLEY COLLEGE, SCIENCE CENTER, 1978. PERRY, DEAN, STAHL & ROGERS. *(below)* *(Photo: Edward Jacoby, courtesy of the architects.)*

Two remarkable science projects, 20 miles apart, constructed within one year of each other, landmark architecture for different reasons. Each can be appreciated as a carefully planned example of laboratory design, and as exemplifying ideas which might be considered in designing other building types.

The Wellesley project serves a college population, is located on a suburban site, and brings together into one area 11 science departments and their library. About 14,000 square feet of new space was joined to 89,000 square feet of renovated space. The juncture, the courtyard of the older collegiate Gothic, was roofed to create an atrium—an awesome gathering space through which and above connecting bridges join new and old. The 1979 facade is a spectacular composition of exposed structural elements, mechanical systems, windows, and portal facing a major campus open space.

Harvard's biochemistry building is laudable for all the important reasons: functionally well planned, with clear directions from the client team; inserted into and organized on a tight site without compromise to interior space requirements; situated to create some beguiling and surprising open spaces, views, and pedestrian circulation; developed with a facade that invites passers-by to see and intuitively understand building purpose; detailing that divides a large and complex building into harmonious parts, human in scale; materials that are reminiscent of older buildings but not diluted copy-cat architecture. Like many masterworks the building does not exhaust its subtlety, grace, and beauty on first glance.

Eminent institutions do not have a lock on innovative building concepts. From the earlier 1960s onward, thought-provoking experiments in architectural configuration could be found in the hinterland, where foundations such as the Educational Facilities Laboratories, Inc., lead by Harold Gores, were willing to risk some seed money on exploratory designs. Ipso facto, Alice Lloyd College, Pipa Pass, Kentucky, was encouraged to construct a science building in form and style not usually found in Appalachia. Architect Jaspar D. Ward and facilities consultant Richard Sames wanted to test the possibilities of a "sandwich concept" for distributing building services to the laboratory floors and increasing "flexibility in interior space configurations; with the objective of being able to optimize space changes in response to curriculum changes." The three-level scheme is framed by a structural grid that provides for nonload-bearing partitions on each floor. Vertical and horizontal utilities are located to serve specialized space on the second level and open laboratories on the upper floor. Typical massing is reversed, the wider base being on top. The fusion of materials and shapes in the articulation of the wall advertise the Modern idiom, including the jutting, metallic upper floor, the masonry vertical elements, and fire stairs separated incongruously, but dramatically, from the main structure. Should the national will to support science and technology be fortified, the hinterlands again will become important venues for experimentation in laboratory teaching and research modes and buildings.

Other considerations should not be overlooked or underestimated: Laboratory buildings should provide inviting and appealing spaces for faculty, researchers, staff, students, and visitors to meet and interact informally. Such encounters help promote the socialization and acculturation of the educational and investigative routines occurring in the building. Friendly and constructive communication helps overcome the obstacles of turf and discipline-based introspection and advances the ideal and reality of science and engineering as a team effort. These exchanges encourage those aspects of intellectual synergy and serendipity which strengthen common interest or reveal new insights and syntheses not previously considered. Such spaces are also useful for groups to meet for progress reports, briefings, and meetings that do not require special preparation or elaborate audiovisual devices. Rooms and spaces of this quality elevate good buildings to the realm of best architecture and can be expressed in the Great Walls.

A HORIZON VIEW. Not all laudable laboratory projects have been new buildings. Tufts University's Science and Technology Center is sheltered in three former warehouse buildings, connected and adapted for exotic subjects such as electrooptics and high-energy physics. Financed by the U.S. Department of Energy, the project was also designed to demonstrate "energy efficient laboratory systems."

DUKE UNIVERSITY, LEVINE SCIENCE RESEARCH BUILDING, 1992. PAYETTE AND ASSOCIATES INC. *(facing page) Stair landing and building juncture designed and furnished as an informal gathering area. Such spaces should be promoted as a common element in all twenty-first-century campus architecture, thus increasing the opportunities for contact and communication outside the scheduled routines and giving programmatic cause for supporting more graceful and spatial buildings than current guidelines, practice, and economy permit. (Source: Payette and Associates Inc.)*

Echoing MIT's mill building paradigm, the warehouse floor-to-floor heights, structural capacity, column locations, and horizontal layout of the floor area "proved ideally suited" for 62,000 square feet of mixed lab and office uses. Big? Of 93 laboratory buildings constructed this past decade (a representative sample), the average size was 127,000 gross square feet and the average project cost $26 million (1993 dollars). Impressive expenditures, but not adequate.

The decline of support for continuing capital investment in laboratory facilities, and the retooling of aging and obsolete buildings, as well as a measurable decline in students entering these fields, has stirred a debate over how and when to revitalize programmatically and physically this segment of higher education. Extrapolations from National Science Surveys (1994) indicate a $5.7 billion backlog in needed new construction and major repairs at 515 "active science and engineering" campuses and a proportionately similar need at other institutions. Decay and obsolescence are intolerable. Though the funding responses are slow to date, it would seem inevitable that the fundamentals of national necessity will overcome inertia and bring about another wave of construction and reconstruction, especially in disciplines where the American polity cannot sustain its status and income without the initiatives stimulated by science, engineering, and technology.

And what happens to good but obsolete older laboratory buildings, heritage architecture too valuable to demolish? Many are Charles Eliot Norton's kind of building: an "ennobling presence, where the architectural atmosphere weakens critical judgment by the spatial and sensual pleasure they immediately offer." Science buildings of intrinsic merit can be functionally and economically adapted to new uses. Constructed in 1927 for chemistry and psychology, Wittenberg University's Koch Hall is now a visual arts building. As illustrated earlier, Beloit College redesigned its 1893 science hall as a campus center. Successful designs avoid cutting up and cramping the original spaces or removing the delightful interior period detailing, with their materials and craftsmanship, seemingly a forgotten art, memory banks from a time when laboratory designs melded utility and beauty without compromise to either.

CAMPUS HOUSING

Compare, for example, the dormitory in which the writer lived as a student with the present-day dormitory generously provided with baths and other plumbing equipment and a modern heating system. The old time dormitory housing fifty to sixty students had for plumbing fixtures two iron sinks and four water closets (which any plumbing inspector today would condemn in even the most primitive structure), and for its heating system small coal- or wood-burning stoves, owned by the students themselves.

Frederic B. Johnson
Yale University, 1936

Because of the prevalent belief that student life in well equipped and efficiently managed dormitories makes a very important contribution to the health habits and to the educational and social development of students, there is rapidly growing tendency to provide more and better dormitories in colleges and universities.

E. S. Evenden, G. D. Strayer, N. L. Engelhardt
Standards for College Buildings, Teachers College,
Columbia University, 1938

A hall of residence is a local habitation with a name where members of a university may live....It is now time to study the material settings which best favor their fulfillment...this study must constantly keep in view the intention and the matter used to express it, the intention being founded, as Vitrivius said, on a conviction that the matter wrought will fully suit the purpose...consideration is first given to three fundamental requirements that a hall should be quiet, sufficiently warm, and well lighted.

University Grants Committee, 1953

In asking deans & architects if they expected basic thinking about college housing to change, over ¾ of architects replied that it would change, not only in technology of materials & construction, but in philosophy of housing as well....They believe that future buildings will be built not just to house & feed students but also to provide them with homes to accelerate knowledge, & will provide them with recreational facilities to keep their bodies in an equally healthy state."

Byron C. Bloomfield, AIA
Bulletin of the American Institute of Architects,
September–October 1956

In our judgment, universities are building too much of the wrong kinds of space. Space needs are too often established parochially without considering campus and student life as a single integrated system of people, activities, and buildings.

Sim Van der Ryn, 1967

The way students live and the way they work intellectually today is different from the past. Colleges need to build new kinds of dormitories for the electronic age, and for achieving the higher retention rate and quality of learning the public now expects.

Earl Flansburgh, FAIA, 1991

Housing goals, philosophy, and policy mold campus design and architecture like the hands of a potter on the clay. The solutions chronicle a fascinating evolution in design concepts at the intersections of educational trends, cultural attitudes, lifestyles, and economics. Anchoring one end of the time scale are the Cambridge and Oxford colleges, originally for bachelor teenagers far from home. At the other end of the time line, Mary Hufford Hall, Texas Women's University, 1995, a traditional dormitory reconstructed for family housing, serving single mothers with children. Both Oxbridge and Hufford are inspired examples of "living and learning" concepts. They demonstrate the impact of demographic changes on higher education, the parallel adjustment in housing objectives, and the resulting physical forms. As to balancing continuity and change, new housing designs can express,

HARVARD UNIVERSITY, HOLLIS HALL. *(overleaf, top) Eighteenth-century architecture reconstructed and restored several times. Dated as to style, but superb in terms of scale and architectural simplicity. (Source: Harvard University)*

WORCESTER POLYTECHNIC INSTITUTE, STUDENT HOUSING, 1989. EARL FLANSBURGH AND ASSOCIATES. *(overleaf, bottom) A polished and sophisticated model of recent student housing. Shapes and materials evoke older architecture but remain clearly contemporary in composition. (Source: Earl Flansburgh and Associates)*

CAMPUS HOUSING: IMAGE AND REALITY. *In the expansion era 1950–1970 undergraduates applying to residential institutions had images of collegiate life and architecture that often ran counter to reality. Some buildings (unfortunately too many), justified as Modern architecture, were not much more than brick-enclosed cells on raw sites, lacking the scale and charm of older traditional styles. The meager buildings—at best, shelter—now require significant restoration and rehabilitation. Where and when useful economic life still remains, and site locations are favorable, then redemptive architecture may be an appropriate solution.*

symbolically and physically without compromise, older ideas worth emulating. Juxtapose eighteenth-century Hollis Hall, Harvard University, and new housing at Worcester Polytechnic Institute. One can appreciate how the art of architecture carries ideas from one era into another without cloning and design degeneration. In this instance the program themes, common to both examples, are suites of rooms, brick architecture, human in scale, with an overall form evocative of time and place.

Seeing these good examples, it is disillusioning to know that too often the image and reality of campus housing are so distant from each other. In the recent past young people arrive expecting a housing stock which will promote campus life and find accommodations which fall far short of expectations. Understanding why this has happened should help generate better designs for this important building type. As to the future, architectural solutions should continue to seek to express diversification in response to demographic factors, inform new designs with the best aspects of previous housing design, and revitalize the large existing housing stock which requires significant reconstruction and regeneration.

Fortunately the tasks to be addressed are in the hands of administrative staffs who are now educated and trained to manage campus housing as a profession, integrating the cultural, social, and financial factors which influence successful housing design and operations. Once these responsibilities were largely the task of the college or university president. Historically their views changed, as did higher education and, in turn, housing concepts. Nineteenth-century presidents at Brown, Harvard, and Michigan thought that students should be treated as adults, and as adults should make their own housing arrangements. Their bias was educational. The university model they were importing was German in origin. Oxbridge was backwater. They noted that living off campus was the typical case with students in Europe, except the "mere remnant of the monkish cloisters of the middle ages, still retained in England." Their opinions prevailed at the start of the university expansion in America, following the Civil War. But, the principle of self-sufficiency in housing, however, soon had to give way to pragmatic events and conditions. The local housing supply could not meet demand. Accommodations were marginal. As in medieval Oxford, town and gown relationships were aggrieved by students' habits and the students' scorn for a community they saw exploiting their plight: the need for safe and sanitary housing at reasonable cost.

Other countervailing forces came from several quarters. Parents and preachers began to fear that living off campus would erode morals, obedience, and respect. An 1876 guide for locating new campuses listed the choices: large city, rural town, state capitol, quiet village. Rural was best, and if such were not possible then "carve out a bit of peaceful countryside within the city," by constructing a group of connected and landscaped quadrangles. Seeking the secure haven of a campus setting, fraternities and sororities rose in prominence, leaving those not so housed isolated and indignant about not being able to participate in campus life. A new generation of college and university presidents then saw political and educational advantages in advocating student housing.

Events at the University of Oregon in 1920 settled a pattern and established a precedent. There an "increasing student body had to accommodate itself as best it could in student living organizations and about town. In many cases the rooming houses were charging high prices for what often was unsuitable services." The University's inability to attract and hold students because of poor housing was seen as an educational crisis in a state that hoped to advance its economy through a strong public university. Pride and purse stimulated a reluctant state legislature "to erect buildings for dormitory housing and boarding purposes and for student activities," and to borrow money for such, and to "pledge the net income from rentals toward the principle and interest of borrowed funds." The act was challenged, tested in the Supreme Court, and given favorable ruling. The six buildings constructed from the first funds were perceptive in several respects. Each unit (40 to 60 students) is designed to be "a separate self-governing social unit...with a separate entrance and distinctive name...(each has its) own excellently furnished living-room on the lower floor, separate telephone room and guest room." Presciently, wrote the University executive secretary in 1928, "the furnishings used have been deliberately set at a level distinctly above that of most college dormitories. It was believed that if substantial and attractive furniture were used, the students would respond by taking pride in their surroundings, taking better care of the building than has been the experience, a consideration of economic importance aside from the educational desirability of providing college students with esthetically and socially satisfying surroundings."

The Oregon scheme would not test well today in terms of density (four students to a room with double bunk beds and access to a study alcove), gang bathrooms and toilets, the extensive application of asbestos for fire protection, and the building style, a modest version of collegiate Georgian. About the same time across the continent Harvard and Yale were building undergraduate accommodations, which in contrast to Oregon, would have about twice the space per student housed, thanks to a donor's benefaction, which moderated the need for housing to "pay its own way." Like Monet painting his hay stack 87 times, by the early 1930s the interpretation of what constituted suitable campus housing types nationwide was impressive in concept and execution, and creative variations.

However, encouraging as that record may be, too often in recent time, during the impressive expansion of higher education, the economics of campus housing compromised program objectives and design response, and when the financing was deficient, the task of resolving the resulting difficulties was left to a later generation. For example, responding kindly to a perceptible need, the Higher Education Facilities Act of 1963 (and subsequent legislation) enabled colleges and universities to construct hundreds of buildings to shelter their enrollment surge. As seen in the 1960 view of the Washington State University campus, the surge was satisfied with heavy-density buildings, minimal shelter. Typically, 6- to 8-story structures were arranged on the campus perimeter, often with few site amenities, and few had perceptible and attractive design relationship to the other campus sectors. The end product was "huge complexes of dormitory residences...with little thought to the ways in which residence life might be integrated into academic life...beset by unwieldy state and federal restrictions on costs per square foot...they seemed to show little regard to the educational life of the students, let alone their personal living space," wrote one observer. Particularly vexing were buildings dependent on elevators, "negative influence on students is clear....With few exceptions, these

UNIVERSITY HOUSING

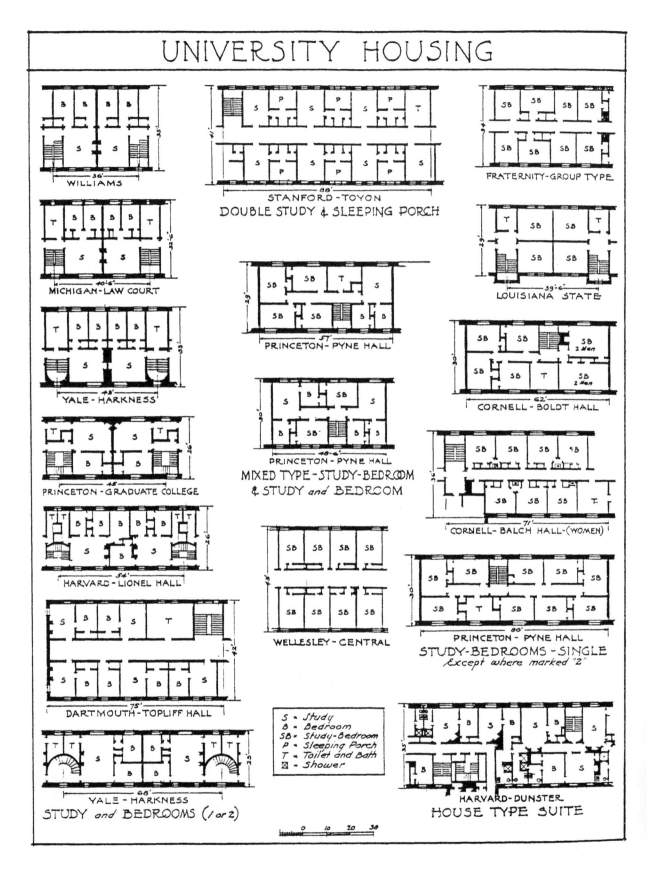

WILLIAMS

MICHIGAN - LAW COURT

YALE - HARKNESS

PRINCETON - GRADUATE COLLEGE

HARVARD - LIONEL HALL

DARTMOUTH - TOPLIFF HALL

YALE - HARKNESS
STUDY and BEDROOMS (1 or 2)

STANFORD - TOYON
DOUBLE STUDY & SLEEPING PORCH

PRINCETON - PYNE HALL

PRINCETON - PYNE HALL
MIXED TYPE - STUDY-BEDROOM
& STUDY and BEDROOM

WELLESLEY - CENTRAL

S = Study
B = Bedroom
SB = Study-Bedroom
P = Sleeping Porch
T = Toilet and Bath
⊠ = Shower

0   10   20   30

FRATERNITY - GROUP TYPE

LOUISIANA STATE

CORNELL - BOLDT HALL

CORNELL - BALCH HALL - (WOMEN)

PRINCETON - PYNE HALL
STUDY-BEDROOMS - SINGLE
Except where marked "2"

HARVARD - DUNSTER
HOUSE TYPE SUITE

ARCHITECTURAL FORUM, JUNE 1931.

buildings are an architectural mistake that needs to be addressed." Smaller buildings were similarly affected and deficient by a seemingly unalterable gap between minimal space standards and cost constraints. Inadequate budgets also left a residue of negative site features which no token landscapes could ameliorate.

The dismal picture at many institutions, stuck with a housing inventory poorly conceived and not yet amortized, worsened through the 1980s as maintenance was deferred and administrators were uncertain whether students would fill the structures. That aspect of campus housing now seems settled. On-campus life is popular, but the residue of neglect remains. Although some new housing is being constructed, and more planned, the thrust of campus housing improvements now and in the near future will focus on rehabilitation and upgrading buildings and sites. Stimulated by alumni pride, trustee concerns, and parental grumbling, elite institutions and public campuses are spending historic sums in restoring their inventory; $75 million at Harvard, $35 million at Brown, $25 million at the University of Connecticut.

Public campuses, and independent colleges less selective academically, are recognizing that housing maintenance deferred is a student exodus accelerated and, worse, a cause for underenrollment. Institutions unable, or unwilling, to plan and fund improvements will discover they are left with draconian choices: rebuild or regret. Obsolescence and decay intrinsically have no cure but sizable capital reinvestment. The size of the renewal is impressive, at least $15 billion, by one reckoning: 1 million beds $15,000 per average bed cost, the latter being about half the cost of new construction.

Given the physical state and cultural status of the campus housing stock in the mid-1990s, not many observers would have predicted that students and their families, institutions, and their administrators would find, promote, and desire residential life once again as an important part and central feature of the American higher education experience. Most of the 15 million college and university students are full-time students, age 22 or less—a significant group demographically, educationally, and architecturally. Of a representative sample (250,000 freshmen students) entering higher education in the Fall of 1994, two-thirds expected to live on campus. Their housing choices were better than that of the preceding generation in terms of type of housing, condition, and architectural character. Slowly, but steadily, the distance between the image of campus housing—domestic in scale and welcoming at the front door, and the reality (sterile, impersonal, brick barracks and cold, seemingly impersonal, filing-cabinet, high-density dormitories) is being shortened as institutions realize that the quality and appearance of campus housing cannot continue to be neglected as they have been in recent decades.

On the bright side of the dismal picture of obsolescence and decay which introduced our scan, the shortcomings and blunders discussed have stimulated social science and design research which has pinpointed cause and effect in developing successful housing programmatically and architecturally. Prompted by the further professionalization of campus housing operations as an institutional responsibility, the past decade has yielded a collection of precepts and principles for planning and designing campus housing which no client and designer can ignore. These include variations in housing programs and designs and the gradual upgrading of housing

from simple shelter to residential halls promoting campus life and educational achievement. For example, *The Journal of College Science Teaching* (September/October 1994) espouses residential learning communities (RLCS) as a contribution to reversing some of "the poor climate and causes for attrition of women in science and engineering." This housing format provides "a cooperative environment beyond the confines of the classroom; integrated and connected academic and social life; (and the) support of like-minded peers to minimize isolation through study groups and collaborative learning; (and) the availability of mentors and role models, such as faculty and older students."

Redemptive architecture is playing a constructive role in banishing blight. Exemplary projects are demonstrating lessons learned from earlier failures, where enlightened rhetoric and good intentions went unfulfilled in cost-cutting procedures that lead to the monotonous, mundane, monoliths now excoriated as academic slums. Recent remedies for high-rise banality have included reducing building density by assigning double rooms as singles; reshaping double-loaded corridor plans into suite arrangements; exchanging housing space for educational space, social space, and apartments for faculty in residence. These measures have been successful at the University of Miami, Florida, where a version of the Harvard-Yale house plan "living-learning" concept has been adapted from space in a conventional high-rise dorm. Brown University's model housing restoration program includes modernizing bathrooms, distributing an equitable share of social and support space in each building, and giving dated decor a fresh and modern look. Other features and factors deserving attention in revitalization plans include provision for reasonable acoustics, temperature, and ventilation; room configurations and furnishings that permit each occupant to express his or her personality; and a site whose landscapes and features are pleasant and functional for informal recreation. Energy conservation and accessibility for the handicapped are issues and opportunities that also need attention. And, not the least, the perception and fact of being in and on a safe and secure campus is today increasingly a meaningful matter for many students and their families. Some locales may need a contemporary equivalent to the grates, walls, and moats of monastic scholastic compounds.

Each generation has its own sense of function and convenience. A leading architect in the 1930s would promote "a pressing room laundry-tub facility, so it will not be necessary for students to do light laundry work in the bedrooms, and so irons can be concentrated in one room, to minimize conflagration." Sixty years later a successful residential hall would have a photography room and a minigym for workouts; another, a bunkhouse for visitors; a third, a dedicated worship room for Islamic students; a fourth, a "country kitchen" for baking birthday cakes. An insti-

UNIVERSITY OF CALIFORNIA, LOS ANGELES, CALIFORNIA MODERN. *(facing page, top) Student housing solutions from the 1960s—stacked shelter, Modern architecture which these days pragmatically and stylistically has few supporters.*

WASHINGTON STATE UNIVERSITY, C. 1960. *(facing page, bottom) Air view. Lower left, cluster of student dorms. Expedient, economical, convenient; presumably a formula which produced satisfactory housing in a hurry, but in retrospect a flawed if not fatal response to student housing goals and objectives. For contrast and emulation see University of California, Berkeley, page 151.*

tution's educational program may dictate housing variations. The residential hall at the Maryland Institute College of Art (1994) provides three- and four-person apartments for housing 350 students. The building includes 17 project rooms which permit students to work late at night in the safety of their own dorm.

Some students, of course, will live in the community rather than on campus, by choice in lifestyle, or because such arrangements seem more economical than campus housing. Housing officials believe that diversification in housing choices raises the level of student satisfaction with dorm choices and "choice is the name of the game." At Cabrini College, shrewdly, students are offered a customary dormitory experience in a traditional or contemporary building (clearly differentiated in plan, materials, and siting) or in one of nine smaller buildings, constructed to look like single-family homes but adapted to house about twenty students. All are located in central campus, near recreation, dining, and social facilities. Site-wise the "houses" are located along what was designed to be (if necessary) a suburban street. Strategically, should the college residential population decline, the units could be leased for a noncollege population, perhaps local elderly families seeking "transition housing" from the estates and large homes in the college vicinity. The 1991 project at Kutztown University melds several objectives—lessons from the past. The project concept, designed to optimize summer use (so as to generate income to lower student room charges), scales down the 400-bed dormitory socially by using 12-person suites (attractively expressed in the cloisterlike site composition, facade, and massing) and provides additional housing choices with 20 beds accommodated in a three-story wing designed to look like a house. Recent projects at Harvard University (conversion of a motel into a law school dormitory) and the Massachusetts Institute of Technology (adaptation of an industrial building into graduate student housing) earn attention as projects worth examination when considering variations and additions to the campus housing stock.

How to proceed with renewal, reconstruction, and new housing? Arguably after a half century of striving and struggling, the patterns of American campus housing have settled down to a predictable and measurable range. Variations in the quality and quantity of campus housing can thus be determined by examining the square footage, distribution, and physical attributes of space available and their relationship to specific institutional missions, educational philosophy, expectations, and peer group comparisons. Less measurable statistically are site conditions—the surrounding ambiance whose visual quality and functions bear directly on student satisfaction with campus housing. Here, problems and opportunities can be summarized graphically. The resulting information—profiles, statistics, and pictorial surveys—can then be used to define actions which will mediate deficient conditions and help project requirements and criteria for new housing and building additions that are tailored to local objectives and resources.

As to standards and criteria, campus housing has more space on most campuses than all other academic functions combined. Interinstitutional and intrainstitutional statistical comparisons also indicate vital differences in the range of undergraduate residential space provided per student housed: 132 net square feet to 190 net square feet in a representative sample taken in 1992. From these and other databases three types of campus housing types can be deduced, with revealing varia-

Sector A
Northwest Quadrangle
North Campus

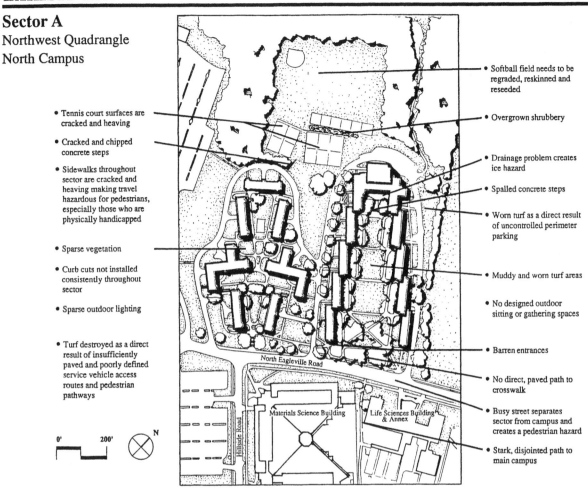

- Tennis court surfaces are cracked and heaving

- Cracked and chipped concrete steps

- Sidewalks throughout sector are cracked and heaving making travel hazardous for pedestrians, especially those who are physically handicapped

- Sparse vegetation

- Curb cuts not installed consistently throughout sector

- Sparse outdoor lighting

- Turf destroyed as a direct result of insufficiently paved and poorly defined service vehicle access routes and pedestrian pathways

- Softball field needs to be regraded, reskinned and reseeded

- Overgrown shrubbery

- Drainage problem creates ice hazard

- Spalled concrete steps

- Worn turf as a direct result of uncontrolled perimeter parking

- Muddy and worn turf areas

- No designed outdoor sitting or gathering spaces

- Barren entrances

- No direct, paved path to crosswalk

- Busy street separates sector from campus and creates a pedestrian hazard

- Stark, disjointed path to main campus

0'   200'   N

North Eagleville Road

Hillside Road

Materials Science Building

Life Sciences Building & Annex

tions. These are the shelter model, the campus life model, and the academic model. In the comparisons that follow, the exact number of net square footage associated with each model—though based on a statistical sample—should be read as an illustrative range of housing types. Size is not necessarily an indicator of problem housing. In scanning a variety of campus housing examples, one can find some residential halls that are spatially small statistically but delightfully proportioned and detailed. And, there are behemoths whose square footages seem favorable on a graph but whose actual designs lack the human scale and visual features expected in an arithmetically spacious and higher-cost dormitory.

The shelter model (less than 150 net square feet per student) provides bedroom and bathroom space and minimal social and support space. Typically a brick box dormitory, designed and constructed cheaply and expediently, these are academe's version of public low-cost housing, with all the social and physical ills the phrase connotes. Parenthetically, many such campus buildings are not beyond salvage, if space is added for functions they do yet contain or their existing exteriors are enlivened with new detailing or the surrounds improved by installing new landscapes. The additions are another example of redemptive architecture, which we

UNIVERSITY OF CONNECTICUT, STUDENT HOUSING RESTORATION STUDY, DIVISION OF STUDENT AFFAIRS AND SERVICES, 1991. DOBER, LIDSKY, CRAIG AND ASSOCIATES, CONSULTANTS. *Example of site conditions documentation; issues needing resolution for a satisfactory housing environment.*

expect could modify considerably the sterile and straitened appearances too often encountered in campus housing sectors.

The campus life model (150 to 200 net square feet per student) includes bedroom and bathroom space, plus support spaces, such as laundry rooms and storage rooms, as well as program and social space for activities that help young people experience the best aspects of campus life in a college-sponsored residential setting. Essentially, the dormitory (or equivalent housing) is seen not just as a place for sleeping, studying, and keeping personal belongings but also as an environment that encourages interaction with peers. This interaction is believed "to contribute to the education and development of the whole person and to the unification of living and learning within that person." With the oncoming, multicultured society, David Reisman's advice seems as cogent as ever. As he noted (1970): "One of the functions of the residential college is to emancipate the young from the inevitable limitations of their home and neighborhood before it is too late."

Interaction is fostered in the campus life model by live-in residential staff and visitors, and through formal and informal meetings, social and cultural programs, and events sponsored by the housing unit. Typical recreational and social spaces found in the campus life model include game room, snack bar, fitness center, laundry, TV room, computer room, designated group study room, and mailroom. Each such function can be located, designed, and furnished to promote the serendipity and synergy of campus life. A good example is the 800-bed Foothill Housing Complex (1992) at the University of California, Berkeley. Here the institution has hurdled the deficiencies of its 1960 high-rise solutions by changing scale from vertical density solutions to the horizontal, with smaller rather than larger building components. A fine ensemble, thoughtfully integrated into a tight site, the project's scale, materials, colors, and furnishings were designed and selected to echo but not imitate the Bay Area's "arts and crafts" domestic style architecture.

The academic model (200 net square feet or more per student) adds space for formal and informal academic experiences to the campus life model. The additional spaces may be developed for faculty in residence, tutor offices, seminar rooms, libraries, and accommodations for visitors who are expected to spend time with students academically. The model precedent is Oxford and Cambridge. The Harvard houses and the Yale colleges are modified American examples as is the most recent version of Oxbridge at the University of California, Santa Cruz. The latter can claim honors for having a diversity of commendable Modern and contemporary architecture interpreting the singular programmatic theme of a cluster of small colleges situated in a larger university context. The Santa Cruz model was intended to help overcome the hazards of "large, impersonal classes, little student-faculty contact, and for many students a computer-card identity crisis." Farther south at the Claremont consortium similar ideals have proved themselves sound and viable. Housing at the earliest colleges in the consortium, Pomona and Scripps, is considered exceptional for the regional architecture and landscape settings.

For success, the architecture of any of the three models must and should reflect local needs, desires, customs, and factors. When designing new housing and revitalizing the old, regional differences in climate, school calendar, traditions, and the nature of surrounding neighborhood are important considerations. Single-sex and

UNIVERSITY OF CALIFORNIA, BERKELEY,
FOOTHILL STUDENT HOUSING, 1991. THE
RATCLIFF ASSOCIATES WITH WILLIAM
TURNBULL ASSOCIATES. *A pivotal example of
changing attitudes about student housing and a
beneficial and attractive architectural response.*
(Source: The Ratcliff Associates)

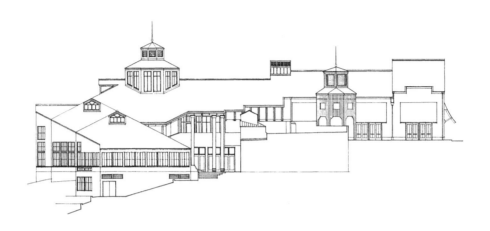

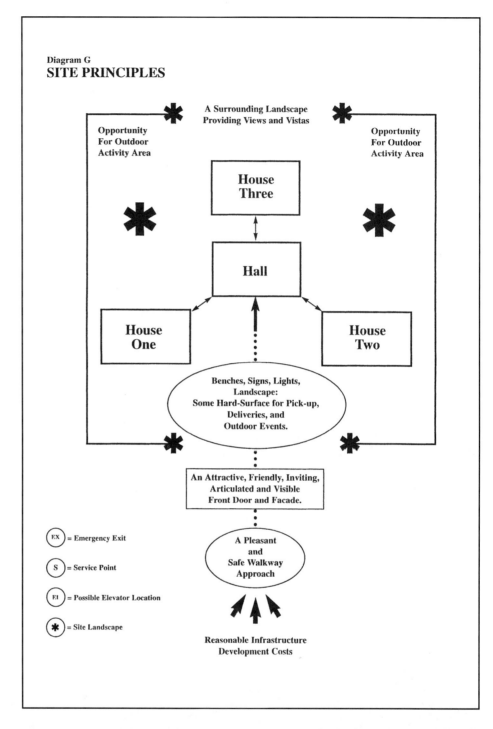

Diagram G
SITE PRINCIPLES

A Surrounding Landscape
Providing Views and Vistas

Opportunity
For Outdoor
Activity Area

Opportunity
For Outdoor
Activity Area

House Three

Hall

House One

House Two

Benches, Signs, Lights,
Landscape:
Some Hard-Surface for Pick-up,
Deliveries, and
Outdoor Events.

An Attractive, Friendly, Inviting,
Articulated and Visible
Front Door and Facade.

A Pleasant
and
Safe Walkway
Approach

Reasonable Infrastructure
Development Costs

EX = Emergency Exit

S = Service Point

EI = Possible Elevator Location

✳ = Site Landscape

BABSON COLLEGE, STUDENT HOUSING FACILITY PROGRAM DIAGRAMS, 1992. DOBER, LIDSKY, CRAIG AND ASSOCIATES, INC. *(this page and facing page bottom) Programmatic diagrams to guide site and building design.*

BABSON COLLEGE, STUDENT HOUSING, FRONT DOOR VIEW, 1992. CBT ARCHITECTS. *(facing page, top) The resulting project. (Photo: Steve Rosenthal, courtesy of Charles Tseckares.)*

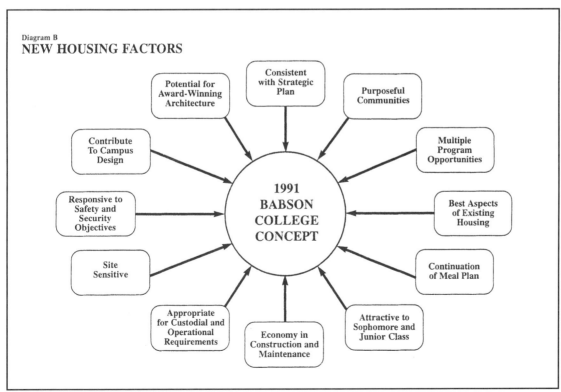

Diagram B
NEW HOUSING FACTORS

Potential for
Award-Winning
Architecture

Consistent
with Strategic
Plan

Purposeful
Communities

Contribute
To Campus
Design

Multiple
Program
Opportunities

**1991
BABSON
COLLEGE
CONCEPT**

Responsive to
Safety and
Security
Objectives

Best Aspects
of Existing
Housing

Site
Sensitive

Continuation
of Meal Plan

Appropriate
for Custodial and
Operational
Requirements

Economy in
Construction and
Maintenance

Attractive to
Sophomore and
Junior Class

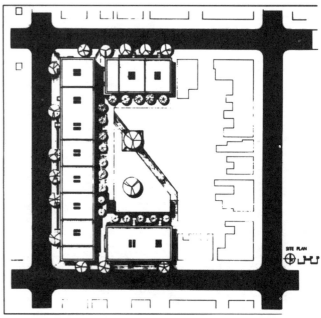

GEORGETOWN UNIVERSITY, VILLAGE B HOUS- ING, 1984. *(above)* *Hugh Newell Jacobson's expressive translation of university housing into a site-sensitive design for one of America's cherished and protected residential districts.* *(Source: Hugh Newell Jacobson)*

AND HOW FAR HAVE WE COME? *(right) Interior view, 1946, Rogers Dormitory Dining Hall, University of Indiana. Exemplary early Modern. See also page 5.*

WESTERN MICHIGAN UNIVERSITY, BRONCO MALL, 1992. *(facing page) Neon signs, food choices, with an ambiance more like a shopping center food court than a military base dining hall—dining that also provides nutritional, eco- nomic, and cultural choices for campus life at the dawn of the twenty-first century.* *(Source: Western Michigan University)*

coed campuses are each different places. Not all campuses will provide housing for single mothers with children, as does Saint Paul's College, Virginia. Executives enrolled in short-term university training programs expect room sizes, bathrooms, and amenities not found in typical dormitories. Fraternities and sororities, graduate student housing, married student housing, faculty housing obviously have their special purposes and architectural requirements.

At the undergraduate level, in principle a varied housing stock is the best response to meeting the generation cycle of changing student expectations—where one age group seeks its identity by being different from the group before. The Babson College facility program diagrams and photos indicate how housing policy considerations and specific site development criteria for a suburban venue merged into a realizable campus life project that broadens the College's housing inventory on a suburban campus. Of urban examples, Georgetown University's Village B student housing is everything the dreaded brick box is not. What might have been a large dormitory is expressed as a series of town houses designed to fit one of America's pleasant historic neighborhoods. Details pick up the Italianate style of nearby buildings in a tour de force of architecture in context.

Most housing sectors have their own associated dining facilities, often architecturally the best spaces, even in otherwise mundane housing compounds. The act of eating together in the institutional dining hall is often remembered by alumni as an act of survival almost leading to sedition or a gracious affair of social and educational benefit. Many existing facilities require upgrading comparable to the resi-

dence halls for similar reasons: decay, obsolescence, and the marketing and economic vitality of the dining experience. The desired objective is to provide a variety of dining choices in an environment that does not conjure up the mental picture of being in a minimum security institution. Conventional cafeteria, serving lines, and large open seating areas are being replaced with food courts and seating areas not unlike those seen in a shopping mall. Where climate permits, outdoor dining areas are popular. All in all, the objective of a streamlined and economic food operation, with an exuberant decor, appealing to students and visitors, is a reachable goal these days. Like housing, college and university dining services have become professionalized. Expert advisors are available on such matters as menu development, methods of food preparation and serving, equipment, health standards, the psychological impact of color and space on the dining experience, and computerized patron identification and charging systems. As to general ambiance and amenities, few institutions can afford the dreary and dismal. Philosophically food services cannot be treated as "auxiliary services," peripheral to the overall educational experience; comprehensive physical renewal of facilities can be expected nationwide.

In scanning several centuries of building types, we have traced an evolution stimulated by function and have indicated and illustrated how function inspires exceptional designs. Clearly, function is a design determinant, but a useful definition of *campus architecture* also requires other discernible distinctions and aesthetic dimensions. These we will now explore as we continue our exposition and examples.

CHAPTER 3

CAMPUS ARCHITECTURE
DEFINED

*Certainly it is not possible to invent a new
kind of architecture every Monday morning.*
Mies van der Rohe, 1961

**UNIVERSITY OF ILLINOIS, CAMPUS PLAN,
1922. CHARLES A. PLATT.** *An Apollonian
campus design, geometric, presumably predictive
in determining building shapes and forms. Platt's
biographer, Keith N. Morgan, writes that the
"trustees were eager to establish an official style
for university buildings. Since Platt found no
appropriate local or campus traditions on which
to base the design of new buildings, he imposed
an architectural vocabulary of English Georgian,
which was consistent with the formality of his
plan and could be expanded easily to accommodate the needs of differing departments and programs." Several such structures were designed,
but several Monday mornings followed, too often
with a pot pourri of styles. Of consequence was
Platt's idea of a regulated development scheme,
honored in principle by subsequent architects,
albeit their own versions.*

CHAOS OR CONTROL: ARCHITECTURAL ENIGMAS

People want the buildings that represent their social and community life to give
more than functional fulfillment. They want their aspirations for monumentality,
joy, pride and excitement to be satisfied.

Sigfried Gideon, 1960

We see our new architecture as an art aimed at satisfying social needs. We
define function not in terms of visual effect but as the arrangement and
enclosures of spaces to make human activities more productive and enjoyable. We
consider materials as tools for enclosure, not as symbolic labels for fixed style.

Phil Will, Jr., FAIA, 1961

The review of building types helps us understand diversity's cause and result but does not establish a structured definition of campus architecture. For that, we have to throw light through a propagating prism. Today a small school such as Carleton College has 63 buildings, a large institution such as Stanford University several hundred, many functionally different as to building type. Diversity is necessary. But, as designer Robert E. Alexander worried in 1963, "such radically different building forms, consciously sought, could lead into chaos unless policies are developed to control them." Writing on the eve of unprecedented growth in American higher education, Alexander was fearful that "Industrial research and salesmanship have opened a Pandora's box of building materials and colors." He believed architectural chaos could be avoided at the University of California, San Diego, where he was working, and other campuses he was studying, by applying certain principles which he saw evident "in the unified and somber buildings of old world" universities. As Alexander and his peers learned, and as we demonstrated in the review of building types, the search for principles to steer architecture through the shoals of function, style, and symbol to solutions that are suitable and relevant to purpose and place is no easy task.

By the time Alexander had completed his buildings in San Diego, old world and new were discombobulated by architectural ideas and philosophies not easily countenanced by Alexander, one of the last masterful interpreters of Modern architecture as it was conceived before and after World War II. How quaint and simple and convincing Gideon's truism, Will's formula, and Mies's convictions, like a flexible sock, one size fitting all. Comforting too, would be Walter Gropius's faith in Modern: "the new building of the future, which will embrace architecture and

---

BROWN UNIVERSITY, JOHN CARTER BROWN EXTENSION, 1990. HARTMAN AND COX, ARCHI-
TECTS. *(facing page, top) The new addition was designed as a stylistically seamless extension in a tour de force of matching new and old. When to invent, when to depart, when to emulate, when to interpret? These are leading questions in defining campus architecture.*

GEORGE WASHINGTON UNIVERSITY, SERVICES AND SUPPORT BUILDING, 1990. KEYES CONDON
FLORANCE. *(facing page, bottom) A clear example of context determining style. The shipping and receiving functions, mail room, equipment storage, and vehicle repair had to be housed near the main building complex, in an urban precinct, and with an architecture that was in scale with and sympathetic to the surrounding residential neighborhood. (Source: Keyes Condon Florance)*

sculpture and painting in one unity and which will rise one day toward heaven from the hands of a million workers like the crystal symbol of a new faith."

Architecture today is an uncertain art. Conflicts in theory, purpose, canon, and convictions exacerbate the tensions between the visionary and the practicable, as they always have in the periodic rise and fall of fashion and function. "Contemporary architecture bathes in the pantheistic limbo of eclecticism," states Demetri Porphyries (1974). "Torn between the dilemma of a frantic search for novelty and an inherited social mission for a popular language, architecture leafs through history caricaturing remembrances." Not so argues Robert Stern (1989), suggesting that the grammar and vocabulary of Classical buildings, the merits of vernacular regional buildings, and the influences and artifacts of industrialization can be melded into an aesthetic that uses the best features of all three.

On campus, commissioning a new building begins with definitions of purpose, size, site, and budget. Once these are settled, the aesthetic adventure is launched. As designs advance, topical vexations and institutional sophistication about architectural matters are immediately exposed in debates such as the merits of gratuitous elaboration versus unambiguous functionalism, or the serenity of a formulated contemporary architectural style versus the panache of design gestures with historical antecedents blended with exterior materials and shapes totally without precedent on the specific campus. This "sweet disorder and carefully careless" may have "merit," acknowledges critic Robert Maxwell (1993). However, "To be acceptable," he says, "modern architecture has to be rendered into a human tradition and subjected to human values." On that score, and to that end, we see campuses as ideal proving grounds for continuous self-determination of appropriate campus architecture, campuses being, as they are, multifaceted congeries of coherence and contradictions. Accordingly, success here may come by first understanding and interpreting some fundamental factors peculiar to building in the groves of academe, where the objective could be conscious design consistency or, where desired, deliberate, though agitating, variety.

FUNDAMENTALS

Knowledge is higher education's prime purpose—utilized in teaching, research, and community service. The three functions are dynamic, the means and modes varied; so too are the physical representations and configurations of the functions. Some campuses are appealing architecturally because they convey the appearance of visual unity, carefully cultivated. The controlled ambiance is cherished through design continuity, such as the three centuries of Collegiate Georgian architecture at William and Mary College, albeit with varying interpretations of that protean style. Other campuses are attractive because they are composites; offering the best architecture of their era. Witness the Green at Brown University, also several centuries in the making, and praised today as a tangible, three-dimensional history book of architectural philosophies, fashions, engineering, and craftsmanship. To use Duke Ellington's superlative, it is "beyond category." Of consequence is Brown's continuing revitalization of these and other original structures; such as the Sayles Gymnasium project cited earlier—inside the building new functions, outside the form preserved.

Such differences are not an East Coast phenomenon but universal in campus design. Visual unity can be found at the University of New Mexico, Albuquerque; composite designs at the University of Washington. Centuries of buildings at Oxford are united by the honey-colored, oolitic limestone, carved, sliced, paneled in older and newer structures, many organized around the memorable quads. In contrast, its intellectual twin, Cambridge University, is remembered as having a larger palette of materials and site configurations. The latest buildings at Lavalle University are joined visually to their earlier counterparts in color, texture, and certain detailing, arranged in veneration to the Quebec vernacular.

Like a geologic cross-section, the buildings at these institutions can be read as economic indicators of good times and bad, as well as swings in the cultural and aesthetic pendulum, from neotraditionalism to avant garde and points in between. Apparent in those cycles is a reality that informs college and university architecture as an exceptional professional challenge, the challenge of discovering, balancing, and expressing the energy of institutional vitality. Pistonlike, these are the push-pull of continuity and change in mission, goals and objectives, size, organizational structure, programmatic priorities, and aesthetic preferences. These forces affect campus architecture at its inception. They are at work in moving a project from concept to reality. Successful architecture must position itself clearly along the spectrum of past, present, and future. Ignorance or indifference to these circumstances has unhinged the complacency of those who would guide campus architecture with a curator's conservatism and goodwill as well as upset the advocates of accelerating a new direction with artistic audacity. In both instances by failing to make a strong case for continuity or change, or for creative solutions for channeling the forces, some ingenious schemes have been sent to the archives unbuilt, concepts which in other circumstances would have survived the test of campus ethos, committee judgments, administrative discretion, board leadership, and the financial officer's concerns about available funding.

Another reality is that whether consciously conceived as a visually unified design concept or emerging as a composite, college and university campuses are never completed. Relentlessly, like the tides, new combinations of teaching, research, and community service evolve as institutions discover, define, and use the corpus of facts and values which is implicit in their missions. The intellectual ferment—evolution or revolution—often requires parallel changes or adaptations in the physical forms that constitute the campus, and, occasionally, for functional reasons will breed fundamental new concepts as to what is appropriate campus architecture. The knowledgeable designer will be alert for and will address these conditions.

Technology influences campus architecture obviously, ubiquitously. The drive-in community college is the product of the auto age. Electricity, and, later, electronics, transformed the use and physical forms of the campus library. Indoor plumbing altered dormitory design. The mechanization of food services impacted dining hall routines, site requirements, and ambiance. The fear of fire gave cause for widespread acceptance of masonry architecture. Cast iron columns helped widen room size. Cheap glass improved natural lighting. Provisions for controlling toxic wastes and gases altered the appearance of science facilities. As they became available, aluminum and poured concrete permitted building forms and shapes previ-

BROWN UNIVERSITY, THE GREEN. JOHN FORASTE. *(top) A living museum of institutional architecture. (Source: Brown University)*

LAVALLE UNIVERSITY, THE OLDER 1920 LIBRARY, THE NEW SCHOOL OF MANAGEMENT. *(left and above) Forms and textures linked for visual continuity and homage to antecedents, a campus worth seeing for good lessons in architecture as heritage, simple landscapes, and clarity in campus design.*

UNIVERSITY OF VERMONT, WILLIAMS HALL. *(facing page, top) (Source: University of Vermont)*
UNITED STATES AIR FORCE ACADEMY, CHAPEL. *(facing page, bottom) (Source: U.S. Air Force Academy)*
Emphatic skyline designs with generational differences in building technology, materials, and aesthetics.

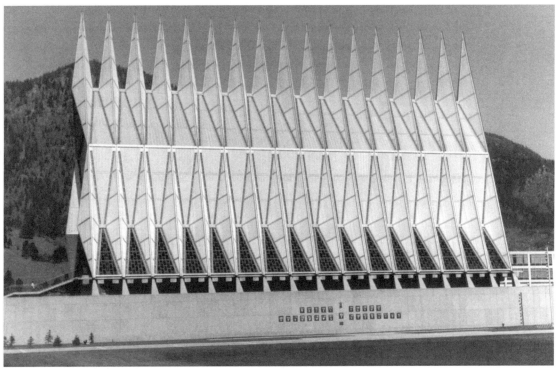

ously unseen on campus, many loaded with design signals that announced the end of one generation's view of good architecture and the arrival of another. Generation differences in materials, technology driven, are easy to read architecturally as signals of change. Compare the elevation of nineteenth-century Williams Hall at the University of Vermont and the Air Force Academy Chapel, both memorable designs pointing skyward. The Williams's building materials and forms are the products of a definable industrial period and architectural style. The Chapel's aluminum framing and construction unquestionably convey modern materials, values, and aesthetic attitudes.

Introducing his concept for the University of Sussex (England, 1964) Basil Spence noted that the Greeks (presumably the classical authority and arbiters of British design values) "welcomed the idea of incompleteness as a virtue, that incompleteness was life itself. It was with that in mind that the first plan was done." Simple and effective conceptually, his designs provided a group of buildings in a landscape setting with expansion directed outward from a stable core.

However, some degree of permanency is also desired philosophically, educationally, physically as campuses mature. The mortmain of achievements and accomplishments should be sustained or reused as heritage. The accommodation of those who are out of step with the times but whose eccentricity finds productive outlet in academe, the enduring qualities of intellectual discipline and rigor, the ideal of governance through collegiality—these are anchors in a sea of change which can be found in campus histories and are often ennobled architecturally. At the least, where desired institutionally, generational continuity can be honored through architectural gestures and genuflections that reflect their surrounding context. Spence for Sussex: "I saw the University now and in the future in pink brick with some arched forms peeping in the trees." The designs of some American campuses are equally compelling in applying that logic. At Virginia Polytechnic University, a traditional local stone is used in the facades of discernible contemporary buildings, manifestations and recognizable signs of change and continuity. Though organized internally by programmatic factors, buildings can stand uncompromised in function, yet be molded by shapes and inflected with details and materials associated with their region, a principle beautifully executed in the 1992 classroom building at Rock Valley College, Illinois. The roof lines, massing, and stone walls are reminders of the surrounding agricultural community. Architectural Rosetta stones, these buildings are alphabets of local design metaphors translatable into signals of continuity and change, of which Vanderbilt University's Psychology Building (shown on page 25) is a sophisticated example. However, as E. H. Gombrich warns, "corruption lurks close to perfection...an overdose of effects produces a hollow and affected style."

Landscapes can also be conceptualized and used to indicate the permanent and the indeterminate. Building sensitively in the groves of academe, using the groves and other forms of campus greenery as campus design themes, is an art worth encouraging, indeed an essential aspect of campus architecture, as discussed below. Poetic or pragmatic, commendable campus landscapes range from the grand classical development schemes (framed and formed by lawns, trees, and flowers) to the nooks and crannies delightful to discover and use (when properly planned, pat-

Virginia Polytechnic University. *Architecture defined by homage to stone. (Source: Virginia Polytechnic University)*

Rock Valley College, 1992. *C. Edward Ware's place-evoking campus architecture. (Photo: A. Sskutans, courtesy of Rock Valley College)*

terned, and planted). Walls and fencing, gateways, ceremonial areas, memorial gardens, sculpture, fountains, and outdoor art are opportunities to raise quotidian designs to a higher level of design achievement. Paradigmatic campus architecture, admittedly challenging by definition, aims to meld all the constituent physical elements into a unified visual statement. How? Again, Spence: unity "comes from internal rhythm, the buildings and materials, and a sensitive appreciation of the site, of using ground in a proper way."

To reiterate, campus design has to ennoble the past, enhance the present, and provide for the future by balancing continuity and change. Campus architecture implements these objectives through specific projects. As will be illustrated, good solutions must meet functional needs on a well-selected site, with creative responses to aesthetics and budget, and gain endorsement among those affected by the design. The last is not least. These days the best designs are not imposed from the top but surface from consensus and participatory planning. Reflecting the forces of continuity and change, it is also understandable that the reasons and rationale which are used in the design processes that create new architecture, or in the plans that conserve and reuse the old architecture, may not be shared by all who have a stake in the outcome. Sometimes collegial reviews and evaluations of the first designs must serve as the occasion for mediating or settling philosophic, cultural, and social differences—not necessarily related to the project under discussion—before a firm concept is approved for design development and construction. That kind of discourse is another institutional reality to be reckoned with in generating campus architecture. Fundamentally, a single model or process for encapsulating higher education physically is as unlikely a proposition as the sun setting in the east. Thus, the search for and expression of diversity and distinctiveness, or a reaffirmation or reinterpretation of design continuity, all through collegial efforts, is an underlying principle in our recommended conceptualization of campus architecture.

There are two other fundamentals which can and should inform and bring all architecture on campus into the twenty-first century—institutional responsibility for demonstrating environmental awareness and the humanizing influence campus architecture can have as computers and communications technology continue to mechanize and accelerate the processes for creating, transferring, and sharing knowledge. The following definitions and commentary are offered in structuring our interpretation of campus architecture.

TROLLING THROUGH THE SEA OF DEFINITIONS

A *campus* is an ensemble of buildings, landscapes, and infrastructure used for higher education, as it exists and as it is planned. The word is occasionally applied to other architectural groupings such as school grounds, government complexes, research parks, and medical and cultural centers. The connotation is favorable and constructive. In these instances *campus* is a cachet implying an ordered design, special and coherent, as in the Rhode Island Hospital long-range development concept. The text and illustrations which follow focus on college and university campuses, though the discussion may have useful application for any large group of buildings and landscapes constructed over time and intended to be mutable environments responding to social and cultural needs.

As to defining *architecture*, a book-length bibliography would be required to introduce the canon. Publications include manifestos sanctioning new directions, screeds on building types, and tropes on designers fashionable, neglected, or rediscovered. Subtitles from publisher Pierre Mardaga's book catalog (Paris, 1994) reveal the range: architecture as a symbolic form, as an expression of realism, as social ornament, as a political statement of power and prestige, as craft, and as patrimony. Each opus offered a universal truth. In that spirit (the search for certitude in an era of paradox and perplexity) the selection of definitions that follow are a sample of those that have had historic influence on campus architecture and, taken as a whole, provide a critical appreciation of causes and effects still at work in determining, shaping, and siting college and university buildings.

Following a tradition dating back to Vitruvius, professionals such as William Halfpenny (*The Art of Sound Building,* London, 1724) and the contemporary Michael Winn (*Architectronics—Revolutionary Technologies for Masterful Building through Design,* McGraw-Hill, New York, 1993) have illustrated architectural purpose and technique for practitioners, their clients, and the interested public. The first such books in English were ubiquitous in application. Treasured by the cultured elite as well as semiliterate craftspeople, these books determined what was acceptable architecture in climes as varied as Northern Ireland and the Southern Caribbean, and in societies as disparate as New England and the Virginia plantations. Some early-nineteenth-century American architectural pattern books, however, soon recognized possible continental differences, the beginnings of transoceanic variations, and architectural regionalism. In publishing his version of suitable architecture, designer Owen Biddle (1810) introduced the matter thusly: "I have experienced much inconvenience for want of suitable books on the subject. All that have appeared, have been written by foreign authors, who have adapted their examples and observations almost entirely to the style of building in their respective countries, which in many instances differs very materially from ours." Biddle's thrust was an unchaining of British influences that produced along the East Coast thousands of watered down versions of Georgian and Neoclassical doorways, fenestration, and mantelpieces—architecture through millwork—which for their age are now justly esteemed and preserved in older college buildings. Decades later, in preparing guidelines for zoning codes and proselytizing architecture as regionalism, John Gaw Meem (circa 1930) would go much further, downgrading all references to European antecedents and upgrading native forms and colors in nourishing and defending the Pueblo style first advocated by William G. Tight for institutional buildings in the Southwest, notably at the University of Mexico.

Designer-writers Andrew Jackson Downing and William Butterfield preached that architecture might be differentiated morally. Downing (1842) advocated country houses be designed "with more chasteness and simplicity than a townhouse; because it is in the country, if anywhere, that we should find essential ease and convenience always preferred to that love of effect and desire to dazzle, which is begotten for the most part, by the rivalry of mere wealth in town life." Thus sympathetic to Downing's reasoning, Frederick Law Olmsted would advocate cottage-

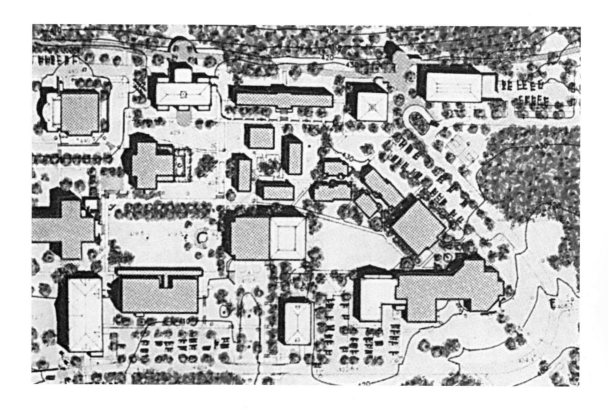

RHODE ISLAND HOSPITAL, 1986. DOBER, LIDSKY, CRAIG AND ASSOCIATES, INC. *(facing page, top)*
ARKANSAS COLLEGE, 1994. DOBER, LIDSKY, CRAIG AND ASSOCIATES, INC. *(facing page, bottom)*
Campus plans: A coordinated view of the future, a mix of new and old buildings, landscapes, circulation, and parking; sufficiently flexible to admit adjustments and changes in specificity during implementation.

SMITH COLLEGE. *(this page) A century of housing, buildings and landscapes engaged, each generation with a style its own but throughout a consistent regard for the Olmstedean programmatic theme. An arboretum defines one edge of the campus and the townscape the other. Residences marked with asterisks are interspersed, a living catalog of architectural motifs and taste. (Source: Smith College)*

style architecture over monumental buildings for his college clients. Olmsted rejected the formality of quadrangles and classical architectural compositions, as well as the housing of students in the "red-brick barrack-like accommodations," with which he was familiar in his tours of eastern seaboard campuses. Domestic scale structures, village and informal park settings—these were most suitable for exemplifying the American character and serving the democratization of higher education, thought Olmsted. His ethical tone resonated with righteousness for the founders of Smith College seeking architectural themes suitable for educating women through and with "every element of their environment—intellectual, spiritual, physical, cultural, aesthetic." Smith College was thus created and maintained as an Olmsted ideal, agricultural in sentiment, producing the first student housing designed as cottages, each with their own dining room. Several generations of buildings track changes in design fashions and styles at Smith, but, the overall purpose and size of campus housing continues—the continuation of collegiate domesticity, the annealing of a Smith tradition of buildings situated in a self-perpetuating landscape.

Campus architecture can serve and signal institutional attitudes about moral issues. Inventing a new style and building plan for Keble College (Oxford, 1868), Butterfield and clients were motivated to end the debauchery, idleness, and indifference to education that they were convinced were too strongly associated with, if not engendered by, earlier Oxford architecture. From the design of brickwork to the arrangement of interior corridors and room sizes, Butterfield departed from earlier Oxonian precedents, producing a version of collegiate architecture that delighted his clients and for a time infuriated critics and peers. Architecture as fashion and architecture as style are two threads that can be woven into a theoretical fabric, fashion being ephemeral, and style being art ossified. The appearance, acceptance, and endurance of the first (fashion) will lead to the latter (a style). Keble was neither, thus a testimony to Butterfield's genius and the strength of the client and architect's joint convictions. Together they fostered and supported the design, eccentric though it was, in a traditional and sometimes hostile educational and social environment.

The history of campus architecture is spotted with such convictions. Explaining his proposed designs—nineteenth-century Classicism for the University of Texas—Paul P. Cret would "conjoin the legacy of the past with the promise of the future" by finding the "character of the building" in establishing its *parti*. The word means "party," he once wrote, "just as in politics there is a Republican, a Democratic party. Selecting a *parti* for an (architectural) problem is like taking an attitude towards a solution." Collegiate Gothic was praised and promoted as the only commendable architectural style for its ability to remind students of the virtues and disciple of monastic education. Such designs were an architectural antidote to late-nineteenth-century "insane secularism," thought its devout propagandist and skilled proponent Ralph Adams Cram. In contrast, Collegiate Georgian was revived several times as a style in memory of the verities and social values of the early New England churches and colleges. Such candles are not easily blown out, witness the recent dormitories at Boston College and Tufts University, echoing nineteenth-century designs, and the library addition at Kenyon College seen earlier—modern in every functional respect, detailed as homage, and built with gestures to nearby historic designs.

Useful are the attempts to rationalize design processes and thus prescribe architecture. Though 200 years apart, Jean-Nicolas-Louis Durand (1802) and Christopher Alexander (1964) share a common approach to defining architecture; first through classifications of forms and functions and then through applying organizing and compositional principles to generate building designs. These coded conventions continue definitional and directional architectural dialogs, of which Leone B. Alberti's *The Art of Building* (1485) is the seminal work in the Western canon. Here, for example, one might find the correct composition and location for design elements as diverse as a vestibule or a town gate. In his pattern-language planning for the University of Oregon (1965) Alexander provides equivalent prescriptions for campus open spaces, path systems, and building elements.

For Robert B. Bechtel architecture is *Enclosing Behavior* (Hutchinson and Ross, Stroudsburg, 1977). He and his counterparts meld human ecology and psychology to infuse design conceptualization and processes with the insights and ideals available in social science research. Their work and points of intervention have significantly influenced design processes such as facility programming and evaluations of the built environment. At the least, they challenged the soap opera of design awards for buildings that were not examined as to functional satisfaction and psychological impact. At their best, they gave designer's methods for stating more clearly architectural intentions and desired outcomes. They moved, for example, concepts of human scale from an abstract Renaissance diagram to descriptive and timely constructs of cultural and generational differences in shaping and experiencing space functionally and visually. As in Robert Geddes's landmark housing scheme for the University of Delaware, designers working this definition sought and applied "sociopetal-anthropophilic" theories to help configure site and building arrangements so as to unite "more fully the social and intellectual life on campus with architectural forms."

Architecture is environment first, some social scientists would claim, as they enrich with disciplined research the intuitive explorations of Richard Neutra (*Survival Through Design,* Oxford University Press, New York, 1954). In his design philosophy and practice, Neutra expanded the definition of modern architecture to embrace and interpret findings from biology and the behavioral sciences. His impact on school design was noted earlier. Sustaining the relationship of man and nature is essential, says Norman Crowe, chastising those who would categorize and isolate environmental concerns and factors from the process of determining the shapes of the built environment. In Crowe's *Nature and the Idea of a Man-Made World* (MIT Press, Cambridge, Massachusetts, 1994), he argues that is an unnecessary dichotomy. He proposes an architectural theory based on return to an historic symbiotic relationship between basic natural environmental conditions and forms induced by functional requisites. He rejects the aesthetic tenets of "postmodernism...which tends to see the built world...through the abstractions of post-enlightenment science."

Christian Norberg-Schulz holds that architecture is a way of giving people an "existential foothold" through a work of art that concretizes and transmits the

meaning of culture and the significance of place (*Genus Loci*, New York, 1984). All campuses have or should have that significance. Peter Eiseman, however, would strip all associational meanings from architecture, "making the plans, walls and elements as valueless as a stack of playing cards." His definition of architecture was first seen in domestic commissions and later given full reign in a controversial scheme for the visual arts (Wexner Center) at Ohio State University. It "shakes us from the complacency of our convictions about campus master planning, traditional architecture, and the notions of what art should be," comments observer Graham Gund. "Spatial gymnastics," writes Carolyn Senft, is an "effort to create perceptual instabilities that displace the subject/viewer within architectural space." For Mies van der Rohe, architecture was less, not more. Iconoclast Robert Venturi advocated the "hybrid" over the "pure," "the inconsistent and equivocal rather than direct and clear" in his savvy and provocative *Complexity and Contradiction in Architecture* (Museum of Modern Art, New York, 1966). Theory is "not a hammer but an *oculus*," thus the concepts of style should be secondary to considerations of site, enclosure, and materials, writes David Leatherbarrow in *The Roots of Architectural Invention* (Cambridge University Press, Cambridge, Massachusetts, 1993). He observes that "the art of building has been transformed into a business of self-display and promotion through the design and construction of figurative motifs, making it an object of consumption." Leatherbarrow would return architecture to "topics and matters that must be worked through before style." He says the "manifest presence" of these form-giving activities has been and will be "the responsibility of the architect who dares to invent something new."

Less mentioned in the annals and bibliographies that trace the evolution of modern Western twentieth-century architecture, and significantly underrated as design influences deserving acknowledgment, are building technology such as high-speed elevators, unitary HVAC systems, artificial lighting, computers, and communication devices. Arguably, a theory of architecture could be formulated as the melding of technology and fashion. As seen earlier, mechanical and structural systems have been expressed in a visually interesting manner on the exterior in some recent campus laboratory buildings, although by 1994 the impulse to do so had seemingly gone dormant.

Thus scanned, definitions of architecture can be found in dense discourses on aesthetic sublimity, ideology, and philosophy, on one hand, and on the other dividing postulation and practice, theories about the manipulation of materials and structure and simple manuals explaining programming, design, and construction as a linked process. Critical appreciations rarely examine these latter factors, which

---

UNIVERSITY OF DELAWARE, STUDENT HOUSING, 1964. GEDDES, BRECHER, QUALLS AND CUNINGHAM. *(facing page, top and bottom left) A pioneering venture in applying social science research to Modern campus housing. (Photo: Jack Buxbaum, courtesy of University of Delaware)*

OXFORD, KEBLE COLLEGE, C. 1870. WILLIAM BUTTERFIELD. *(facing page, bottom right) The architect gives the client a refreshing design palette to announce and symbolize significant changes in educational philosophy and housing arrangements. Coeval opinions: Nickolaus Pevsner ("actively ugly"); Kenneth Clark ("one of the finest buildings of its date in England").*

affect answers to such questions as: How well does the building work? How well was it built? The last is not to be neglected. As Bruce Durie reminds us "Hadrian built the Pantheon to the glory of Gods and Art, but it only went up because of concrete and some good arithmetic." Ironically, the *Penguin Dictionary of Architecture* (New York, 1977), a standard work, has no entry under *architecture*.

Trolling through the canon, some aspects of all the definitions cited apply to some extent to college and university buildings. Required then is the architectural equivalent of the cosmologists "General Theory": an all-embracing definition that accounts for shifting horizons, the heat and light of an expanding universe, black holes and bright stars, the waxing and waning of observable phenomena that inspires poets and physicists, and, to stretch the metaphor further, a definition that sets in motion the best efforts of the preachers, patrons, and producers of campus architecture.

CAMPUS ARCHITECTURE

Our objective in suggesting a general theory is furthered by joining and treating the two words (*campus* + *architecture*) as a descriptive entity. The definition we seek must apply to microscale designs (specific college and university projects) and macroscale concepts (area designs that organize the campus, or campus sector, as a functional and visual unit).

At the macroscale, architecture is an amalgam of context and relationships. The desired result is an overall area design concept, creating both the image and specificity of a memorable city, district, campus, or site. Here, through *place-making* and *place-marking* techniques, the art of civic design comes into play, generating large-scale architectural effects that are seen and remembered as the essence of the particular area. *Place-making* objectives are realized through the articulation, classification, and differentiation of building groups and significant structures, landscapes, and circulation elements and then their arrangement and positioning in response to site conditions, climate, programmatic and functional relationships, and desired visual sequence. *Place marking* strengthens the overall design structure and inflects it with perceptible physical character. Take, for example, Bath, England, with its honey-colored stone, the brick edifices of Back Bay, Boston, the white stucco of historic Seville—in these instances the consistent use of regional materials in new and old architecture are visible place markers reinforcing the sense of place.

As to microscale architecture, some version of the ancient *utilitas, firmatas, et venustas* would cover the essentials. Campus buildings are understandable objects, from the outer walls inward, with characteristic features associated with the building type. These characteristics are revealed in floor plans, cross sections, elevations, details, fittings and finishes, the sizing and relationships of spaces to meet program requirements (including, these days, safety, accessibility, and energy conservation), and the introduction and installation of necessary building technology to sustain and support building activities and for economic operations and maintenance. But above all else, a building declares itself as architecture through clarity of purpose, logic in plan, perceptible and enjoyable vertical and horizontal circulation patterns, the dimensioning and flow of space to be experienced as volume, and the selection and arrangement of exterior materials and motifs as a conscious, congruous demonstration of building function, structure, and style.

Admittedly, the result for some may be a yawn, or a yelp, or elation—reflecting the merging of client intentions with the designer's ability to produce a persuasive design and the inevitable reckoning of objective critical judgment and peer standards and expectations. Nonetheless, whether from the hand of Pugin or Aalto, Wren or Wright, such architecture gains the approbation "masterpiece" when the design and crafting of the interiors and furnishings echo and sustain the building concept and when the siting and kindred landscape extend the aesthetic experience of the structure into the environs for use and pleasure.

So far the definitions of architecture—macro and micro—have universal application. To assay the particular in this book, we define *campus architecture* as buildings and landscapes synergistically engaged and integrated as projects which are situated in paradigms planned and designed for higher education. As illustrated more abundantly later, *paradigms* are areawide designs, created through place making, such as the overall form of the campus or the design of a campus precinct. The paradigms may be perceptibly geometric, such as the original quadrangular plan for the Duke University West Campus, less fettered site arrangements such as the Texas A & M campus, or composites that include both formal and informal campus precincts. In all three instances, campus greenery helps establish, embellish, and "emblematize" the broad-scale campus design and its constituent parts.

The paradigms thus created for campuses can be further strengthened through place marking, i.e., an additional transfer of civic design techniques into campus design methods, and their application to campus venues. The desired outcome is location and orchestration of certain physical attributes which give a campus a visual uniqueness appropriately its own. Place-marking elements include the consistent use of building materials (such as the cut limestone associated with the image of Kansas State University), continuity in aspects of style (such as variations of Collegiate Georgian associated with images of William and Mary College), a heritage building serving as an institutional symbol (Old Morrison, Transylvania University), or a mnemonic landscape element (such as the clock tower and surrounding lawn, University of California, Riverside). In varying combinations these image-imprinting, place-making features will be found in abundance on campuses with a strong sense of place. However created, eventually honored and recognized, these design strokes provide beneficial links to the past, a Proustian continuity, bearing "unflinchingly in the tiny drop of their essence, the vast structure of recollection."

Projects are specific designs, admirable in scope and execution, which help realize the paradigm or are consistent with the paradigm themes and purposes. Projects selected for this book as campus architecture are thus clustered and illustrated by types of paradigms. The selection is skewed toward designs that resonate with a confident interpretation of their surrounding history and natural context, respecting, but not in thrall to, antecedents and precedents, designs that celebrate diversity and variety. The best overcome the curse of "time out of joint…the instinctive dissatisfaction with formula driven designs…they catch the atmosphere and tradition of the district with inherent artistic perception or even the rarer response of poetic grace."

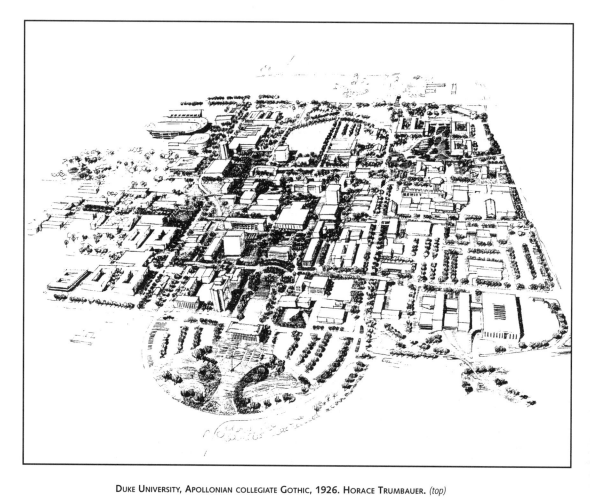

DUKE UNIVERSITY, APOLLONIAN COLLEGIATE GOTHIC, 1926. HORACE TRUMBAUER. *(top)*

TEXAS A & M UNIVERSITY, DIONYSIAN CONTEMPORARY CAMPUS DEVELOPMENT CONCEPT, 1986. MND, INC. *(bottom)*

However exemplary our selection may be for explaining how the past can inform the future, for didactic and illustrative purpose, Freya Stark's comments on the untranslatable aspects of artifacts and architecture are a caution also to be contemplated. Observing and experiencing centuries of classical buildings, she wrote: "copy not the forms," but understand "the traditions and impulses behind them. These alone can be handed on, to be assimilated, to be nurtured and reborn in a new shape, alive and different in new hands. Unless such a process takes place the mere imitation is dead."

BUILDINGS NOT CAMPUS ARCHITECTURE

Colleges and universities have some structures and many buildings, but not all are campus architecture. Occasionally, there may be legitimate reasons to construct an edifice out of context and only vaguely related to site history and the visual character of the immediate environs. Erected as icons of aesthetic supremacy, stylized elegance, the uplifting *grand projects* are usually intended to signify institutional advancement, solemnize special causes three dimensionally, ennoble benefactors, and provide publicity, if not prestige, to the sponsoring college and university. They may be individual structures, such as Frank Gehry's Fine Arts building at the University of Minnesota, or a group of buildings, such as Frank Lloyd Wright's West Campus of Florida Southern College.

The same impulses can have an opposite effect: giving birth to structures with convoluted shapes, fractured forms, ambiguous floor plans, and incongruous materials—all this stitched together in the name of modernity and plopped on the land with minimal regard to terrain, climate, or locale. With well-aimed disdain, Porphyries labels such buildings as "evasions...the illusion of authenticity cherished by collectors of reproductions...industrial kitsch...violent jerkiness of advertisement...architecture with no discourse."

Both kinds of buildings animate the campus visually and philosophically. Like certain spices added to a stew, these buildings may be welcomed for their flavor, but they are not needed for nutrition. Eccentric and idiosyncratic, these structures sometimes end up happily as campus landmarks, recognized as treasured testaments to the vagaries and vanities peculiar to higher education. Whatever their fate or critical regard, in principle, the approbation *campus architecture* is, however, best applied to facilities that contribute to their surrounds by helping to generate a sense of place worthy of posterity's respect as a contribution to a unifying campus design concept rather than astonishment as a singular act of architectural audacity.

CAMPUS AS LANDSCAPE

Some aspects of campus development other than buildings merit attention. Their efficacious planning and design will contribute to achieving the institution's mission, improve operations and reputation, and strengthen the desired sense of place, for example, site sensitive solutions to circulation, parking, and infrastructure. Functional outdoor areas such as play fields, gardens, and arboretums can be designed and placed for convenience, maintenance, and appearance. The selection

FLORIDA SOUTHERN COLLEGE, 1946–1950. FRANK LLOYD WRIGHT. *(top) Idiosyncratic architecture. A bold statement, not repeated, set no direction, enjoyed and celebrated as the unique work of a master designer.*

CONCORDIA UNIVERSITY (CALIFORNIA), CENTER FOR WORSHIP AND PERFORMING ARTS, 1993. THE BLUROCK PARTNERSHIP. *(bottom) The punctuation mark on a linear campus design, with appropriate contemporary materials—a solo, soaring structure designed and sited to serve as a symbolic campus building. (Source: Concordia University)*

UNIVERSITY OF MINNESOTA, FREDERICK R. WEISEMAN MUSEUM OF ART, 1993. FRANK GEHRY. *A bravura performance with few precedents on campus or elsewhere. The building as an art work for art, thus commendable, but not campus architecture.* (Source: University of Minnesota)

and location of outdoor furniture, lighting systems, art works, or a bridge can also contribute to place making and place marking. A campus is well designed when the interface area between campus and community is consciously articulated, and attention is given to the sequence of visual experiences (including signs) which brings and guides people to and from the environs to the campus gateways and interior destinations. Good buildings and bad become better architecture when every aspect of their surrounding environment has been consciously designed. And without question, a campus is not a campus without suitable landscapes; as at the University of Nebraska (pictured on page 184), they generate for many people the ultimate and all-embracing campus design experiences.

The absence of landscape on campus is as telling as a sweet smile with a missing front tooth. Some campuses are as memorable for their landscape as they are for their buildings. The physical development of Pomona College radiates with the founder's doctrine that a "garden setting," rather than architectural style, should be the overriding campus design theme. Arguably, the presence and quality of the full range of campus landscape elements, ensemble, would be sufficient to produce a distinctive and distinguished campus design. The point is well-illustrated in Ralph Cornell's landscape imprint on Pomona College and the beauty he encouraged. Hofstra University markets its sense of place by advertising the campus as a 6000-tree arboretum. Whether indicating the college and university boundaries, announcing the passing seasons, epitomizing a new fashion in garden design, channeling circulation, embellishing the sites for rites and rituals, commemorating people and events—nature shaped by dialogue, dictum, and diligence—these kinds of landscapes and campus design effects are understandably linked to architecture.

Campus *as* landscape is a subject deserving a magisterial treatment. After all, Eden, the perfect environment, was a garden, not a building. Open the lens on the history of campus design and one finds landscapes framing evocative renderings of facades or positioned to carry the eye into picturesque greenery, or through botanical detail suggesting a specific locale—polar differences, such as pine trees for Maine, palm trees for Florida, evergreens in the Northwest, and cacti in Arizona. Variations in landscapes can signal changes in cultural attitudes and style. The passion for change, which is a driving force in architectural innovation, has its equivalent in campus greenery. Mavis Batey cogently illustrates cause and effect in her pioneering book *Oxford Gardens* (1982)—"pioneering" because she treats campus landscape as a major campus design influence, not subsidiary to building design. As our definition of campus architecture includes campus greenery, some additional comments about landscape as an art are timely, and Batey's work is a good guide.

In seeking the causes of change, Batey's illuminating assessment can be deconstructed as a docket of the transitory factors that have shaped and reshaped Oxford's physical forms over a thousand years. The factors include modifications in college size and modes of teaching, changes in subject matter and disciplines, the arrival of women and their gradual rise in status and influence, the introduction of new building technologies (from indoor plumbing to computers), mutable artistic determination about what kind of architecture and greenery is best for new conditions and requirements, and the occasional nostalgia for the return of a design

UNIVERSITY OF TEXAS AT DALLAS, CECIL AND IDA GREEN CENTER, 1992. F&S PARTNERS. *(top) A catalog of contemporary "hardscape" design components, including variations in paving, fountain, and lighting fixtures. (Source: University of Texas)*

POMONA COLLEGE, CAMPUS CENTER, 1995. ROBERT A. M. STERN. *(bottom) Another piece added to the "college in the garden." The design concept reinterprets earlier Pomona buildings and paradigm of soft landscapes. (Source: Robert A. M. Stern)*

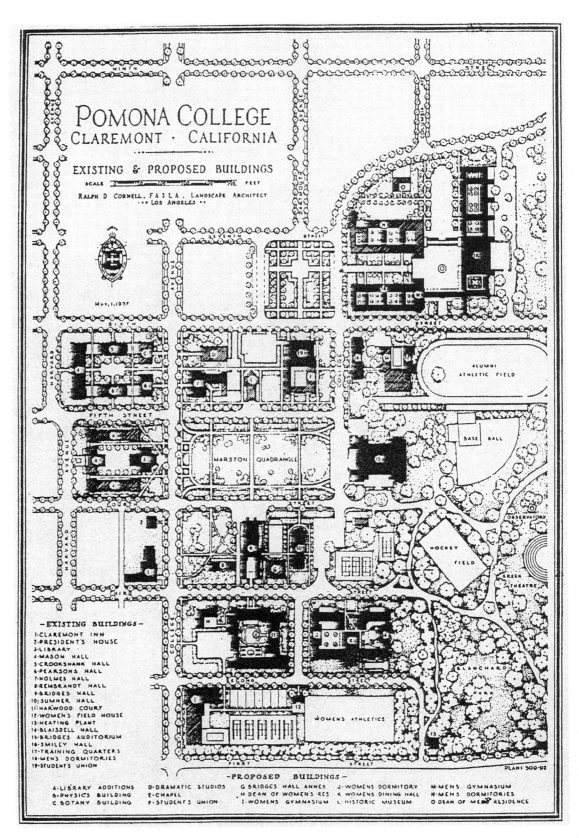

POMONA COLLEGE, DEVELOPMENT PLAN, 1957. RALPH D. CORNELL. *A strong statement of campus as landscape, providing a graphic rendition of the founder's vision of "college buildings as architecture in a garden." Several building sites have been changed and functions differ, but the spirit of the concept continues to guide development at one of America's superior campuses.*

expression discarded by earlier generations. The knowledgeable observer will see in Oxford similarities and analogies in tracing the development of campuses elsewhere.

Whereas the significant place-making form at Oxford is the quad, the place-marking gestures taken together—facades, roof lines, towers, gates, fenestration—are stunning chronicle of design convictions and then-changing directions. A litany of those once at work at Oxford makes the point: Wren, Gibbs, Hawksmoor, Ruskin, Butterfield, Lutyens, Jacobson. As a group, the Oxford designers produced buildings in 22 styles. Oxford's landscapes are equally rich in their marking of time, taste, and locale. In attempting a summary one appreciates Nathaniel Hawthorn's observation: "…it is a disappointment to see such a place…for it would take a lifetime, and more than one, to comprehend (Oxford) satisfactorily." Each gyration in building style (formal to informal and back) has had its equivalent in greenery.

Legendary are the confrontations between those supporting the formal Dutch and French gardens and those favoring the picturesque and romantic. Of the former, a 1732 print shows New College's four lawns: an historic masterpiece now lost, with its embroidered flower gardens and palisades of green hedge, reinforced linearly with stilted, pollarded Dutch elms. Early on St. John's College would embrace both aesthetics. In contrast to a formal garden, an adjacent arbor was laid out as a "wilderness," 4 acres of contrived countryside, squeezed onto the college grounds, in a design attributed to Capability Brown. Later, seemingly insulted by the presence of a formal green lawn, one proctor presented a case for turning the grass into a monastic turnip garden; another argued for a bowling green. Neither prevailed. "Not in my time," ruled the reigning don. Oxford's historic oscillations in landscape design, overall, are settled in recent years by favorable memories and respect of antecedents and precedents, greenery to be preserved and honored.

Landscape's impact as a form-generating factor can be seen in many illustrious American campus designs. Jefferson's and Olmsted's ideas were cited earlier. Recent versions include William Turnbull's dormitory design for Arizona State University and the BOORA Architects development plan for the Oregon Graduate Institute of Science and Technology. At Arizona, the distant buttes inspired the massing concept, accented by a tower that marks the front door. The adjacent courtyards planted with distinctive indigenous materials are configured to provide optimum shadow and light effects. The building colors and textures recall the sedimentary southwest land forms, strengthening the visual unity of a commendable project. In Beaverton, Oregon, the stands of firs and deciduous trees and a large grassy park were utilized both as a green foil for the site composition and as a natural preserve and outdoor science observation park. The laboratory buildings were configured to fit the edge of the wetlands.

The respect given historic campus buildings in the United States is now beginning to find its equivalent in campus landscape. For some places, unfortunately a little late, important aesthetic ideas—cultural evidence as revealing and enlightening as a building design—have been destroyed or altered through expediency or ignorance. Thus the restoration plans at Vassar College (Sasaki and Associates, 1989) and the University of Virginia (EDAW, 1994) are commendable. The Virginia strategy removes mature plantings to return the views and vistas along the

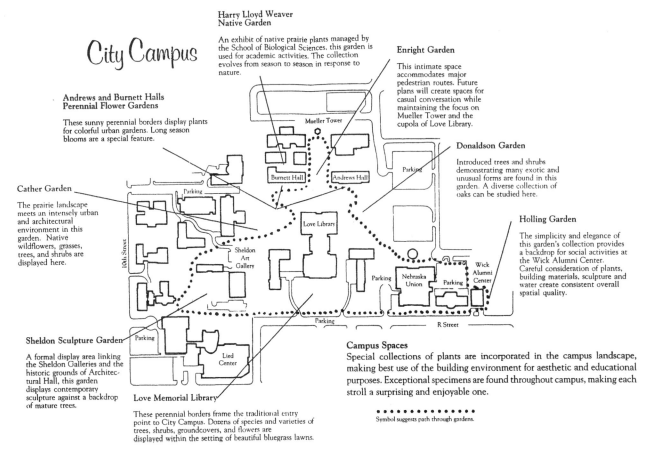

City Campus

Harry Lloyd Weaver Native Garden

An exhibit of native prairie plants managed by the School of Biological Sciences, this garden is used for academic activities. The collection evolves from season to season in response to nature.

Enright Garden

This intimate space accommodates major pedestrian routes. Future plans will create spaces for casual conversation while maintaining the focus on Mueller Tower and the cupola of Love Library.

Andrews and Burnett Halls Perennial Flower Gardens

These sunny perennial borders display plants for colorful urban gardens. Long season blooms are a special feature.

Donaldson Garden

Introduced trees and shrubs demonstrating many exotic and unusual forms are found in this garden. A diverse collection of oaks can be studied here.

Cather Garden

The prairie landscape meets an intensely urban and architectural environment in this garden. Native wildflowers, grasses, trees, and shrubs are displayed here.

Holling Garden

The simplicity and elegance of this garden's collection provides a backdrop for social activities at the Wick Alumni Center. Careful consideration of plants, building materials, sculpture and water create consistent overall spatial quality.

Mueller Tower

Burnett Hall

Andrews Hall

Parking

Love Library

Sheldon Art Gallery

Parking

Nebraska Union

Parking

Wick Alumni Center

10th Street

Parking

Parking

R Street

Sheldon Sculpture Garden

A formal display area linking the Sheldon Galleries and the historic grounds of Architectural Hall, this garden displays contemporary sculpture against a backdrop of mature trees.

Lied Center

Love Memorial Library

These perennial borders frame the traditional entry point to City Campus. Dozens of species and varieties of trees, shrubs, groundcovers, and flowers are displayed within the setting of beautiful bluegrass lawns.

Campus Spaces

Special collections of plants are incorporated in the campus landscape, making best use of the building environment for aesthetic and educational purposes. Exceptional specimens are found throughout campus, making each stroll a surprising and enjoyable one.

• • • • • • • • • • • • • •
Symbol suggests path through gardens.

"One plans not places, or spaces, or things; one plans experiences."

John Ormsbee Simonds

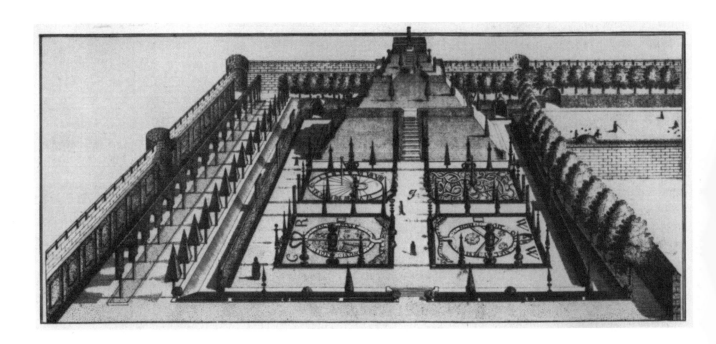

UNIVERSITY OF NEBRASKA, CAMPUS AS LANDSCAPE, 1994. *(facing page, top) An epitome of Dionysian campus landscape experiences arranged to complement building designs. (Source: University of Nebraska)*

OXFORD, NEW COLLEGE GARDEN, C. 1730. *(facing page, bottom) An Apollonian design. Just as buildings can be read and deciphered as signs and signals of values and tastes, so too can campus landscapes. Significantly, the Oxford landscapes are not available to be experienced in sequence; the American campus, being more open, provides that possibility—beautifully so at Pomona College and the University of Nebraska, cited earlier.*

ARIZONA STATE UNIVERSITY, 1990. WILLIAM TURNBULL ASSOCIATES. *(this page) The architect's sketch which inspired a building concept for a 410-student dormitory. The large tower reflects the forms of the distant buttes and marks the main entry and commons areas. The roof design is striated concrete, suggesting the color and texture of the sedimentary rocks in the vicinity. An epitome of campus architecture and campus housing. (Source: William Turnbull Associates)*

Lawn so they approximate Jefferson's concept—the horticultural equivalent of peeling contemporary vinyl siding from a nineteenth-century building.

Existing campus landscapes are often undervalued. Recognizing the contribution trees make to campus design, The College of Saint Catherine (Minnesota, 1993) "surveyed their landscape to determine appropriate management." The College discovered a $2 million campus design asset. The survey identified 523 campus trees, thirty-eight varieties, some rare, including several dozen over 2 feet in diameter. Unfortunately, overall, nationally, campus landscape maintenance is getting worse. In lockstep with building maintenance budgets, funds for grounds upkeep are being reduced. New landscapes, in the main, seem feeble in concept, penny-pinching in budget, far short of what the design professions could do were there as many advocates and donors available for the art and science of campus greenery as there are for buildings. At the least, while awaiting the grand revival of a great tradition, campuses could increase their tree cover in areas not likely to be building sites. The new landscapes could include miniarboretums for science, greenbelts for noise control, bosks for contemplation, gardens for art, and a few exotic specimens for visual interest and enchantment.

The built and natural environments should be conceived and developed, with beneficial regard to each other, as a unified design. In principle, the budgets for such development must include a reasonable allocation for implementing the full scheme. Landscape is not a contingent item to be reduced or eliminated from an inadequate construction budget but an essential component of campus architecture.

We have acknowledged the presence of good and bad buildings on campus. We recognize the many ways to design and position physical elements that are not buildings to structure and inform campus designs. We show the influence of campus landscape on campus design. We will indicate through examples below that the melding of buildings and greenery, above all else, is the distinguishing mark and province of *campus architecture* physically. Those relationships—built and natural—are also significant symbolically, philosophically, and instructively. As qualifying attributes, these aspects merit further though brief comment as affecting factors in our definition of campus architecture.

SYMBOL

Historically institutional architecture has been charged with symbolism, producing objects with cultural and social significance. Creedal forms such as pyramid, cathedral, palace, or town hall can signify the power and presence of personalities, history, time, and place. A campus possesses many such symbols. The semiotics of campus architecture is a subject untapped as a systematic intellectual inquiry. Though not evident at all institutions, certain public images of campus and their physical forms are place-related and thus amenable to design. In the fall, spectator sports, the sounds and sights of animated play, and cheering crowds are heard, seen, and remembered nationwide through telecasts from the collegiate and university stadiums. In the spring, processions, orations, and ceremonies on the campus green celebrate the end of the school year. The months between conjure up quotidian routines in classrooms, libraries, dormitories, campus centers—formal

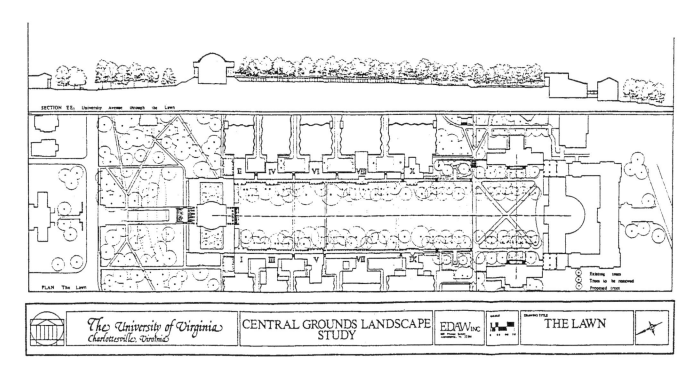

OREGON GRADUATE INSTITUTE OF SCIENCE AND TECHNOLOGY, 1995. BOORA, ARCHITECTS. *(top) Site composition and building plan are informed by and integrated with the surrounding landscape. (Source: BOORA, Architects)*

UNIVERSITY OF VIRGINIA, RESTORATION PLAN, THE LAWN, 1994. EDAW. *(bottom) A significant design project in which the concept of sensitive restoration of historic campus buildings is applied to campus landscapes. (Source: EDAW)*

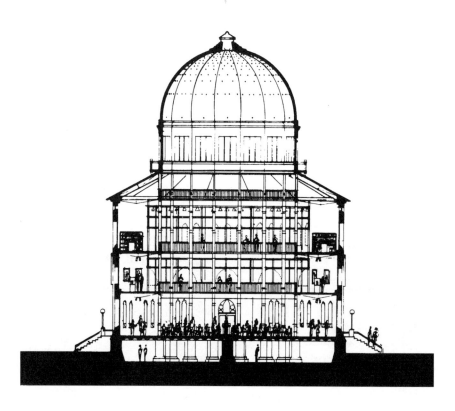

UNION COLLEGE, NOTT MEMORIAL.
FINEGOLD ALEXANDER+ASSOCIATES. *The restoration plan (cross section) gives new life to a landmark building while maintaining views and vistas from the historic surrounding green. The engagement of the two into a singular design (building and landscape) defines campus architecture. (Source: Finegold Alexander+Associates)*

and informal activities which the best campus architecture recalls and represents as the essence of collegiate life.

Buildings and landscapes conjoined as campus architecture may also be read as a symbol of institutional ethos and organization, as the Vatican is for Catholicism, or Capitol Hill for national government. Library Field at Union College scintillates with history and homage. Here a legacy building and symbolic landscape are wonderfully situated. The greensward was defined in Joseph Jacques Ramée's 1813 design, said to be the first coherent campus plan in North America. Nott Memorial (1858) celebrates the life of Eliphalat Nott, the college president and significant academic leader who engaged Ramée. The landmark building was given extended life in 1995 as an assembly hall, museum, and classroom study by restoration experts Finegold Alexander and Associates. There are, of course, many campus design elements which serve as institutional emblems, and, if not at their genesis, they later become associated with a particular campus. Thus the cupola at Saint Joseph College, Connecticut, and the domes that punctuate the Massachusetts Institute of Technology's Charles River skyline are remembered as marking and symbolizing a specific place. In Webster's dictionary the word *ivy* equates with academic, reflecting "the prevalence of ivy-covered buildings on the campuses of the older U. S. Colleges." As suggested earlier, regional plant materials can be used and treasured as a campus symbol. At the macroscale or microscale, good campus architecture uses these design inflections to define, display, and symbolize a sense of place.

PHILOSOPHY

In an era of accelerated degradation of the physical environment, an architecture that embraces nature kindly is a welcomed demonstration of an ethical view about our relationships to the living world. Architecture thus fostered may also help counter possible indifference to the varieties of human experiences when one is immersed in, almost mesmerized by, the new and emerging forms of knowledge production and utilization, the electronic-driven computer and communications technology. In both situations, campus architecture could satisfy deeply rooted, instinctive emotions and interests about landscapes and the built environment perhaps genetic in origin.

At the dawn of our modern university, these sentiments and insights were the preserve of artists and pedants. Several from the eighteenth century deserve citation for their influence on campus design historically. Stephen Switzer (*Iconographica Rustica*, London, 1742) raised a banner under which many a theoretician and practitioner, from Humphrey Repton to Ian McHarg, would happily march. The designer should "submit to Nature, and not Nature to his design," wrote Switzer. In providing human satisfaction, the color green (and hence greenery) was the "most agreeable and necessary" part of the aesthetic spectrum, expounded David Hartley (1749) in defense of landscaped university quadrangles. Nature's harmony (a salutary state of mind) could be found in applying certain optical laws, thought William Hogarth (1752). His codification of aesthetic principles rationalized the serpentine lines that shaped the location of paths and plantings at Exeter College, which at that time was a revolutionary design concept in collegiate England.

These historic musings were encouraged, if not launched, by Oxonian Joseph Addison (1672 to 1715). In his *Spectator* articles, Addison claimed to see in nature the sources of imagination from which unwavering empirical principles governing the physical world could be deduced and appreciated. His college environment (Magdalen) inspired this cognition, Addison later related, especially the walks and meadows, where he perambulated through grounds "unalienated" by the formal Dutch and French modes of landscape then in style at other colleges.

As our age seems to be, so was Addison's. His was a time when the rich menu of information, intelligence, and ideals was a diet not all found palatable. At many an eighteenth-century Georgian college, the continuing secularization was a vexing threat to some who resisted change, especially change accelerating with the onset of investigative science, with the arrival of new knowledge from the colonies, and with the rapid dissemination of information through cheaper and more accessible books, pamphlets, and newspapers. During an era of intellectual stimulation, whose future and bounds could not be ascertained, how comforting to many was Addison's conviction that certain forms of campus greenery fill "the mind with calmness and tranquillity…(laying) turbulent Passions at Rest…and (giving) great Insights into the Contrivance and Wisdom of Providence."

Stripped of their eighteenth-century language, and questionable intellectual underpinnings, are these ideas and intuitions relevant for our time? Some contemporary scientists at Yale University think so. Their *Biophilia Hypothesis* holds that "Eons of evolution, during which humans constantly and intimately interacted with nature, have imbued Homo Sapiens with a deep, genetically based environmental necd to affiliate with the rest of the living world." Lacking affiliation with, or not having a sufficient appreciation of, nature (bio-indifference) gradually erodes psychological health, limits aesthetic appreciation, constrains altruism, and leaves us potentially seduced and sedated in our "electronic cocoons." No proof of "biophilia" has yet been offered as convincing as the law of gravity, but the concerns expressed in the hypothesis, especially the "electronic cocoons" metaphor, are significant given the existing and emerging presence and use of campus computers and their connected communications technology.

Speculative thought or design imperative? Not since books were unchained from the library walls and Thomas A. Edison's lighting devices changed the sites and times for learning has there been a more substantial shift in the methods, modes, and means of conducting higher education. Via the new technology, a student living in a dormitory or residing off campus can "…check the library's card catalogue, consult primary sources and a professor's lecture notes, contact experts at distant schools, draft a major research paper, send it to a teacher, get it back graded, rewrite it, resubmit it, debate a point electronically with a teacher in his or her den, and then have the final grade sent to the registrar's office…" (*The New York Times,* February 26, 1991).

Through computers, classroom presentations, laboratory experiments, and studio exercises can be conducted with data and information, sounds and images, observations and hands-on activities once thought experimental in scope and delivery. Distant as well as on-campus information formats and sources are accessible 24 hours a day, potentially throughout the campus. The technology is transforming other aspects of college and university operations, such as admissions, administration, alumni affairs, fundraising, and placement. The technology has an extraordinary capacity to extend knowledge across disciplines and to integrate knowledge production and knowledge application. Temple University, for example, operates a worldwide network that enables performing artists to find and link up with professionals offering help with physical and psychological problems. The network includes an electronic bulletin board, electronic mail, and access to a database of over 20,000 abstracts, research papers, and clinical findings. The system is organized to inform students, assist music therapists, and to advance and share knowledge in a subject area once limited by conventional means of communication.

The technology is sifting downward to elementary and secondary schools, with eventual consequences for higher education when students arrive "computer literate." Here the application and utilization is expanding at a phenomenal pace. The first expenditure from a $325 million school bond reconstruction fund (Jefferson County, Colorado, 1994) provides "...at least one computer in every room, classroom sets of laptop computers, TV monitors and video hookups, laser disk readers, digital cameras...a simple telephone in the classroom, complete with voice mail...a gateway to cyberspace and all that implies..." (*Denver Post,* August 15, 1994). In Colorado and elsewhere, students will enter higher education with abilities and expectations heralded by a few technology pundits and prophets several years ago but not expected by many people to be so pervasive and prevalent until well into the twenty-first century. Self-evidently, campus architecture must be responsive to the specific requirements of the technology, such being a necessary utility, and as fundamental in building design as heating, lighting, ventilation, and plumbing.

Arguably, the mechanization of knowledge transfer should also accelerate the need for face-to-face discourse and dialogue, especially exchanges which elucidate ideas and values with the nuances, subtleties, inventiveness, connectivity, and speed of the human brain. Well-designed campus environments, inside and outside the building, can facilitate and nurture those human and personal exchanges without losing the efficiencies and economies of information technology or other impacting shifts in education philosophy, modes of teaching, and events from cyberspace. For most of its history, that kind of environment has been Pomona College's legacy and lesson for higher education. Intended by its first president to be "a college in a garden," the Pomona landscape (see illustration on page 182) was given definitive shape by Ralph Cornell, and extended and reinforced by succeeding generations exercising an informed stewardship. The beasts of technical change and intellectual uncertainty were tamed by greenery's beauty.

The philosophic basis for campus architecture, as defined, can thus be summarized as having these imperatives: the presence of nature as a life-sustaining force; the utility of green settings (buildings and landscape intertwined) to encourage and facilitate contact and communications among those participating in campus life; and the mediation of the knowledge machines' hermetic and artificial attractions by nature's edifying presence. "Presence" includes the horticultural clocks that announce the color and texture of the changing seasons, the sensing of regional differences in plant materials, an appreciation of the art of landscape through views, vistas, embellishment, the observation, studied or otherwise, of botanical gardens and arboretums. Landscapes of this quality enrich campus architecture. But they cannot be accomplished casually and as an afterthought and cannot be neglected once created. The definition of where the landscape begins and the building ends is not a moot point. Each discipline (architecture and landscape architecture) has its special techniques, routines, skills. In principle, these are best applied in coordinated collaboration—another aspect of symbolism, generating campus architecture as a collegial enterprise.

INSTRUCTIVE

The instructive value of campus architecture, process and product, deserves comment, being congruent and complimentary with higher education's central purpose—to teach and to learn. At the University of British Columbia, the Institute of Asian Research Building was designed purposively to demonstrate "new standards for sustainable design, construction, and operations." From the reuse of old timbers (reclaimed from a nearby demolished armory), the installation of energy-efficient and waste-reducing building systems, and the selection of Gingko Bilboa trees "as a filter for carbon monoxide," the project continues the tradition of environmental stewardship associated with northwestern colleges and universities.

"Stewardship through demonstration has three elements," says campus designer Rolfe P. Kellor, "the conservation of limited natural resources, the avoidance or mitigation of environmental impacts, and the preservation of campus and community character." As to the latter, campuses are testimonies to authenticity. Their form, function, and appearance serve and reinforce determinable purposes occurring in specific places. Campuses need not, and should not, be facsimiles of each other but genuine environments, locally determined. That demonstration of the genuine is critical in a world that often distorts reality by conflating, simulating, and cheapening experiences, of which the Grand Slam Canyon (Las Vegas, 1994) is a late example. The Nevada entertainment complex includes roller coasters, water rides, laser tag, dinosaur bones, archeology exhibits, and American Indians. "All under a pink glass dome. Admission is $10, all ages." Historian Anne M. Butler trenchantly unmasks the weakness of such indulged fantasies: "tolerated and encouraged misrepresentations of history…varnishing over problematic expressions of race, class, gender…in the willingness to buy into a…myth in almost any form." Campus architecture should not, need not, disguise and distort real life.

UNIVERSITY OF IOWA, TERRITORIAL CAPITOL BUILDING, 1874. *(facing page, top) Restored as the University's main administrative building and serving as a three-dimensional memory of state and higher education history. (Source: University of Iowa)*

KENT STATE UNIVERSITY, TAYLOR HALL, 1963. *(facing page, bottom) Designed to preside over the campus, like a "Parthenon," and to introduce "a feeling for Greek architecture." Counterpoised, the two examples of Great Walls are instructive for different reasons, philosophically and aesthetically. In their clarity and faithfulness to their idioms they demonstrate again how a building (Kent) differs from architecture (Iowa). (Source: Kent State University)*

Stating a belief held by many, Chancellor Larry N. Vanderhef (University of California, Davis) desires and sees the campus as a venue where "students are exposed to a range of principles, ideas, and ethics at a time when they can mature and come to their own conclusions." Attitudes and values among the young can be molded as they experience campus design first-hand. Amateur architect and savant, Henry Aldrich (Dean of Christ Church College/Oxford) encouraged his pupils to find in his design for Peckwater Quadrangle (1704) ideas worth emulating. The seeds sprouted later, gloriously, with an exceptional group of country houses and public buildings, erected by those who once occupied Aldrich's inspiring Palladian collegiate architecture.

Recognizing a teachable moment and an instructive process, Howard R. Swearer (president of Carleton College and later Brown University) often appointed students to campus building committees. He believed they would thus learn about how institutional architecture is determined, contribute to its conceptualization, and be encouraged to participate in comparable undertakings later as responsible and active citizens involved in life beyond the campus precincts.

New functions, new forms, and new styles may communicate instructively changes that announce institutional vitality. Supporting this view, one often finds in letters soliciting building funds, in facility program statements, and in brochures commemorating the start of construction and the dedication speeches that open new facilities the heralding of a time-tested benefit: campus architecture as the omnipresent intimation of institutional purpose, character, and commitments.

The idea of architecture as a silent teacher, of course, has an important precedent in American higher education. Thomas Jefferson arranged the details of his "academic village" (University of Virginia) as an ever-present reminder of styles he considered suitable for a democratic society.

At the least, by their visual impact certain Great Walls, such as Kent State University's assertively Modern Taylor Hall, should not fail to stir some thoughts about design genesis and purpose. Labeled the "Parthenon," the architect believed it "introduced a feeling of Greek architecture—from the year 483 B.C.—to the campus." Preservation of heritage, in contrast to new construction, may also instruct by its presence, as does the 1874 Territorial Capitol Building now used by the University of Iowa as an administration office. On inspection of the two examples, each meant to crown their site, one can readily detect the differences between a building and architecture. Perhaps the Kent students also sensed that a "Parthenon" of this subtlety was not quite right when, it has been reported, they "staged a small and good-natured protest when the hill (assigned for new building) was taken away." The demonstration set a precedent for a more significant protest later, centering on war or peace.

The lines of reasoning that inform the definitions of campus architecture—landscape, philosophy, symbol, instruction—could be multiplied and thickened into a richer theoretical treatise, an objective this book does not further pursue. Rather, the definition of campus architecture as stated and qualified should suffice to serve as a framework for introducing paradigms and projects.

CHAPTER 4

PARADIGMS
AND
PROJECTS

...a connotation of
infinity
sharpens
the temporal splendor
of this place....
e. e. cummings

A PRINCIPLE REITERATED

The older colleges have passed through periods of style, each new building being
added to the then current architectural fashion....Such heterogeneous collections
have not been found pleasing even though they have given us an historical
record, and the tendency at present is to establish definitely a style in the inter-
ests of coherence and unity.

Architectural Forum, *1926*

The fundamental principle reiterated: The conscious and inspired intertwining of
buildings and landscapes is the essence of accomplished campus architecture. This
sign of excellence is evident in America's oldest surviving collegiate building grouping (College of William and Mary, 1693) and one of its newest institutions (The
College of Staten Island, 1992). The principle has informed campus development
at the country's largest institutions (the University of Minnesota, 45,000 students),
and one of its smallest residential schools (Scripps College, 800 students), and com-
muter campuses at both ends of the higher education spectrum (Santa Fe
Community College and City University of New York). Flexible in application, the
principle will yield the necessary variety in design—in response to institutional mission, history, resources, site conditions, climate, and other influential factors, not
the least of which is the diversity of American higher education itself. Each academy, institute, college, school, seminary, and university comprising that cultural
universe called higher education has both the reason to expect and the capability

to induce an image and reality specifically its own. Thus the conceptualization and design of paradigms—buildings and landscapes mutually engaged for a common result—can help extend to infinity the realization of a campus being or becoming a splendid place.

If the past offers any experience, it is likely that each generation can be expected to exercise or initiate its own judgments as to what constitutes good architecture, either freestanding structures or ensembles. Arguably, with Modern having run its course, and the styles that followed rapidly exhausted, one senses a renewal of earlier aesthetic debates. In settling a direction, the principle outlined above can be applied in several ways: loosely for those advocating diversity and variety, or strictly for those seeking to establish and maintain a dominant visual order, or as a mediated position that provides continuity with latitude for skillful divergence when conditions permit or encourage, via paradigms and projects.

PARADIGMS

Paradigms are configurations, frameworks, and molds which shape, structure, and contain the campus or campus sector, i.e., macroscale campus architecture. Architectural and institutional histories chronicle pendulumlike swings in taste and preferment among the forms, from the Dionysian to the Apollonian, and back again, in no predictable sequence. For those comforted by contemporary analogies, the differences are as striking as the contrasts between a painting by Ad Reinhardt and a late-phase Jackson Pollock.

Apollonian paradigms (Reinhardt) tend to be linear, rectangular, and hard-edged, immediately perceptible in their organization, with connected beginnings and ends. The composition shows a hierarchy of dominant and subordinate architectural elements. Massing, elevations, and interior spaces are informed by functions. The overall building designs are generally marked with facades of consistent materials, with motifs, and detailing richer or reductive as the style would command. Thus, the Collegiate Gothic ensemble at the University of Chicago and the Modern idiom at State University of New York, Purchase, provide a visual unity for buildings functionally different. In both instances the adjacent landscapes are geometric and muted, reinforcing the ordered site compositions. Easy to achieve at the start, when significant construction is completed at one time, Apollonian coherence is difficult to keep intact stylistically. As one university president was reported to have said, when asked to select a style and set some firm design guidelines, "He could not, because he did not believe in prejudicing the future."

What style cannot command, consistent use of building materials (or related versions of color and texture) will produce some degree of visual unity where such is desired, as discussed earlier. Good examples are the brick architecture at the University of Virginia, the palette of gray to white masonry at Pomona College, Pennsylvania fieldstone at Swarthmore College, and sandstone and red-tile roofs at that paradigm of campus design, the University of Colorado, Boulder. There, following Charles Z. Klauder's lead, successive generations of architects have utilized the palette for consistency and coherence in external appearance, while exercising some latitude in massing, configuration, and detailing. The University design guidelines aim for "a serendipitous mix of open space and building mass, attention to human scale," and the preservation and extension of "the architectural design themes and building materials," so as to allow the architect to "bend the rules with care when needs arise."

Dionysian paradigms (Pollock) are generally looser in site composition. Few buildings are connected. The site design is less hierarchical. There is greater variety in styles and materials, the kinds of campuses that apparently gave classicists such as Ralph Adams Cram artistic dyspepsia. "A harder (design) problem...assimilating the heterogeneous repast of varied types of aesthetic food [Princeton University] had wolfed down during her formative period, with scant attention to gustatorial harmonics or the possibilities of a normal digestive system." So burped Cram (1906), engaged by Princeton to create "ultimate unity" from "congeries of subordinate units (so as to) tie the anarchy of the past into the order of the present."

In terms of plantings, the Dionysian is a richer fabric. The landscapes tend to be more informal and picturesque. Seemingly natural, the matured landscape, is, of course, a design invention, often with superb results, as at Mount Holyoke College. There, the idea of purposeful gardens, functional and horticultural landscapes, bits and pieces, woven by generations into a campus design theme, started early and has continued thereafter. A student writes on opening day (1837): "There were no trees, no fence, not a blade of grass, but a deep bed of sand around the (building)." Two years later nurseryman Samuel Wells, seeking to sell plant materials and a design concept, inquires of founder Mary Lyon, "As your building is a plain one and the ground perfectly level, I suppose you would not think of rusticating the area in the present most approved fashion." A century later, a cluster of clearly modern buildings by Hugh Stubbins and Associates are pleasantly ensconced by a Mount Holyoke landscape, a collegiate ambiance of Dionysian rustication which has few equals. Playfields wrapped in groves, the lakes, quads, nooks and crannies, courtyards, and the views to Prospect Hill—Mount Holyoke's informal beauty transcends critical judgments of the constituent elements of the college's architectural ensemble, including some buildings, inevitably in older institutions, that Cram probably would have called "the indiscretions of the munificent but misguided."

The categorization, "geometric versus loose" is an approximation, of course. Some site development schemes, which in their derivation would be the typical Apollonian progeny of T-square and right triangle, are sometimes broken and arranged eccentrically, with Dionysian results. The slanting and odd angles produce unexpected effects in building plan and ground plane, as in Paul Rudolph's Southeastern Massachusetts University development (1963), or Le Corbusier's Carpenter Center for the Visual Arts (Harvard University), with the structure pivoted from the street, and the pedestrian ramp slashing through the site, physically and esoterically. These *le dernier cri* go unappreciated, perhaps, if one is not tuned in to the designer's philosophy or knowledgeable about generation fashions. Evaluating Corbu's building, Graham Gund writes that Carpenter Center stands apart from the University's historic architecture, announcing to visitors and students "avant-garde exploration and visual comment." Rejecting the "tight orthogonal arrangement of formal Georgian buildings which line Harvard Yard...(the design) is diagonal and different from its surroundings as if art itself is slightly outside the regular academic life."

UNIVERSITY OF CHICAGO, COLLEGIATE GOTHIC, 1893. HENRY IVES COBB. *(facing page, top) (Source: University of Chicago)*
STATE UNIVERSITY OF NEW YORK, PURCHASE, MODERN, 1971. EDWARD LARRABEE BARNES. *(facing page, bottom) (Source:*
State University of New York)
Apollonian consistency and visual unity in both a traditional style and Modern idiom.

KLAUDER IN COLORADO. *(above) Versatile and imaginative, Charles Z. Klauder's accomplished work represents the continuing and eventually successful attempts to define an appropriate architecture for American higher education. His work with traditional styles, his explorations in form (such as the skyscraper Cathedral of Learning at the University of Pittsburgh), his informative book (College Architecture in America, 1929) were all preludes to his masterwork at the University of Colorado. There Klauder introduced a style of architecture that expressed variations in function with variations of forms, cloaked with regional building materials, and arranged with diversified open space patterns and landscapes. The ensemble produced paradigm campus architecture, an approach which permitted reinterpretation and continuity by later generations. To the left, above, original Klauder. To the right, an interpretation. Since the late 1950s an aware and wise campus stewardship has guided new development with the principles established by Klauder, creating an epitome of American campus design.*

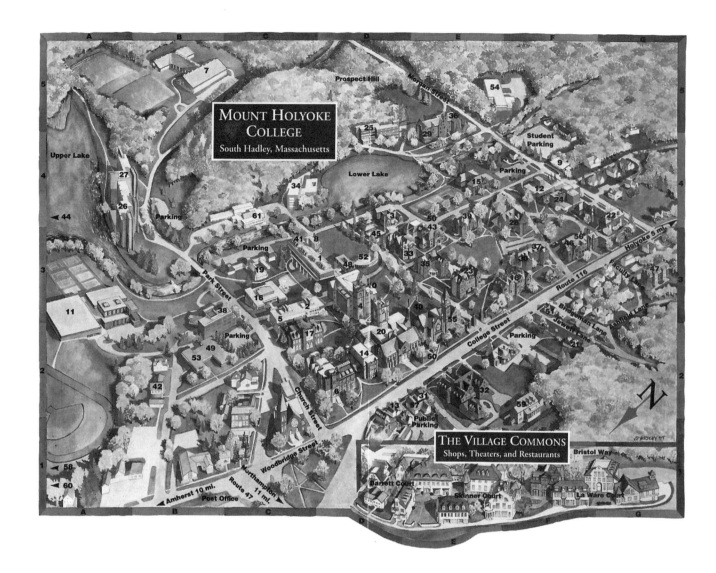

MOUNT HOLYOKE COLLEGE. *(above) Founded in 1837, the 800-acre site is a fascinating example of the mature Dionysian campus. Groves, hills, lakes, play fields, courtyards, lawns, views, and vistas in all directions—the campus design is a rich fabric of landscapes and buildings. The Willets-Hallowell Campus Center and the 1837 residential hall (The Stubbins Associates, Inc.) demonstrate how commendable Modern architecture could be fitted into generation-binding campus design pattern. (Source: Mount Holyoke College)*

WILLETS-HOWELL CAMPUS CENTER. THE STUBBINS ASSOCIATES, INC. *(facing page, top) (Source: The Stubbins Associates, Inc.; photographer: J. W. Molitor)*

1837 HALL. THE STUBBINS ASSOCIATES, INC. *(facing page, bottom) (Source: The Stubbins Associates, Inc.; photographer: J. Green)*

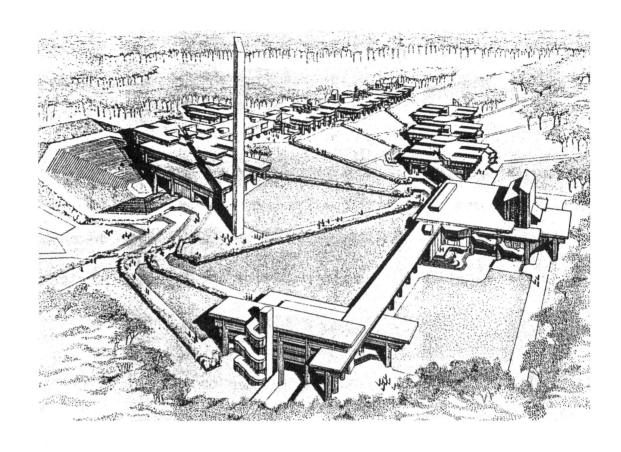

SOUTHEASTERN MASSACHUSETTS UNIVERSITY, 1963. PAUL RUDOLPH. *(facing page, top) Apollonian into Dionysian. Rudolph's rendering defines a site development pattern consistent with his manipulation of interior spaces and architectural expression, a classic from the 1960s. The skewing of open space, greensward, and buildings creates distinctive campus architecture. (Source: Paul Rudolph)*

DESIGN STUDY, 1983. *(facing page, bottom) A geometric Apollonian university courtyard design concept from the Middle East, with buildings using a limited palette of materials on the facades, takes on a Dionysian characteristic with its variegated arches, pavings, fountain, and landscapes. (Source: CRS)*

FOOTHILLS COMMUNITY COLLEGE, 1958. ERNEST KUMP, MASTEN AND HURD, SASAKI, WALKER AND ASSOCIATES, INC. *(above) Shown under construction is the landmark design. For site sensitivity and functional architecture, collaborative efforts made it a paradigm of campus architecture. The creation of a hilltop precinct, free of automobile traffic, the melding of buildings and landscapes, set a standard emulated worldwide.*

PALO ALTO COLLEGE, SAN ANTONIO, TEXAS, 1987–1991. JONES KELL AND DELARA ALMOND, ARCHITECTS. *A creative variation of the open-plan campus with building shapes and forms expressing the region's Spanish-American heritage. The space-defining landscape elements however are in crude contrast to the sophisticated building designs, thus diluting the paradigmatic effect.* (Source: Palo Alto College)

New buildings are occasionally inserted into loose schemes so as to bring several buildings into visual alignment, the Dionysian gravitating toward the Apollonian, with site organization disciplined and the outlooks channeled to and from predetermined vistas. The resulting site design is strengthened in its perceptible geometry when nearby circulation elements are also clarified and become armatures for additional landscape.

Contemporary buildings of this character (variegated Dionysian) have left Apollonian designs from the 1960s (with their somber and structured facades and their predictable geometric open spaces) apparently in the dust bin of history. "When you think Florida State University, think arches," said its President Modesto Maidique, announcing the 1995 plans for the University expansion. "Departing from the school's stark Modern architectural vision, hundreds of arches will appear on new buildings over the next decade; part of an effort to achieve a visual unity and image as FSU becomes one of the top 25 urban research universities in America." Exploratory design studies by CRS for a new Pakistani university (page 202) a decade earlier give a fair impression of the possible scale and beauty—and another revealing example of ideas and concepts that designers seek, find, and share.

Less satisfactory are attempts at loose or tight compositions which ignore topography, i.e., the campus design equivalent of the Ordinance of 1785, the gridding and calibrating of physical development irrespective of undulations in terrain and related site influences. Good campus architecture begins with an understanding of the character of the earth's surface, as in Frederick Law Olmsted, Jr.'s advice (1906) for the Amherst College grounds. Lacking site sensitivity, he believed the results could only be additional "crude, ill designed and poorly built structures of an unfortunate period in American Architecture." The successful melding of land and building demands adequate site information, the skill and training to handle or create changes in topography, and the experience and judgment to know how best to work with nature's fundamental contribution to the resulting design, Apollonian or Dionysian. Foothills Community College, California (1958), became a paradigm because a team of talents was able to find in the natural setting the clues for arranging and joining buildings and site into a landmark design.

CHOICES AND DECISIONS

> *Jacob C. Harper (college agent and lawyer, 1925–1940) was without any doubt the guiding spirit behind the physical development of the Scripps Campus. The record shows him to be a man of diverse talents, amazing energy and attention to detail. He was instrumental in the choice of architect for the Scripps College. He was involved in the setting of educational policy and in the developing of a vision for the new campus and its buildings; he questioned aesthetic or pragmatic planning and design decisions with a great deal of curiosity and firmness. Neither the architect nor the supervising engineer escaped constant probing."*
>
> Stefanos Polyzoides
> The Design of the Scripps College Campus, 1992

To set the terms for defining paradigms, and to flesh out our definition of campus architecture, we will pick up some historic strands left dangling in the prospectus and weave a tighter mesh of influence and interactions among people, ideas, and the built environment.

No campuses are designed at their inception or extension to be inferior, second-rate, or out-of-touch with the aesthetic of their time. What that aesthetic might be, or should be, is never universally conceded, particularly not during the advent of the new American colleges and universities in the late nineteenth and early twentieth centuries, when wealth and wisdom would combine to afford an unusual moment for elevating campus development from a cluster of disparate buildings built over time to grand schemes, visually unified, and completed expeditiously. Some of the heroes were designers, others were administrators, trustees, and counselors. When they worked in tandem, good things happened.

Although the styles under consideration might contradict each other in philosophy, the manifestos that announced the eventual selection were reiterative in suggesting that the projected academic excellence would be encapsulated in distinguished architecture. Presidents and trustees would travel and study, debate and discuss choices and options while searching for convincing arguments to adopt the old or experiment with something new. Most believed they had unparalleled opportunities to fashion an overall plan and an architectural character that would help transform stodgy and still-born academic programs, curriculum, modes of teaching, and campus life. The principle goal of a new aesthetic excellence was not strong enough, however, to cast out the architectural past.

Nonetheless, grand plans were conceived and nurtured. Among the notable and enduring results from those inquiries were Collegiate Georgian, chosen for Southern Methodist University, Johns Hopkins University, and the Duke University East Campus; Collegiate Gothic, favored for The University of Chicago and the City College of New York; and Richardsonian-Romanesque, appropriated for Leland Stanford Jr. University. In retrospect, all were safe choices, with precursors and precedents acceptable to preceptors and patrons. The last was not least. Noted the *Architectural Record* (1899), "nobody who knows the campus at Yale will be disposed to dispute that Mr. Cornelius Vanderbilt was happily inspired" when choosing Charles Coolidge Haight for the proposed dormitory complex (1894). Haight was, said the magazine, "the most successful designer of college buildings in this country, the man who more than any other succeeded in making a college building look like a college building." That look was Collegiate Gothic, which Haight had implanted successfully in such disparate locations as Trinity College, Connecticut, and the University of the South, Tennessee. Haight would continue a streak of "architecturesque" successes at Yale, which in its variety after the Civil War was a vivid expression of the historical fact that Yale was, "in the intention of its founders, a non-conformist institution." With apparent delight, the *Record* critic crowed: "Thirty years ago there was nothing to be seen on the (Yale) campus but the bleak works of the Puritanical artisan who had expressed his contemptuous disregard for the looks of things, the same 'honest bricklayer' whom Professor Huxley so warmly commended to the trustees of Johns Hopkins, what (sic) time he warned them against the wiles of the delusive bricklayer."

Later annotating Haight's Vanderbilt Hall, Russell Sturgis noted: "welcome for a man of taste who does not aspire to be original, who looks in many places for what suits him, changing his styles with his needs, and who is as sure as anybody we have of an exact appropriateness to the work at hand." Around the corner, on Temple Street, facing New Haven Green, lies Bruce Price's Welch Hall (1891), imitative of Henry Hobson Richardson, and another example of Yale seeking release from its colonial heritage. Price had that skill. His American Surety Building in downtown Manhattan was high-class wedding cake office architecture. Price's designs for Chateau Frontenac (Quebec) were the work of genius, functionally and in terms of evoking a regional architecture for the peak of Canadian railroad expansion. His Japanese Cottage in Tuxedo Park (New York) was one of forty different residential structures he designed and built on the estate in a six-month period. "An engineer was in charge of the grounds," said Price retrospectively, "but the architectural requirements were naturally permitted to dominate all essential matters." These were the people and the times, then, when Yale's "architecturesque" adventure was all plums and no pudding, leaving the college treasurer, William W. Farnham, the task of sketching a campus plan that would rationalize and integrate the building placement.

Not atypical then in the search for suitable campus architecture was the Rice University experience (1910). "I reassembled all the elements," wrote Ralph Adams Cram, "creating a measurably new style" for buildings and the campus plan. As traced in David Dillon's conspectus, architects Cram, Goodhue, and Ferguson's concoction included Mediterraneanlike loggias and arcades to ameliorate the swampish Houston environment. They paid homage to their client's version of academic history, utilizing medieval cloisters and quadrangles in devising their long-range site development concept, and married selected elements of the Gothic with "details cribbed from dozens of picturesque sources" to give the buildings a texture and color that became uniquely Rice.

Ironically, it was the founder's intention for Rice to emulate Cooper Union (New York City), by providing Texans with science and engineering coursework encased within the humanities and arts. Arguably, as we will see, an architecture that might have been suitable for such was 20 years and 2000 miles distant at the Illinois Institute of Technology. What constraints existed to imagine that kind of architecture, or a solution as simple and dramatic as Don M. Hisaka's 1972 buildings at Cleveland State University? Materials? Constructon technology? Fashion? Institutional ethos? An architect's reputation or persuasion? No mind, the quibble is hindsight. The fortress of style was seemingly impenetrable at the century's hinge. As discussed earlier, the new campus for Massachusetts Institute of Technology (W. W. Bosworth, 1913) was wrapped in a Roman toga. Outside symbol, inside function and technology. This would be the fate of many buildings in the first half of the twentieth century, where traditional styles ruled in a dreamland that ignored oncoming reasons for aesthetic change. In mid-twentieth century, the succeeding designs at Rice were slack versions or crude reminders of the original work. Recognizing the differences, the University began corrective measures. In the commissions that followed, buildings and a revived campus plan aimed "to fit in rather than take over." The latest buildings succeeded in echoing aspects of the earlier design principles, whether as attachments to existing buildings or freestanding structures. Especially commendable are renditions of the Rice's first

CLEVELAND STATE UNIVERSITY, ATRIUM, 1972. DON M. HISAKA. *The engagement of building and landscapes defines campus architecture, a tour de force of Great Walls and great spaces. Questionable in terms of energy conservation and maintenance, nonetheless a dramatic and audacious concept.* (Source: Don M. Hisaka; photographer; G. Cesrna)

masonry architecture, new Great Walls such as the Cambridge Seven's George R. Brown Hall (1991).

At Rice, and other strong-image campuses with lengthy histories, places where strong styles prevail, the mix of acceptable creative reinterpretations, the occasional elegant mockery, and the dispiriting imitation is as evident in appearance as it is perplexing for cause. For example, in succeeding versions of Collegiate Tudor, a once popular and dominant style, one can find and appreciate successive, subtle variations in detailing and substance. Categorized critically, one can then position the specific building at the beginning, middle, or the end of that fashionable run. The last phase—a kind of design entropy—can be seen by contrasting two functionally sound buildings at Loyola University. The facade and composition of Marquette Hall (circa 1920) is a rich composition of materials, fenestration, doorways, and roof lines. The 1960 library is a feeble imitation, with the two vestigial lanterns at either side of the main entrance, a declarative statement announcing a vibrant style gone bankrupt. Modern and contemporary designs are not, intrinsically by the nature of their style, free from this disabling tendency to distill the essence of a style until it looses flavor, strength, and defining character. Some such projects were illustrated earlier, including failures that are worthy as efforts, efforts now seen as failing against contemporary criteria, and projects easily dismissed for their patent and visible indifference to architectural standards.

With little interest in invigorating a dead style, such as Tudor, and weary and wary of the Modern movement's simplistic formulas, *contextual architecture*, as noted earlier, gained prominence in the 1970s. The canon was easily codified; the new designs taking their clues from older buildings in their environs. Here was a way for disputing the myth that all significant designs must strike out in a new direction and invigorating the reality of cultural attitudes and professional practice that all new buildings cannot all be different from each other. Where once the directions for giving a building a Modern look were often expressed in unmeasurable moral statements (e.g., Adolph Loos's "Economical space is beautiful"), the rules for context were readily ascertainable. Response to five criteria would yield an acceptable solution. Thus, the building size and mass should be in scale and proportion to its progenitor; contour and form should be reminiscent; the texture and colors on the exterior should either imitate or recall the older materials; the design of doors, windows, and selection of detailing should restate or evoke an impression of the building being emulated. This is not eclecticism, argue its proponents, since the borrowings are specific to the inspiring archetype.

Context solutions came in two packages: the staid and studied interpretations and exaggerated forms and polychromatic stylization. Given the variations of expression in the other plastic arts, from the same period, might some of the resulting architecture be a generation equivalent of pop-art, color field painting, and assemblage sculpture, and thus another example of unity in creed and caprice among the plastic arts, an echoing of societal values and cognoscenti preferment? Such judgments may be best left to historians and philosophers. If memories of discussions in the drafting rooms are reliable, the attraction of context architecture, and all that followed, has a simpler explanation, we think, i.e., generation shifts in designer interests and attitudes.

RICE UNIVERSITY, LOVETT HALL, 1908. CRAM, GOODHUE AND FERGUSON. *(top)*
RICE UNIVERSITY, GEORGE R. BROWN HALL, 1991. CAMBRIDGE SEVEN ASSOCIATES. *(bottom)*
Paradigm campus architecture with the blending of green lawns and the Great Walls. (Source: Rice University)

LOYOLA UNIVERSITY OF THE SOUTH, MARQUETTE HALL, C. 1920. *(top) (Russ Creson.)*
LOYOLA UNIVERSITY OF THE SOUTH, LIBRARY, C. 1960. *(bottom) (Russ Creson.)*
Over time without creative reinterpretation, the fate of all styles: design entropy, changing tastes, new values, indifference? (Source:
Loyola University of the South)

Arguably, young designers were attracted to Dionysian with its richer design expression. Their creative agitation catalyzed new approaches to problem solving and began to affect and inform designs that were coming out of firms that were growing stale in working up Apollonian variations of Modern. Sensing change in critical regard, and aware of economic necessity, firms had few choices but to promote the emerging aesthetic. There were generation shifts in clients, also. Architecture is not a mail-order business or the end product of robotics manufacturing. Personal interaction between client and designer, individually or in teams, affects design innovation and acceptance. With little memory or experience with projects as they were developed before Word War II, the rising senior administrators and trustees, and faculty and student committees—many more immersed in new culture than old—were both willing and ready to consider something new. The process was furthered by institutional planning officers, or consultants, trained to see, appreciate, and advance, where appropriate, the new architecture.

Thus, on many campuses in the 1980s, architects working the context approach were able to detach themselves from the relentless search for inventing another version of Modern, whose dogma was suspect and whose visual appearance seemed dated. If the floor plans provided the spaces desired by client representatives, if the buildings were intelligently sited in accordance with a campus plan, and if the preliminary budget was reasonable, then polemically the faux aspects of context were not troublesome. If needed for precedent, designers could cite Christopher Wren's painted-like-marble columns in the Sheldonian, Sansovino polishing Istrian stone to resemble Venetian marble, or the vocabulary of High Victorian, with its delightful transferring of color and texture of Byzantine churches and Arabian vernacular buildings to the sober and somber institutional buildings of smog-ridden England. Acceptance of the new style gained momentum as peers followed one another in emulation, as they had in utilizing traditional styles.

Pragmatically, context concepts fitted well the design profession's continuing quest to try something new, rather than copy and imitate something established. This habit, of course, is the essence of the art, the dividing line between repetitive banality and creative emulation. The mode is encouraged in schools that train architects. Differentiation is highly prized. It is honored by awards from peers and encouraged by the resulting publicity which then helps gain commissions for further innovation. Instinct matched with opportunity is the fuel of architectural progress. As Jacob Bronowski observes, "The most powerful drive in the ascent of man is his pleasure in his own skill. He loves to do what he does well, and having done it well, he loves to do it better.…You see it in the magnificence with which he carves and builds, the loving care, the gaiety, the effrontery." Amen, notes Washington University Chancellor William H. Danforth (1978): "Dr. Bronowski's insights are corroborated in the building of our great educational institutions by their architects and their trustees."

To be caught at the intersection during changes in styles can be hazardous. Early in Modern's ascendancy (1950), critic Frank G. Lopez saw the challenge of proceeding a "half step at a time, the blending of the new 'style' so imperceptibly into the old forms of existing buildings that an unappetizing architectural sawdust, much like unseasoned, crumbly hash, results. This is probably the toughest architectural form the campus problem can take, but it can be licked. To make good hash one must season with both vigor and compassion." Those cooking Modern architecture made good hash—assisted by professional societies who promoted the menus of the new architecture shrewdly, with spicy and tantalizing seasoning by influential newspapers and magazines that gave significant space for architectural criticism and scrumptiously served up by museum shows that celebrated both completed projects and ideas not yet proved. On some campuses, the excitement generated by some of the new architecture provided a stimulating diversion from the expediency induced by rapid growth, a tonic still savored today at some campuses immersed in the economic and demographic trials and troubles now afflicting higher education.

KLAUDER'S CLARITY

Accepting those understandable sources of creativity and opportunity, and their relationship to nurturing a professional practice, will there be another shift in design attitudes in the near future? Are there fundamental principles that can be (or have been) followed which would rationalize a design direction, say formal Apollonian versus informal Dionysian, with particular regard to designing paradigms, and in preferring one approach over the other? America's most accomplished campus designer, Charles Z. Klauder, thought so.

Charles Z. Klauder (1872–1938) was responsible for the University of Pittsburgh's "Cathedral of Learning," several fine buildings in the collegiate Gothic style at Ivy League campuses, and the masterwork of seminal, regional architecture that graces the University of Colorado, Boulder campus (shown on page 199). As a coeval commentator said in nominating Klauder for work at the University of Texas, he "was a really first-class architect—an expert in campus planning and more than that a creator of noble buildings."

Assisted by office partner Herbert C. Wise, Klauder wrote *College Architecture in America* (Charles Scribner's Sons, New York, 1929). Their purpose was "to define standards, to make comparisons, to aid, if possible, in envisaging a completed work of art that will win approval as nearly as unanimous as may be." For Klauder site influenced style, there being only two choices, the "Formal" and the "Informal." The first included "Classic, Renaissance, Georgian, Colonial"; the other was "Gothic." Perhaps reflecting Klauder's then-current work (the University of Colorado commission, his major contribution to posterity, had not yet blossomed), he favored the second. Klauder believed that Gothic forms, with their "adaptability and elasticity" could be molded to any terrain and their interiors shaped for any function. In doing so, Gothic would also remain "hospital to a few classic motifs if skillfully introduced." Klauder stressed the virtues of "an integrated whole…that permitted expansion." Such schemes were "conducive to beauty of the scene and architectural effect, to convenience of daily use and to economic and affective administration." His sketch plan for the University of Chicago expansion (1927) was a brilliant rendering of Collegiate Gothic's best features: connected courtyards, animated roof lines, textured facades, vertical and horizontal elements composed to read independently and ensemble.

For Klauder style would breed unity, but equally important, he thought, was "joining top and bottom." Subsurface, the nuisances of inclement weather and accessibility for repairs and additions to infrastructure were problems "that should be bravely faced and solved by constructing connecting tunnels....Above ground there should be contrived (sic) a planting composition sympathetic with the architectural composition, whether the grouping of buildings be open and park-like or more closely *knit* and *arranged*." Klauder's quote and our italics reinforce the principle espoused: campus architecture as buildings and landscapes engaged and melded for function and effect. But Klauder's work at Colorado or elsewhere settles no preference as to Apollonian or Dionysian paradigms. Might aspects of architecture more modern than his clarify choices and offer direction?

NEW FORMS/NO APOLOGIES

Klauder's views echo the convictions of his period and peers, cognizant of but not embracing the new aesthetics then crossing the Atlantic in the 1920s. The incoming aesthetics, promoted with passion, persistence, and diligence by its advocates, would topple giants in campus design, such as the formidable classicist Ralph Adams Cram, whose vivid writing, much quoted herein, made and make an informative sounding board for contrary opinions. In the academic world, the Beaux Arts proponents would be replaced with faculty that would preach and practice the new idiom. "An open invitation to aesthetic chaos and expediency," thought some. For others, the necessities of institutional purpose and size occurring with the unprecedented expansion of higher education after World War II would rationalize "New forms of architecture...with no apologies." The quotes are Paul V. Turner's. He captures the tension and explains the results in his epic history, *Campus* (MIT Press, Cambridge, Massachusetts, 1984). Turner begins his encyclopedic work on the "eve of American Colonization."

We pick up our account of contemporary choices, drawing on his and other sources, at the dawn of contemporary campus architecture. And, it was, truly, a new day with the arrival of seminal figures and the resulting significant events at the Cranbrook School (Eliel Saarinen), the Illinois Institute of Technology (Mies van der Rohe), and Harvard University (Walter Gropius). Educators, promoters, practitioners, creators of college and university architecture—these were the three giant trees, to continue our earlier metaphor, in the forest called Modern architecture. Their roots were nurtured by a dismissal of traditional architecture as *ancien regime*, blossomed through an interest in rationalizing forms and shapes by their interior functions, and reached full leafing with the utilization of the materials created by advanced mechanization of industrial processes. They had a firm grasp on how and why parallel artistic expressions in painting, sculpture, and crafts could be blended into and inform their building concepts. They were comfortable in an America that was being stirred by political and cultural events that ripened expectations for novelty, innovation, and experimentation.

Acknowledging differences but synthesizing their commonality, might not the three trees and their arboreal companions be arranged as a hierarchy of preferment, thus offering some rules for variations of campus architecture, paradigms and projects, within the general definition established earlier? A series of design secessions and new sects have usurped their once solid role as givers of form and arbiters of taste. But in quantity alone, and in the clarity of their doctrines, the work of each is nonetheless worth examining; not for contemporary justification or *post facto* condescension but for the clues and cues they offer in launching new campus architecture in the twenty-first century. Nearing, we believe, the end of contemporary architecture's version of classical eclecticism (the string of words compresses today's semantic and design confusion), might not campus architecture now be on the threshold of taking creative repossession of the fundamental reasons that Modern architecture was appealing in the first place? Can such architectural concepts be recast to avoid earlier and later deficiencies and excesses? The examination is propitious for an additional reason. How much of the heritage these concepts inspired is worth resuscitating and saving as age and obsolescence take their inevitable toll on buildings whose construction quality may have been reduced originally by inadequate budgets or by artisans unfamiliar with ways to craft and build the style? What do colleges and universities owe history as owners and stewards of an extensive architectural patrimony labeled Modern architecture?

The vocabulary of Classical architecture applied to domestic structures was once explicit, with its application channeled by rigid rules that no aesthetic broker dare violate. Ionic porticos were associated with the aristocracy, the middle class and landed gentry had Doric doorways, and the housing of the poor was usually left unadorned. The Tuscan order was deemed appropriate for farm buildings and barracks, the Corinthian for religious edifices, and the Composite for palaces. So much is now familiar about the Modern, that, looking backward a crude sorting out can be argued for the three trees based on principles espoused, patronage attainable, commissions completed, and influences on others.

Mies's work would seem right for schools of science and engineering, being measured and exacting, favoring function and simplicity. Saarinen's ideas would appear well suited for schools sheltering the creative arts and campus housing, with designs scaled down and textured on one hand and on the other, sited and arranged to fit, as he said "the next larger thing." In this group, Gropius and company would hold the middle ground, with concepts growing from program analysis, with exteriors that have limited detailing and materials, and the whole conceived in collaboration with the planning and plastic arts.

Each had their devotees. "I was invited to Mies's house, and with other aspiring architects, sat at his feet with my eyes watering from cigar smoke, knowing I was in Mecca. At 25, I was ready to sell my soul and all I had for a Barcelona chair. I believed that simplicity was holiness and less just had to be more," reminisced Bruce Abrahamson, 40 years later. Each had their critics. Groused one editor in compiling a list of projects from Harvard-trained designers: "Gropius is proud of the fact that it is difficult to tell the work of one of his pupils from another...what is this anonymity that the Chairman of the Harvard Department of Architecture admires in his pupils' work."

MIES

The Illinois Institute of Technology (IIT) was founded in 1892 to "stress the importance of technical training to industrial progress." Thirty years later the trustees thought the school had "lost its way architecturally," diverted by the seductive, emotional architecture of Chicago's World Columbian Exposition and the eclecticism it stimulated through the City Beautiful movement. To reverse course, Mies van der Rohe was hired "to lead without fail to a clear and unequivocal spiritual orientation," reported *Architectural Forum*, October 1938. Under his guidance architecture at IIT was to be a school where students "will tackle...the nature of materials...the nature of functions...(engage in) actual creative work in architecture." The Mies appointment inaugurated an aesthetic progression that would strip Chicago, metaphorically and literally, of "the romantic notion of architecture as an art of embellishment and ornamentation."

As his sponsors expected, Mies soon planned the IIT campus extension. The geometric plot plan drawing and model were calibrated essays in imposing on the site an Apollonian scheme devoid of references to its surroundings. Its simplicity was appealing to critics, and convincing with the buildings and spaces organized to reinforce Mies's aesthetic. One enthusiast saw the approach as a useful way to sanitize an adjacent 6 square miles of aging Chicago real estate. In varying ways the design was a precursor and model for the extensive urban renewal that destroyed wholesale sectors of the American city in the 1950s. For many years, in its rejection of classical motifs and regional idioms, in its manifestation of the new and open versus the old and closed, versions of IIT were a popular pattern for new campus development throughout the world, of which Skidmore, Owings & Merrill's Air Force Academy exemplifies the Miesean disciples and discipline.

In the design of his first building at IIT (1942) Mies demonstrated a rationalized building method that used steel framing, glass, and a few materials, exquisite in their simplicity, seemingly machine-made and assembled, but nonetheless requiring crafted tolerances and masterful joinery. Successive buildings have faithfully emulated the style at IIT, and sometimes elsewhere, producing a campus design image honored for its creator and followers, though the style is now considered dated and passé. In some instances the imitations are functional disasters, out of scale and poorly detailed, and in the instance of several midwestern college buildings, the elegant glass facades were replaced with energy-saving masonry designs. As Reginald R. Isaacs has concluded, "his lasting impact was Mies's concern with theoretical concepts; clarity of image, careful attention to detail, and rightness of proportion."

GROPIUS

During the same period that Mies rose to prominence in Chicago, Bauhaus colleague Walter Gropius was appointed (1937) to lead the architecture department at Harvard's Graduate School of Design. Through astute faculty appointments he would enlist a cadre of teachers and attract a host of students that shared his view that "architecture can be rational without being dogmatic, experimental without yielding to design tricks, and socially responsive."

ILLINOIS INSTITUTE OF TECHNOLOGY, AIR VIEW, 1990. MIES VAN DER ROHE. *(left) (Source: Illinois Institute of Technology)*

UNITED STATES AIR FORCE ACADEMY, C. 1960. SKIDMORE, OWINGS & MERRILL. *(bottom) (Source: U.S. Air Force Academy)*

Like Mies at IIT, Gropius was able to build an example of his philosophy early in his tenure at Harvard, via his office, The Architect's Collaborative, soon to be known worldwide as TAC. Parenthetically and importantly, and not sufficiently appreciated historically, was Gropius's attitude toward women practitioners. Two of the seven TAC founders were female, Jean B. Fletcher and Sarah P. Harkness.

TAC's first work, the Harvard Graduate Center complex (1949), was for its time a refreshing demonstration of clarity in building forms and simplicity in materials; of the integration of interior design, landscape, and architecture as a holistic concept; and of a site plan that promoted the idealization of an academic community through its circulation and space relationships. Unlike many campus buildings, the presence of art was planned and anticipated from the beginning, not added as an afterthought. In color, texture, and exterior detailing the facades made little reference to historic and nearby Harvard buildings. "How can we expect our students to be bold and fearless in thought and action," Gropius once asked, if we encase them "in sentimental shrines feigning a culture which long has disappeared?" The Harvard scheme was significant for being a trial run at applying a design process, for its attempt to implant a design direction previously unacceptable to university officials, and in providing a group of young designers the prominence and experience needed to gain college and university commissions in the modern mode. As to the latter, Gropius's career was crowned with enormous success. TAC became a breeding ground for hundreds of planners and designers, who at TAC and in their own firms would fill the American campus with an extraordinary range of Modern and later contemporary architecture. Regretfully, the office closed in 1995.

Where Mies's followers were notably Apollonian in their aesthetic, with his principles applied, with a few exceptions, through corporate practice such as Skidmore, Owings & Merrill (SOM), the Gropius graduates seem to be more personal and less formula-driven in their designs and site arrangements, perhaps influenced, one thinks, by the presence of Harvard's landscape and city planning department and a schoolwide design philosophy that encouraged the three disciplines to collaborate. "My intention," Gropius once wrote, " was not to introduce a [style from Europe], but rather introduce a method of approach which allows one to tackle a problem according to its peculiar conditions." If diversity and variety are the ultimate proof of his influence, then these names among many, and their campus architecture, are testimony to his teaching: Edward L. Barnes, Ulrich Frantzen, I. M. Pei, Paul Rudolph, Hugh Stubbins.

SAARINEN THE ELDER

For sometime Eliel Saarinen's work has been shadowed by that of his prolific son, Eero, whose buildings at Yale University and the Massachusetts Institute of

CRANBROOK ACADEMY OF THE ARTS, ELIEL SAARINEN. *(facing page, top) View of central campus area, 1994. Buildings and landscapes conjoined for campus architecture. (Photo courtesy of Eugene J. Mackey III.)*

HARVARD UNIVERSITY GRADUATE CENTER, 1949. THE ARCHITECT'S COLLABORATIVE. *(facing page, bottom) Building elevations and landscape Spring 1995, an historic example of campus architecture as defined.*

Technology have few parallels and no equals. Finnish-born, and unlike Mies formally trained as an architect, Eliel arrived in the United States in 1923, heralded by a body of honored work that included the Helsinki Railroad Station and a second-place design concept for the 1922 Chicago Tribune Tower competition. Settling near Ann Arbor he taught at the University of Michigan and then the Cranbrook Academy of Arts, where he eventually became president. He helped institutionalize its founder's vision (George G. Booth) of "integrating arts and crafts into contemporary culture." The complex includes elementary and secondary schools, a science museum, and a higher education design school, whose graduates in reputation hold their own with IIT and Harvard. Saarinen's crop range from the urbanist Edward Bacon to the authoritative stylist Charles Eames.

From 1925 through 1945, the elder Saarinen designed for Cranbrook what was and still remains a lovely case study of building designs and integrated site planning. The ensemble respects many modern-day principles of function fashioning form. Heavily landscaped, the composition is inflected with continuity in materials, with detailing that soothes the eye rather than irritates the imagination. Cranbrook combines the logic of the Apollonian and visual delights of the Dionysian. "Architecture," wrote Saarinen (1933), "is not necessarily building, but it includes everything which man has created as a practical organization of his relation to his environment....There is no assembling of stylistic forms for the solution of a problem, but dependence upon common sense." Students were not given a set piece or program to be designed but brought with them a design problem of their own choosing. The Cranbrook milieu did not breed and propagate designers and concepts as did the Mies and Gropius venues. As a place, however, recent opinions would give Cranbrook high marks for visual consistency and a self-confidence that appeals to those rejecting the rapid oscillation of architecture as fashion. Where Jefferson's academic buildings at the University of Virginia are considered the best American work from the nineteenth century—so voted the American Institute of Architects on its one-hundredth anniversary—the diadem for twentieth-century campus architecture may eventually be Cranbrook's.

The intersecting influences of these three design teachers, the status conveyed by their institutional affiliation, their own commissions, and their student's work after graduation, and the enormity of their productions, which proceeded in lockstep with the impressive growth of higher education after World War II, is a subject that deserves a history of its own, an architectural equivalent of Gibbons's *Rise and Fall of the Roman Empire*. For good reasons, we have isolated Gropius, Mies, and Saarinen as progenitors. Also meriting significant attention in that inspection of cause and effect would be Pietro Belluschi (Massachusetts Institute of Technology), William C. Caudill (University of Texas), Louis I. Kahn (Yale University and the University of Pennsylvania), Ralph Rapson (University of Minnesota), and Gropius's successor at Harvard, Jose Lluis Sert. How much of their views and work remains valid and useful today?

Although one hesitates to generalize from such a large compendium of completed work, at this writing those works which are Apollonian in site planning and building execution seem less attractive to today's patrons and practitioners than the Dionysian. Hard-edged buildings, stripped and septic, tough concrete, a limited

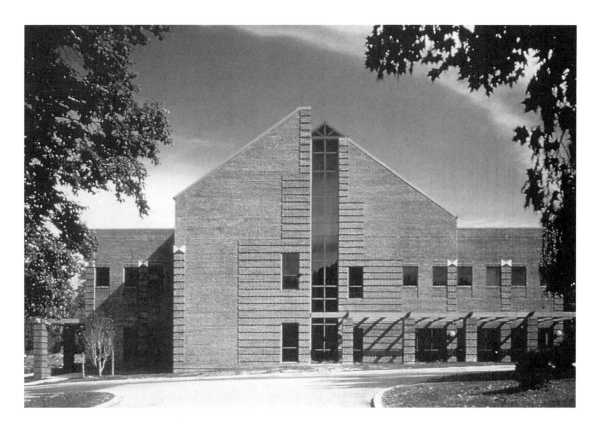

range of colors and textures, geometrically arranged glass and aluminum—the trademarks of Modern campus buildings are out of fashion. As indicated, more appealing and prevalent in journals and critical articles are buildings with articulated forms, loaded with texture and color, with detailing excerpted from traditional Collegiate Georgian and Collegiate Gothic styles, and cobbled with signaturelike visual effects associated with the designer. Should a name be required, Collegiate Modern should do, and Perkins & Will's felicitous design for Mount Vernon College Library (1988) serves as a surrogate for numerous good examples. The machined exterior look is not uncommon in recent projects either, a kind of Neo-Functionalism descended from the Constructionivist movement and early-twentieth-century Modern architecture. Regionalism still inspires good work in New England, Florida, New Mexico, and California. On the horizon may be the return of Classical architecture, signaled by the 1992 University of Notre Dame design curriculum and nostalgic stirrings for a style with a formula that can be used to measure and evaluate an architect's creative bent for finding something new in older paradigms.

MOUNT VERNON COLLEGE LIBRARY, 1988. PERKINS AND WILL, ARCHITECTS; AND DOBER, LIDSKY, CRAIG AND ASSOCIATES, SITE SELECTION AND CAMPUS DESIGN CONSULTANTS. *Campus architecture in the post-Modern style. (Source: Mount Vernon College)*

DEMISE AND RESURRECTION

If it is fair to describe universities as the country's depositories of learning, it is obvious, too, that a large number have not learnt enough about architecture and planning. Although some are using modern architects, they do not necessarily appreciate the full meaning of modern architecture. Many appear to think of it

OKLAHOMA STATE UNIVERSITY, NOBLE RESEARCH CENTER, 1989. TAC. *Dedicated to the "wise stewardship of the land and sustainability of the environment," it expresses time and technology. Aspects of early Modern are clearly evident (flat-roof, hard-edge, simplicity in materials) as well as contemporary design gestures (indented facade and atrium). The minimal landscape, however, denies, if not dilutes, the ideal of campus architecture, a situation not beyond redemption by filling the foreground with suitable plantings. (Source: Oklahoma State University)*

merely as a style which is more fashionable than traditional styles. They do
appreciate—and it is up to the younger members to bring this home to them—that
they cannot get the efficiency of performance they require from their buildings, at
a price they can afford, save by accepting modern, functional, architecture.

Editors
The Architects Journal, *January 9, 1959*

For two decades after 1945, an architecture flexible enough to include a Mies, a Gropius, and a Saarinen, and their second-generation interpreters, would seem like the logical conclusion to a Darwinian progression in architectural theory and practice. At high water the style floated an enormous fleet, with commanding admirals. "I will give you the soul of technocracy," promised Mies. But not everyone wanted to take that voyage. Prescient, Henry-Russell Hitchcock licensed the search for a "new proper pattern and program" in his 1951 critique, *The International Style, Twenty Years After.* The style was "not intended to be the whole of modern architecture, past, present and future," wrote Hitchcock: "Many docile architects, and even builders outside the profession, have followed the rules dutifully enough, but their buildings can hardly be considered aesthetically sound...now we are ready, probably too ready, to extend the sanctions of genius widely once more."

With his 1962 rallying cry—"less is a bore," Robert Venturi encouraged those seeking a revived orthodoxy for older ideas. Multivalent visual effects, ornamentation, the conscious suppression of structural elements as indicators of style—thus post-Modernism and variations that followed. The popularity of context architecture was noted earlier. Enervated and demoted. Modern is now seen as another shift in fluctuating taste. Trend-chaser and explicator Charles Jenkins dates Modern's demise: July 15, 1972. On that date the American Institute of Architecture award-winning Pruitt-Igoe housing project, in Saint Louis, was blown up, demolished as being beyond salvage, having been designed "in a purist language at variance with the architectural codes of the inhabitants." Ironically, a high-rise dormitory at the University of Cincinnati, in a similar style, was demolished in 1990, being a campus housing design philosophically, physically, and operationally beyond salvage.

Modern architecture, as defined, has few champions on most campuses these days. If some physical plant administrators had their way, additional demolition could be expected. They argue logically that for many Modern campus buildings, "the cost of repairs to fix original deficiencies and/or adaptation for functionality" exceeds the cost of new construction. Especially vulnerable are buildings from the Korean War period, when a shortage of materials and labor, and pressures for additional space at lowest possible cost, sired expedient architecture. Unfortunately, because the style did not require embellishment and could be imitated in crude and cheap variants of the original, many such structures were essentially faux Modern. Flat roofs, simple brickwork, walls punched out for windows, scaleless boxes—these trite simulations gained few friends for the Modern movement. On cost and aesthetic grounds, few have cause for continuance.

Leaving aside the fatalities induced by expediency, where then did "Modern architecture" go stale, sour, fade into insignificance? The constant push for design invention is one explanation; the inevitable erosion of creative reinterpretation of the first-tier designs is another. A third factor is shift in cultural attitudes and expectations. The Apollonian conviction that function shapes forms and that the technology of structure and materials determines appearance generates buildings which in their simplicity run counter to the contemporary desires for the instant impact of Dionysian expression. Our time constantly seeks novelty, and in finding something new it is quick to discard the old or to treat it with disdain as out of fashion. Think of art museums with their survival now dependent on "blockbuster shows" or the reformatting of newspapers so text and graphics can be read for content and meaning in short bursts of attention.

The dismissal of Modern architecture as an institutional style appropriate for our time may also relate to the style's general indifference to campus landscape as a design factor. Few of the Modern masterpieces are remembered also for their greenery. The conscious integration of buildings and landscapes—apparent in work such as Jefferson's University of Virginia and its spawn, and the grand plans of nineteenth-century college and university expansion—was diminished and trivialized in the Modern movement, despite Gropius's plea for collaboration and integration and the self-evident charm of Saarinen's Cranbrook masterpiece. Retrospectively, and in the main, landscape architecture was not stirred in the 1920 to 1950 period by the equivalent changes occurring in architecture. Jens Jensen, the Olmsted Brothers, and Charles A. Platt were the historic figures. As recorded in Norman Newton's standard account, *Design on the Land* (Harvard University Press, Cambridge, Massachusetts, 1971), the notable achievements were estate gardens, parks, highways, and subdivisions. Despite campuses having enough greenery to fill a century of calendar art, apparently landscape designers played subsidiary roles in campus development. Some, sympathetic to Modern art and architecture, available and talented, were largely ignored. Presumably synoptic, Newton's history, for example, overlooks James Rose (circa 1939), who saw in abstract art the possibilities of using in landscape designs forms, colors, and textures free of historic references and unencumbered by regal symmetry or the nostalgic picturesque. Where once they helped lead the charge in shaping the campus design, landscape architects now followed. Lacking interest and status, with few exceptions, their contributions to early Modern campus design were marginalized. Compare project credit lines from architectural magazines prior to 1950 and those in the subsequent years.

How contrasting, then, the eventual emergence and welcomed work of the succeeding generation. With skill, acumen, and professionalism, landscape designers such as Thomas Church, Ralph Cornell, Dan Kiely, and Hideo Sasaki demonstrated the benefits and delights of campus architecture as a collaborative endeavor in the Modern idiom. "The ideal campus design," wrote their peer, Garrett Eckbo, "contains, in various ways, equal inputs from architecture and nature." Many a stark Apollonian campus design would be softened and made human in scale with regional plant materials, in varying combinations of ground covers and paving, outdoor furniture, and related landscape site elements. At the University of California, Santa Cruz, Church would inspire an epitome of Dionysian contemporary campus designs, clusters of buildings tucked in the redwood forests, approached through meadows and fields.

As to the future, the kaleidoscope is not yet in focus for predicting what aesthetic philosophy will take hold, through which leaders and practitioners, and at which college and university campuses. At the end of the twentieth century all directions seem possible. Stylistically, we see four trends, as noted above, Collegiate Modern, Neo-Functionalism, Regionalism, and Classicism—thus participating in the "great naming game," which critical speculation inevitably engenders. Steady-state preferences have clearly given way to multiple choices. And, as in the college classroom, one may also argue, in response to the question of preferment, "none of the above." An agreeable and productive base for departure into a new realm would, we believe, include the form-to-function simplicity of Mies, the processes and multiartistic collaboration advocated by Gropius, and the concern for scale, site, texture, and surrounds manifest in Eliel Saarinen's screeds and best work.

Back, briefly, to the beginning. Unlike IIT, where Mies and Mies-like buildings would continue to fill the campus to the master's pleasure, the Graduate Student Center project was not, however, an aesthetic which Harvard would emulate in buildings that followed, even those by TAC. Constructed on a tight budget, difficult to maintain, with mechanical systems designed for cheap energy, on land that might be used more intensely, the building's survival in the future may be determined by its status as an icon of ideals and ideas more than as an example of work perfected. As a depository of knowledge, the university's obligation to keep the building as a memory of a pivotal moment in the history of campus design seems self-evident.

ORIGIN OF SPECIES

Some retrospection, further grist for the mills of definition and emulation. Those seeking certitude and comfort about the fundamental and desirable characteristics of college and university architecture will find in these probings no formulas or absolutes other than diversity and variety as the alphas and omegas of campus development—architecturally, that is the origin of species. Campuses are cauldrons of ideation, invention, and innovation, and at the same time conservators of knowledge past and societal values as signified in architecture. To serve and remain vital, architecture must respond to initial needs and functions and provide the capability to adapt to later change, when necessary, without losing the physical attributes which made the buildings noticeable at inception. Good campus buildings, as old as Harvard's first dormitories or Jefferson's academic village or the spawn of late-nineteenth-century "architecturesque," and many Modern landmark edifices have demonstrated that physical capacity and solidity for renewal.

Campuses are proving grounds for celebrating place and aspiration through architectural styles—sometimes leading, sometimes following the trends, fashions, and aesthetic convictions of their period and locale. Where the ethos favors diversity, the results can be a delightful, museumlike collection of buildings, such as Brown University's main campus. Where unity is considered important, continuity in interpretation, not repetitive emulation of style, will produce high-quality campus design. Thus, at Pomona College and the University of Colorado, Boulder (pictured on page 199) decades of buildings have a beguiling resemblance in their use of masonry materials but individual distinctions expressed in the elevations that are generated by interior functions and time and taste-related detailing.

DRAFT CAMPUS PLANNING MODEL AND PROCEDURES. *(over, facing pages) Definitions, purpose and structure, campus plan objectives. Ten-step process. Prepared for the 1994 Society for College and University Planning Annual Meeting by Richard P. Dober, AICP, and Clinton N. Hewett, ASLA.*

DISCUSSION DRAFT - CAMPUS PLAN - SCUP STANDARD MODEL

Definitions

A campus plan focuses on and is concerned with the physical resources—buildings, grounds, and infrastructure—that serve and symbolize an institution's existence. Three–dimensional and mutable, these resources should be periodically examined and evaluated as to their condition, utilization, and functional suitability.

Based on those assessments, proposals should be articulated to improve existing facilities, and where justifiable and feasible, to add those facilities which are required to support and advance the college or university's missions.

The individual proposals should be coordinated and integrated into an overall physical development concept, i.e., the campus plan. Occasionally, where warranted, some facilities may be declared redundant and eliminated. These proposals, too, should be noted in the campus plan.

Purpose and Structure

As a steward and advocate of planning, the Society for College and University Planning (SCUP) urges all institutions to prepare and keep current a campus plan.

To foster that objective SCUP has established a Standard Model Campus Plan. The Model can be adapted to the specific sites and circumstance which make each college and university distinctive and different. *Circumstances* here means such affecting factors as institutional history, current and projected missions, priorities, and enabling resources. Operationally, the campus plan does not stand alone as a beacon and guide for action, but reflects and is concordant with other institutional planning efforts.

The SCUP Standard Model consists of 12 objectives and a 10-step procedure. The former describes the desired campus plan content and coverage. The latter outlines a process that encourages collegial participation in plan preparation. Both are intentionally flexible so each institutional campus plan will reflect (as it must) local conditions, priorities, emphases. The intertwining of product and process is deliberate. A process without sufficient coverage is a vision without substance; a comprehensive plan without campus participation lacks credibility and certitude.

Campus Plan Objectives

To provide the physical setting for supporting and advancing the campus's mission and existence as a distinctive institution of higher education, and employing a participatory planning procedure, a campus plan will:

01. identify and use beneficially site realities such as climate, topography, infrastructure, site aesthetics, boundary conditions, and the surrounds;

02. determine and delineate the desired shape and size of the campus property and articulate appropriate campus land use patterns;

03. ascertain and facilitate the optimum utilization of existing and proposed physical resources;

04. promote contact, communications, and collegiality, among the campus constituencies and visitors by positioning buildings, outdoor areas, circulation systems, and modes of transportation so as to nurture institutional goals and foster participation in campus life;

05. establish an accessible, ecologically sound, physically and psychologically safe, and energy conserving campus development concept;

06. define actions for reducing deferred maintenance, blight, decay, obsolescence;

07. justify the location of new construction programmatically, functionally, aesthetically, and operationally;

08. designate specific actions for conserving, embellishing and extending the campus landscapes;

09. celebrate the campus heritage, natural and constructed—buildings and grounds—by recognizing and integrating significant historic features in the campus plan;

10. coordinate, integrate and phase capital investments so each project contributes to the overall campus design concept;

11. promote beneficial development at the institution and community interface, and in the environs;

12. depict and document a comprehensive and aspiring view of future development.

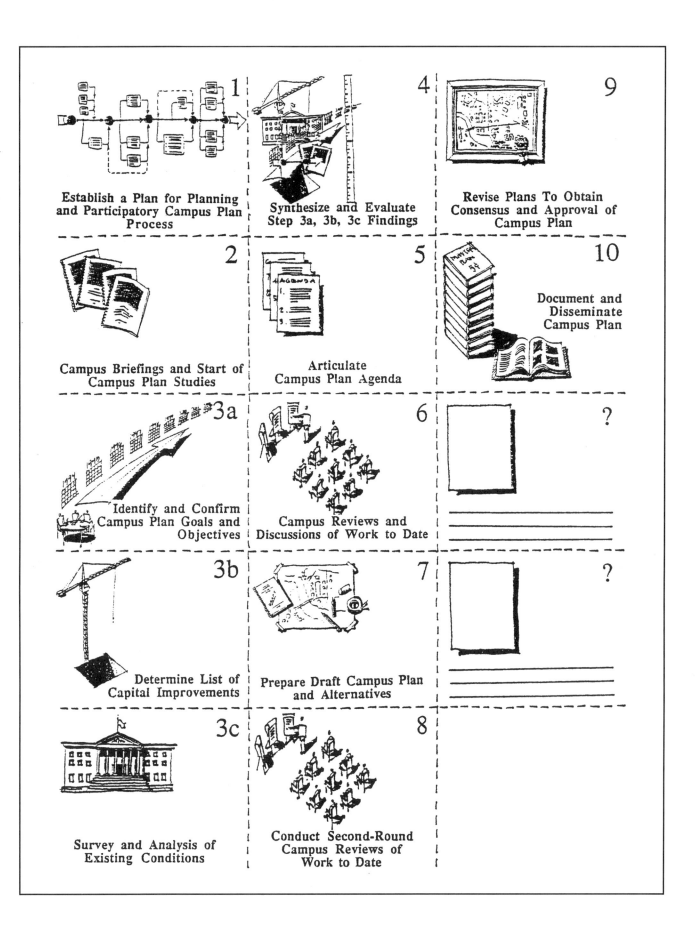

1 — Establish a Plan for Planning and Participatory Campus Plan Process

4 — Synthesize and Evaluate Step 3a, 3b, 3c Findings

9 — Revise Plans To Obtain Consensus and Approval of Campus Plan

2 — Campus Briefings and Start of Campus Plan Studies

5 — Articulate Campus Plan Agenda

10 — Document and Disseminate Campus Plan

3a — Identify and Confirm Campus Plan Goals and Objectives

6 — Campus Reviews and Discussions of Work to Date

?

3b — Determine List of Capital Improvements

7 — Prepare Draft Campus Plan and Alternatives

?

3c — Survey and Analysis of Existing Conditions

8 — Conduct Second-Round Campus Reviews of Work to Date

Campuses are political arenas for powerful and persuasive presidents, deans, donors, and trustees to impose their views, sometimes with singular and beneficial results. Klauder thought: "Fortunate indeed is the institution the development of whose physical plant is long in the hands of a wise and wide-visioned autocrat who brooks no detours in reaching the goal of a fine architectural plan." The preferred route to excellence these days is a well-lead consensus, with a clear goal and a consistent effort to obtain appropriate campus architecture. At the least, the process requires a campus plan and a facility program. The first identifies the project location, thus ensuring that building and landscapes relate and contribute to the broader development scheme, or a mediation thereof. The second is a disciplined description of the specific building characteristics, space requirements, criteria, and budget targets. The document provides the design team with a level of specificity for which there is no substitute in achieving accomplished campus architecture.

Campus plan and facility program are the double helix of viable campus architecture. Whether Apollonian or Dionysian at inception, they help overcome the shortcomings of expedient process, the dissemblance of aesthetic plutocrats, and the musings of misfired genius. Campus plans will vary in intention, scope, and detail. The campus planning process and product has to be tailored to the needs and resources of the individual institution. Typical coverage is noted in the routines suggested by members of the Society for College and University Planning, page 226.

PARADIGMS AND PROJECTS: A TAXONOMY APPLIED

The earlier scan of definitions and illustrations of the canon indicated abundant theories about design methods and desired results but few references to the specific challenges of college and university commissions. As one comes closer to the history and reality of campus development, some broad outlines of theory and practice can be detected, which provide a conceptual route for moving good buildings into the realm of exemplary campus architecture. These are *paradigms,* ideal forms, the terra firma of the designer's voyage of discovery and invention. As indicated earlier, however, a single physical form for all higher education institutions is neither likely nor appropriate and historically has slender justification. Like cities and towns with a vibrant life and distinctive physique, most campuses are multigeneration developments whose current expression is an accumulation of earlier work. The accumulative forms are thus categorized by perceptible prototypes of macroscale campus architecture, i.e., paradigms, some Apollonian, some Dionysian, some mosaics of both.

Paradigms are both symbolic images of place and dimensioned prototypes of macroscale campus architecture. As templates in a design process, paradigms can be used to examine, decipher, evaluate, and critique an existing campus or campus sector. The inspection would yield an appreciation of what exists, expose opportunities to strengthen a paradigm, and/or give cause to protect, preserve, and enhance physical features which might otherwise be neglected or diminished by new development. Such surveys and scrutinizing will help avoid ad hoc, expedient architectural conceptualizations and elevate building and site design to the desired level of campus architecture. Not all buildings are great architecture. But in principle, however constrained by pragmatic matters, the spirit and execution of even quotidian campus improvements can be charged and excited when they contribute to the paradigm within which they are situated. A rising tide lifts all the boats.

Though higher education reigns as a kingdom of knowledge, there are no formulas for shaping the campus and its architecture that apply to all places. Campuses are not towns configured, as were Spanish colonial cities, by edict from a central authority, nor are they the result of mandate and custom as were Roman precincts established in the empire's borderlands. Nonetheless, Klauder's book can be read as a design manual whose certitude, problematical as to style, is illuminating in its comments on site composition and convincing in its plea for unity. Batey and Oxford offer insights on how tastes change and landscape forms can respond by melding greenery and buildings. Turner and others provide a fine exposition on the history and significance of campus design paragons. All affirm the principle of diversity and multiplicity as the defining characteristic of the American campus. One finds no apparent priority given to formal versus informal campus design concepts. Apollonian campuses may be sprinkled with Dionysian designs. Dionysian campuses, pentimento, may have sectors laid out in classical geometric configurations, those being the commanding aesthetic at the time they were developed. Accordingly, using these sources, experiences, and observations, our objective of describing and defining campus architecture is constructively concluded by distilling that rich history and categorizing the essence of campus architecture through a taxonomy of paradigms. Some are Dionysian, some Appollian, some take on the characteristics of both. They are *groves, closed quadrangles, courtyards and atriums, plazas, lawns and greens, open quadrangles.*

The paradigms are illustrated with specific projects, i.e., microscale designs which help create and extend the paradigm design concepts. As examples of campus architecture, the projects are not just buildings but structures and landscapes engaged in a unified concept that informs and advances the sense of place inherent in the paradigm. Projects can be likened to the end product of a healthy food chain: campus plan (place making) → campus design (place marking) → paradigms (macroscale campus architecture) → projects (microscale campus architecture).

The examples selected below demonstrate the paradigm-project relationship, buildings and landscapes intertwined, and thus define campus architecture. Given more than 3500 colleges and universities, and probably 10 times that number of examples of campus architecture, opinions will differ as to what projects might be shown to make the desired point. The bias in selection leans toward projects we have seen and enjoyed or works-in-progress which we expect will eventually be recognized as fine examples of campus architecture. We include a few older places whose accomplishment recalls a legacy worth remembering. The taxonomy begins by acknowledging the primacy of precedence, honoring the place where campus architecture began, buildings in the groves of academe. We end with lawns and greens, paradigms universally seen in admirable campus designs, seemingly transcending time, style, and geography.

UNIVERSITY OF WASHINGTON, BOTHELL CAMPUS DEVELOPMENT CONCEPT—1992. UNIVERSITY OF WASHINGTON FACILITIES PLANNING COMMITTEE, SIMON MARTIN - VEGUE WINKELSTEIN MORRIS, ARCHITECTS, HANNA OLIN, LTD., LANDSCAPE ARCHITECTS. *A satellite campus, the Bothell site will offer upper-division and master's degree courses in selected disciplines. The design was expected to foster a sense of tradition through a landmark architectural concept and a symbolic association with the Northwest region ethos and cultural traditions. The concept aims at a dense building group, with a strong form that can be phased, each segment carefully inserted into the existing landscape, i.e., buildings in the groves of academe. The University intended that the "physical environment of the campus should explicate the qualities of the natural environment of the region, and promote stewardship of the land." (Source: Simon Martin - Vegue Winkelstein Morris, Architects)*

GROVES. Founded by Plato (378 BC), closed by Justian (529 AD), and situated in a botanical garden or grove, near Athens, the Greek academy is considered the direct ancestor of all Western colleges and universities. For centuries young people in classical times would travel to Greece to complete their education. Those who gained that experience were valued as advisors to political leaders, served in the civil service, were engaged by the states or wealthy to create, promote, and propagate the arts and science. A mosaic uncovered in Pompeii provides a view of the site: library, residential hall, outdoor places for instruction and discourse, and the all-embracing epic Groves of Academe. A nineteenth-century etching of Exeter College, Oxford, communicates the image of sagacious exchanges in a tranquil grove backing up to the College's Great Walls. Another variation on the theme are the groves encircling Meyers Hall (1846), Wittenberg, Ohio, which have matured to define the site and building relationship, a landmark hilltop temple of learning.

Of recent accomplished epochal works, benchmarks, two are polar paradigms. Apollonian, Simon Fraser University is a geometric megastructure strung across a site created by carving into the dense hilltop groves of British Columbia. In contrast, the development at the University of California, Santa Cruz, Dionysian, consists of clusters of buildings inserted into the redwood forest. At the University of California, Los Angeles, a smaller-scale grove has been created as an outdoor, landscaped sculpture gallery, helping to humanize the scale of surrounding buildings. Hardy, Holzman, Pfeifer plant and use a grove to define and embellish a central campus space, an Apollonian embracement of their proposed octagonal library— University of Kentucky, 1995. At the University of Nebraska, cited earlier for its landscapes, an existing mature grove of white oaks helps mark the library site, and in the surrounds the "inviting walks winding through masses of shrubs and trees grows ever more appealing as the landscape matures."

The Bothell campus (University of Washington, 1994) resonates with a skillful and dramatic engagement of contemporary building forms and the surrounding groves, including a clever scheme for campus expansion and the parking concept. The new hilltop campus for the College of Integrated Science and Technology (James Madison University, 1994) supplements the existing site landscape with a grove of broadly spaced hardwoods. Planted to form a high canopy, the tree massing accentuates the topography and scales the buildings to human dimensions. The grove plantings are not intended as barriers or screens but veils through which views outward and inward can be glimpsed day and night.

CLOSED QUADRANGLES. *Closed quadrangles* are the oldest extant campus architecture. Buildings and walls are connected to frame the interior landscapes. Early, the greenery would include flowers for the altar, herbs for healing, and vegetables for the kitchen. Later, horticultural effects would be the prime objective. Quad entry is limited and controlled. Epitomes are found in Oxford and Cambridge. Less publicized but highly prized is Trinity College in Dublin. Designed for defense in an era of town and gown acrimony, the value of enclosure now is the repelling of swarms of tourists attracted to superlative campus architecture and the tranquility offered by being removed from the noisy surrounding city development.

WITTENBERG UNIVERSITY, MEYERS HALL, 1846. *(facing page) Perhaps the best extant example of the early American hilltop campus, situated in a grove. The landmark building was rescued and reconstructed for housing in 1972. (Source: Wittenberg University)*

OXFORD, THE GROVES AT EXETER COLLEGE, C. 1860. *(right)*

SIMON FRASER UNIVERSITY, C. 1968. *(below) Now a classic of Modern architecture, truly a campus in a grove. (Source: Simon Fraser University)*

PROPOSED GROVE-SETTING FOR UNIVERSITY OF KENTUCKY LIBRARY, 1995. *(bottom) The symbol and beauty of the groves of academe are given a renewed expression in the Hardy, Holzman, Pfeifer concept for the landscape surrounding the projected new library. (Source: University of Kentucky)*

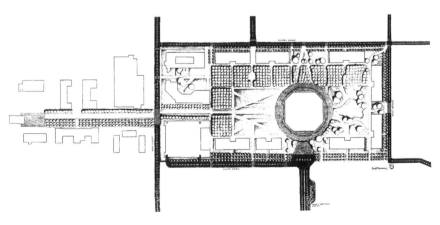

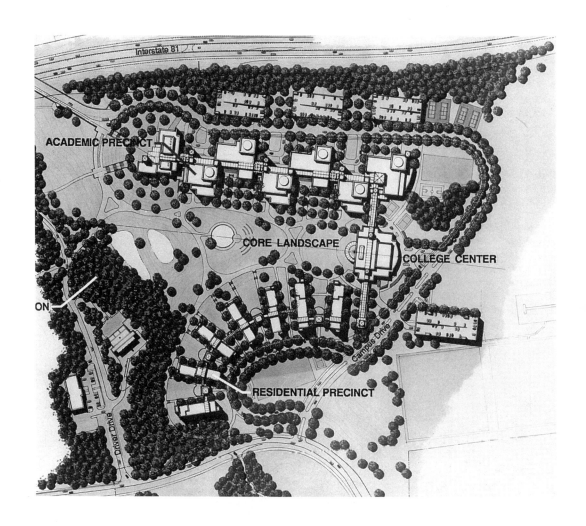

Usually Apollonian rectangular, the longer the construction period, the more likely the expression of the architecture within the paradigm will change, though not necessarily the overall form. The inevitable results can be seen and appreciated in Holabird & Root's 1984 physics building (University of Chicago). The project completed a multiphase quad concept, faithful to the original collegiate Gothic campus plan concept, which thus affected the building site configuration; at the same time the last building was designed to read as contemporary architecture, manifesting purpose, period, and technology unchained from the influence of the earlier style. Recent Oxford quads are also instructive examples of that continuity—contemporary buildings in a traditional site configuration.

The closed quad paradigm has stimulated imaginative Dionysian variations, such as the Aston Webb and Ingress Bell concept for a bastion of learning at the University of Manchester. Their 1900 design concept called for six quadrangles radiating from a Byzantine style central tower. Domes then being a popular place-marking element, ten were proposed. Six were built, along with a mediated version of the design, which ended up being more courtyard than connected quads. Of jewels conserved and sensitively modified, Paul Helpern's remedy for "benign neglect" at General Theological Seminary (New York) sums up challenges and opportunities for revitalizing historic landmark closed quads. His approach included removing incongruous sheds, renovating dated interiors, and strategic in-filling for requirements that cannot be otherwise satisfied.

Of modern American idiosyncratic schemes, Eero Saarinen's Morse and Stiles Colleges (Yale University, 1962) is one of higher education's best. The site drawing has become a campus design icon, with the authoritative interlock of buildings, walls, paving, and greenery. Sarrinen's melding of forms, spaces, and materials has medieval ancestors. Ironically, his Yale design has no progeny. Little & Associates development for the University of North Carolina, Greensboro (1993), brings the closed quad into the twenty-first century: responsive to security, radiant with its site configuration and open space pattern, reasonable in cost of construction, responsible in recalling but not mimicking regional Collegiate Georgian architecture.

COURTYARDS AND ATRIUMS. *Courtyards* and *atriums* are extended architecture, settings for campus life, configured, defined, enclosed by a building or buildings. Often neglected because of expedient cost-cutting measures, these are superb opportunities for creating significant designs—places were people can gather to participate in institutional life informally during daily routines. Should there be a will to generate a significant surge in the quality of campus architecture in the near future, courtyards and atriums would be a productive area to achieve such effects, adding Great Spaces to the Great Walls. For good reason there is a reluctance to build and operate more space than required by statistical norms. But such norms

JAMES MADISON UNIVERSITY, COLLEGE OF INTEGRATED SCIENCE AND TECHNOLOGY, 1993.
METCALF, TOBY & PARTNERS; SHEPLEY, BULFINCH, RICHARDSON & ABBOTT; DOBER, LIDSKY, CRAIG AND ASSOCIATES; EDAW. *(facing page, top and bottom) A new hilltop college in a landscaped grove, with facades and siting arranged for vistas and views. (Source: James Madison University)*

TENTH AVENUE

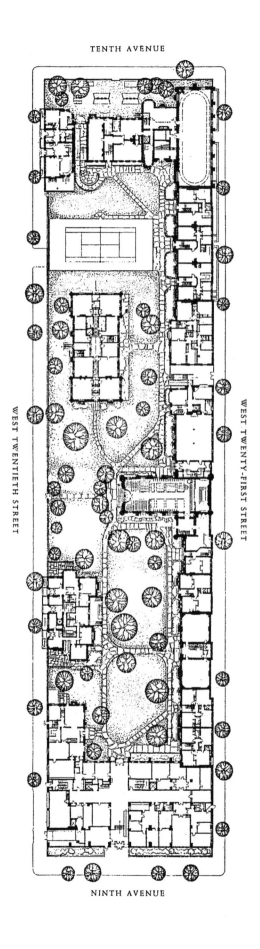

WEST TWENTIETH STREET

WEST TWENTY-FIRST STREET

NINTH AVENUE

GENERAL THEOLOGICAL SEMINARY, DEVELOPMENT PLAN, 1994. PAUL HELPERN & ASSOCIATES. *(left) A landmark closed quadrangle, a New York City rarity, designed by Charles Haight and constructed between 1883 and 1900. Helpern's task involved cleaning out extraneous structures that cluttered the original design, interior restoration work, and inserting building additions to meet space requirements not otherwise satisfied. (Source: Paul Helpern & Associates)*

YALE UNIVERSITY, MORSE STILES COLLEGE, 1962. *(facing page, top) Eero Saarinen and Dan Kiely's paradigm courtyard, an idiosyncratic version of Yale's closed quads. The scheme produced troubled criticism and was a startling departure from the designer's earlier work. Though not a landmark in campus housing pragmatically, it is a landmark of design in context.*

UNIVERSITY OF CHICAGO, PHYSICS BUILDING, 1984. HOLABIRD AND ROOT, ARCHITECTS. *(facing page, bottom) By this date the University has given up collegiate Gothic and imitations thereof. The idea of quadrangular development, however, prevailed as a campus design theme. The Holabird and Root building exemplifies contemporary period campus architecture, neither copycat context nor audacious departures into a new realm but a convincing completion of a major campus open space. (Source: Holabird and Root, Architects)*

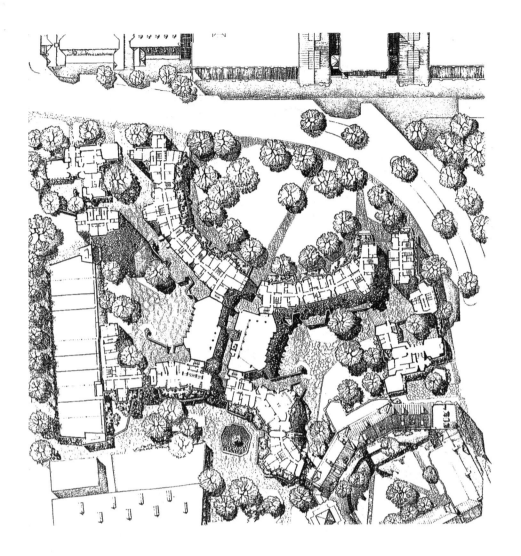

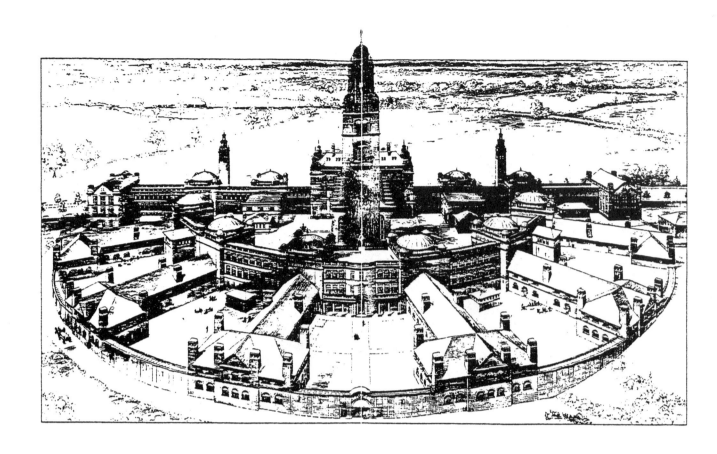

UNIVERSITY OF MANCHESTER, C. 1900.
(above) Webb and Bell's delightful reminder that the Apollonian quadrangle could be expressed in a canon-stretching Dionysian variant.

UNIVERSITY OF NORTH CAROLINA, GREENSBORO, CLOSED QUAD HOUSING, 1993. LITTLE AND ASSOCIATES. *(right) As is now popular, the site composition breaks the geometric grid to achieve some beguiling spatial and visual effects. A fine example of campus architecture with paradigmatic open space and late-twenty-first-century interpretation of Collegiate Georgian. (Source: Little and Associates)*

have to be interpreted with an occasional allowance for informal activities and interactions which promote communications and collegial exchanges. Grandiose designs are not necessary as evident in two contrasting projects at Colorado College and The Claremont Colleges. The first an interior space with art, plants, and scientific objects displayed (vide Chandler Hall) also yields on entrance an immediate sense of building purpose and spatial organization. The second shows a small courtyard and simple sunscreen animating an austere building.

Wallace, Roberts & Todd's Engineering II Apollonian courtyard (University of California, San Diego, 1993) demonstrates how visual experiences can be orchestrated in the paradigm: the landscaped approach to the Great Wall, the emphatic and inviting portico, and then the courtyard itself, with attractive views outward. Whether Robert Alexander would find the building "chaos or control" cannot be ascertained, but the design unequivocally confirms a university's willingness to build an instructive example of contemporary campus architecture.

"Cobblegate"—less structured, symbolically rich, an ingenious Dionysian design in concept and execution—is the eponym courtyard at West Hall (Portland State University, Oregon, 1992), giving new life to adjacent quotidian architecture. Basalt paving stones from the old city thoroughfares, circa 1880 to 1910, were recovered and used sculpturally to transform the courtyard into a "topographic and kinesthetic experience, metamorphosing the region's man-made urban and natural/geological history." The Santa Fe Community College courtyard is a grass carpet with trees and sculpture; an exquisite contrasting landscape setting for the adjacent adobelike buildings, in an otherwise arid setting.

Don M. Hisaka's atrium at Cleveland State University (shown on page 208) melds the atrium and courtyard spatial effects into a singular dramatic composition, creating a convincing and persuasive example of late-Modern twenty-first-century campus architecture.

PLAZAS. In civic design, a plaza is a public square in a city or town. Associated with palaces and halls of dynastic empires, and thus suspect, plazas did not become a prominent campus design feature in the United States until the colleges and universities adopted and adapted the formal design concepts of the City Beautiful movement. Plazas at the University of California, Berkeley (Sproul), and Columbia University (Low Library) are remnants from that era. Low is an extension of the building; Sproul is a nexus space. These are the kind of spaces which by size and location and history—City Hall plaza in New York City and Trafalgar Square—attract participants during momentous times and celebratory occasions.

In campus design today a plaza is a significant space, geometric in configuration or informal, hard space or soft greenery, at the campus entrance or portal of a major building or at the junction of several campus path systems. The academic precinct plaza at the University of New Mexico is an attractive combination of several such features, serving also as a centroid for pedestrian traffic moving in and out of the adjacent buildings. Nearby is Garret Eckbo's incongruous but inspired "New England pond." In tandem with the paved plaza, the yin and yang of dry and moist, creates memorable campus architecture on the desertlike arid Albuquerque mesa.

COLORADO COLLEGE, BARNES SCIENCE CENTER, 1987. CLIFFORD S. NAKATA & ASSOCIATES. *(over) The four-story atrium symbolizes the openness of the science curriculum and the commitment to encourage students and faculty to engage in cross-disciplinary activities. Symbol and service aside, the spatial effects are stunning, particularly with the play of sun-shadow through the day and the beckoning light through the oculus at night. (Source: Colorado College)*

CLAREMONT COLLEGES, COURTYARD, J. M. KECK SCIENCE CENTER, 1991. ANSHEN+ALLEN, ARCHITECTS. *(over, facing page) The courtyard between two wings serves as an informal meeting area and social area for the faculties and staff of the four colleges sharing the science teaching facility. (Source: Claremont Colleges)*

UNIVERSITY OF CALIFORNIA, SAN DIEGO, ENGINEERING UNIT I, 1992. WALLACE, ROBERTS & TODD. *(this page) Building and courtyard, engaged for campus architecture. (Source: Wallace, Roberts & Todd)*

SANTA FE COMMUNITY COLLEGE, 1985. *(facing page, top) A courtyard gem waiting to be recognized nationally.*

PORTLAND STATE UNIVERSITY, COBBLEGATE, 1992. *(facing page, bottom) Jerry Mayer's homage to time and place. (Source: Portland State University)*

ALBERTOPOLIS, SIR NORMAN FOSTER, 1994. *(right) (Source: Imperial College of London)*

ARIZONA STATE UNIVERSITY, LIBRARY PLAZA, 1988. SASAKI AND ASSOCIATES. *(bottom)*
(Source: Sasaki and Associates; photographer: Bob Freund)

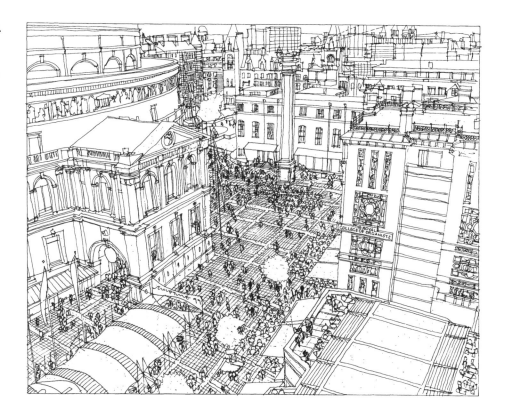

WASHINGTON UNIVERSITY, DETAIL, 1900. COPE AND STEWARDSON. *(top) (Source: Washington University)*

WASHINGTON UNIVERSITY. *(bottom) 1995 view of Cope and Stewardson's entrance plaza, an enduring example of campus architecture. (Source: Washington University)*

Norman Foster's Albertopolis plaza serves and symbolizes the converging programmatic interests of several institutions and the cooperative use of their buildings and land (including Imperial College, the Royal College of Art, and the Royal College of Music). The plaza concept, suitably urban, establishes a pedestrian precinct and a festive air for an institutional conglomeration extraordinary in its architectural variety. The library plaza at the Arizona State University, Tempe, ingeniously reads like a formal landscaped campus open space, and like Albertopolis, provides a pleasant traffic-free zone. On closer inspection the Sasaki and Associates design reveals the main entrance to the library via a small plaza in a sunken courtyard. Paving, landscape, architectural gestures combine to shape and animate a superb campus design concept.

At Washington University, open space, greenery, and the steps traversing a subtle rise in topography are an integral part of the 1900 Cope and Stewardson quadrangular plan—a soft plaza. Their full scheme was never completed, but the Brookings Hall side is a splendid version of the architects' intention. Edging and enfolded into the informal plaza, the crenellated towers and archway punctuate the Great Wall and lead the eye and the visitor to the inner quad. The concept is an elaboration of the architect's Blair Hall at Princeton University (1896).

GREENS AND LAWNS. Swards, swatches, nature's outdoor carpets, typically grass, sometimes edged with shrubbery and flower beds, and planted with trees, ever-inviting for rest and relaxation and informal games, fabled venues for rites and rituals—these legacy landscapes and adjacent buildings are enduring emblems of higher education worldwide. Green carpets can be found in the fourteenth-century Mob Quad (Merton College, Oxford) as well as late-twentieth-century campus precincts. Our focus here is a paradigm of specific architectural effects, the greensward sweeping up to the Great Walls and surrounding groups of buildings.

Greens and lawns conjoined are treasured symbols linking America's first colleges and the institutions that followed. American architecture continually uses "the past to redefine the present, to make things that solve *our* needs, and to make an extraordinary dialogue with things that went before," comments designer Robert A. M. Stern, lecturing on his work at St. Paul's School (1988). Though not addressing college and university architecture specifically, Stern's insights underline cause and effect in the associational appeal and linkage between campus greenery and an evolving American culture. The list of grasslike artifacts is impressive: the village green, town common, cemeteries, city parks, play fields, small plots in front of Victorian row houses, median dividers along early parkways, suburbia. The campus lawn fits well into that spectrum, icon and analog of aspiration and achievable campus architecture, each generation adding another gesture, sustaining "the vast structure of recollection."

No account of lawns and greens would be complete without reference to Harvard Yard and Thomas Jefferson's University of Virginia scheme, circa 1817. Jefferson designed the Charlottesville campus to avoid the dullness he thought evident at William and Mary. With his lawn, Jefferson established a design pattern that he thought, philosophically, might overcome the deficiencies he saw in the closed English quadrangles, places which Edward Gibbon disparaged as physical environ-

UNIVERSITY OF LOUISVILLE, C. 1910. *(top) Jefferson's paradigm reinterpreted.*

TSINGHUA UNIVERSITY, C. 1925. *(bottom) An American campus paradigm, lawns and building constructed in mainland China.*

University of Helsinki lecture hall, 1958. Alvar Aalto. *(top)*
Haverford College, campus center, 1992. Dagit-Saylor, architects. *(bottom)*
Campus architecture, paradigm elements: a distinctive building and green lawn setting, a tradition expressed in two place-marking projects.

ments "stagnated in a round of college business, Tory politics, personal anecdotes, and private scandal." Of equal consequence was Jefferson's faith that a grand scheme would draw, from the power of its imagination and invention, financial and political support at a time when coeval institutions were as impoverished architecturally as they were operationally.

Jefferson's building and linked greenery is a revered and pervasive model; as indicated in the Southern Methodist University concept, and the late-nineteenth-century version at the University of Louisville, and the 1926 rendition at Tsinghua University, Shanghai, which was configured to look like an American campus. Alvar Aalto's lecture building, University of Helsinki, bows to no tradition but his own genius, but the green lawn, again, evokes a universal image of campus. "Traditional ideals and simple settings form the basis for college expansion," writes architect Charles E. Dagit, explaining how the terrace at the rear of the Haverford College building serves as an outdoor cafe in good weather and becomes a defined edge to a new green lawn. The green and building in combination sustains the college's Quaker tradition of a visually unpretentious academic precinct.

Are lawns and greens, an ever-present companion to good campus buildings, an appropriate paradigm for future college and university architecture? With one of those statistics intended to be awesome and alarming, one economist has estimated that turf management is a $25 billion business nationally, with millions of acres under cultivation as recreational and aesthetic grass. Ecologically, grassy lawns and greens are suspect by those who fear their financial costs and environmental impact, including water charges, grounds maintenance, artificial fertilizers, herbicides, and expedient disposal of brush, leaves, and clippings. Preferable to the "Industrial Lawn," so-called by landscape architect Diana Balmori and colleagues at Yale University (1993), would be the "Freedom Lawn," their phrase for a landscape not dependent on technology and artificial sustenance. In the Yale screed on weeds and natural ground covers, the designer's desired color and texture would come from locally determined species and combinations of nonstandard materials such as timothy, crabgrass, dandelions, violets, and bluets. Serendipitously, in campus design terms such lawns would be reminiscent of medieval scholastic enclaves, grasses and flowers, wild and cultivated, which later were denuded and lost in favor of manicured grass. The prospect is favored by those seeking a relief to boring greensward. Others would regret losing an emblem of higher education.

With traditional lawns, it may be difficult to get an institution to adjust its tune, however persuasive the ecological premises. Since 1989, head gardener Simon MacPhaun (Trinity College, Cambridge) has been advocating "an environmentally sympathetic attitude" toward lawns and adjacent gardens. "You are turning gardeners into sprayer operators not skilled gardeners," he warned the Fellows. In a reasonable compromise, the faculty determined that Trinity's great lawn and framing buildings, truly campus architecture, would be left intact as the chief amenity of an ancient place, but modern ecological principles would be applied to all the other campus greenery. Though focused on landscape, the debate is, itself, a metaphor for determining why and how campus architecture must change through the resolution of four affecting factors—tradition and technology, function and appearance.

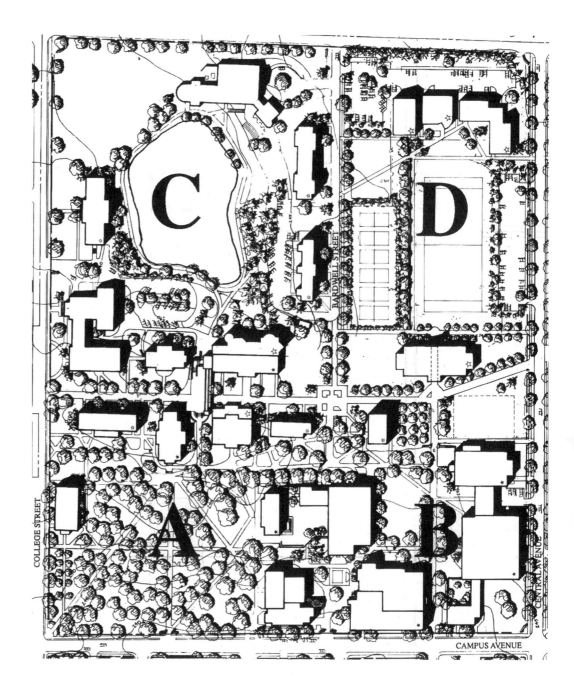

BATES COLLEGE, CAMPUS PLAN, FOUR QUADS EQUAL FIFTH QUAD. DOBER, LIDSKY, CRAIG AND ASSOCIATES, INC.
(Above) Central campus (the fifth quad) evolved in four phases. Quad A was configured in the nineteenth century. Quad B was
formed with a new library and science building in the 1980s. Quad C was anchored with the TAC fine arts building at the north end of
the College pond. Quad D was shaped by the 1992 campus plan, which relocated the stadium, provided a site for the 1994 housing,
and clarified parking and automobile circulation routes to create a central campus pedestrian precinct, i.e., the fifth quad. (Source:
Dober, Lidsky, Craig and Associates, Inc.)

BATES COLLEGE, OLIN ARTS CENTER, 1986. TAC. *(facing page, top) A landmark building for several reasons: the engagement*
of building and landscape to generate campus architecture; a building whose form and shape establish a strong sense of place on a
critical site; and one of the last college buildings designed by TAC, and thus a symbolic ending to an era and a design philosophy.
(Source: Bates College; photographer: B. V. Brink)

BATES COLLEGE, CAMPUS HOUSING. 1994. WILLIAM RAWN AND ASSOCIATES INC. *(facing page, bottom) Buildings and land-*
scapes intertwined, with a contemporary style that honors the older Bates buildings. (Source: Bates College; photographer: Steve Rosenthal)

OPEN QUADRANGLES. The old Bates College in ancient New England, or new Palo Alto College, San Antonio, Texas—both use the open quadrangle as a particularly American paradigm. Fear of fire and contagion if individual structures were connected, the requirements for ventilation and daylight prior to mechanical means, slow-paced development, the wishes of donors and architects to keep their edifices apart from others, the symbolism of a landscape that could be immediately seen from streets and road—all these were factors and conditions that affected the configuration of early American campuses. As the progenitors matured, the design forms were codified as epitomes of collegiate architecture, more Dionysian than Apollonian in their mix of different architectural styles and greenery. New England examples were carried south and west in the migration and growth of higher education. When purged of parking and through traffic, the open quadrangles are attractive pedestrian precincts. As in the instance of Bates College, the concepts can be enlarged and enhanced beneficially generation by generation, without compromise to expressing period architecture. Palo Alto College (1994 view) illustrates the paradigm's vulnerability when the landscape falls short of the architectural quality (pictured on page 204). Palo Alto's evocation of mission-style shapes and forms can be considered a grand interpretation of regional design themes. The panoramic view, however, is diluted by the awkward and seemingly incongruous site development.

*   *   *

As with a Stradavarian cello, age in time imparts a music of its own. Taken together the paradigms, projects, and commentary point the way to future campus architecture: buildings and greenery creatively conjoined, the conservation and continuing use of heritage buildings and landscapes; the commitment to explore and experiment with new ideas through collegial design processes; and the willingness to confront and redefine architectural traditions when new knowledge, technology, and the craft of construction presents opportunities to do so.

And fear not,

> *The uncertain glory of an April day;*
> *Which now shows all the beauty of the sun,*
> *And by and by a cloud takes all away...*

Campus architecture has and will have its Shakespearean Aprils but also designs that will hold fast in their integrity and visual appeal through all seasons in all places.

BIBLIOGRAPHY

Campus Architecture is a book of opinion, advice, and encouragement for those responsible for determining and designing college and university buildings and landscapes. It contains examples and references gathered during many years of professional practice and brought up-to-date through some delightful hours spent at the Loeb Library, Graduate School of Design, Harvard University. There, Ms. Hinda Sklar and her colleagues were very helpful in identifying and obtaining reference sources and materials. It was a pleasure and privilege to work with an outstanding collection and a dedicated professional staff. The provenance for most of my quotations are given directly in the text. In addition, the following are listed as the bibliographic map of the author's recent journey through the fascinating literature of campus planning and design.

Architectural Record. *Architecture of American Colleges.* New York: 1909–1912.

Audrain, Calvert, with William B. Cannon and Howard T. Wolff. *A Review of Planning at the University of Chicago.* Chicago, 1978.

Batey, Mavis. *Oxford Gardens.* Scholar Press; Amersham, England, 1986.

Brolin, Brent C. *Flight of Fancy, the Banishment and Return of Ornament.* St. Martin Press, London, 1985.

Brooke, Christopher, with Roger Highfield and Wim Swaan. *Oxford and Cambridge.* Oxford University Press, Cambridge, 1988.

Bunting, Bainbridge. *Harvard, an Architectural History.* Harvard University Press, Cambridge, MA, 1985.

Cheney, Sheldon. *The New World Architecture.* AMS Press, New York, 1930.

Crook, J. Mordaunt. *The Dilemma of Style.* Architectural Press, London, 1987.

Davey, Norman. *A History of Building Materials.* London, 1961.

Dober, Richard P. *Campus Design.* John Wiley and Sons, New York, 1992.

———, *Campus Planning.* Van Nostrand Reinhold, New York, 1963.

———, *New Campus in Great Britain.* EFL Publications, New York, 1964.

"Dormitories at Smith College." *Architectural Forum*, 1923.

Downes, Kerry. *Hawksmoor*. Praeger, London, 1979.

Encyclopedia of Architecture, Design, Engineering and Construction. Wiley, New York, 1990.

Gombrich, E. H. *Style, Vol. 15, International Encyclopedia of the Social Sciences*. New York, 1968.

Granger, A. *Architectural Style of the College Group*. American Landscape Architecture, New York, 1930.

Harrison, W. K. *School Buildings of Today and Tomorrow*. Pencil Points, New York, 1931.

Hayes, Harriet. *Planning Residence Halls*. Columbia University Press, New York, 1932.

Hibbert, Christopher, with Edward Hibbert. *The Encyclopedia of Oxford*. London, 1988.

Holden, Reuben A. *Yale, A Pictorial History*. Yale University Press, New Haven, CT, 1967.

Jenks, Christopher. *The Language of Postmodern Architecture*. Rizzoli, New York, 1977.

Klauder, Charles Z., and Wise, Herbert C. *Campus Architecture in America and Its Part in the Development of the Campus*. Charles Scribner's Sons, New York, 1926.

L'Architecture D'Audjourd'hui—Écoles. France, 1934.

Macmillian Encyclopedia of Architects. New York, 1972.

Morgan, Keith H. *Charles A. Platt as Architect*. MIT Press, Cambridge, MA, 1985.

Morrison, Hugh. *Early American Architecture*. Oxford University Press, New York, 1952.

Munby, Alan E. "Design of Science Buildings," *R.I.B.A. Journal*, 1929.

Newton, Norman T. *Design of the Land: The Development of Landscape Architecture*. Harvard University Press, Cambridge, MA, 1971.

O'Donnell, Thomas E. *University of Illinois Campus Plan*. Western Architect, Champaign-Urbana, IL, 1929.

Parsons, Kermit C. *The Cornell Campus*. Cornell University Press, Ithaca, NY, 1968.

Proceedings of the Thirty-Third Annual Meeting of the Society of Directors of Physical Education in Colleges. Rice Institute, 1929.

Rashdall, H. *The Universities of Europe in the Middle Ages*. Oxford University Press, Oxford, 1936.

Roos, Frank J., Jr. *Bibliography of Early American Architecture*. University of Illinois Press, Urbana, 1968.

Rudolph, Frederick. *The American College and University*. Knopf, New York, 1962.

Smith, F. A. C. *Selecting the Site for the Small College*. American Landscape Architecture, New York, 1930.

Shurtleff, A. A. *Program for Campus Development of Mount Holyoke College*. American Landscape Architecture, New York, 1930.

Thomas, Mary Martha Hosford. *Southern Methodist University, Founding and Early Years*. SMU Press, Dallas, TX, 1974.

Thompson, Paul. *William Butterfield*. Architectural Press, London, 1971.

Tishler, William H., ed. *American Landscape Architecture, Designers and Places*. National Trust for Historic Preservation, Washington, DC, 1989.

Turner, Paul Venable. *Campus, An American Planning Tradition*. MIT Press, Cambridge, MA, 1984.

"University Buildings Reference Number," *Architectural Forum*, 1925.

"University Buildings Reference Number," *Architectural Forum*, 1926.

INDEX

About the Author

Richard P. Dober, AICP, is a principal of Dober, Lidsky, Craig, and Associates, a design group of long-standing experience in campus development. He is the author of several previous books on campus planning and design. A graduate of Harvard University, Mr. Dober has consulted on the physical development of over 350 colleges and universities worldwide and is the recipient of numerous awards in the field.